NEW STUDIES ON CIVIL-MILITARY RELATIONS AND DEFENSE POLICY IN BRAZIL

Octavio Amorim Neto
EDITOR

NEW STUDIES ON CIVIL-MILITARY RELATIONS AND DEFENSE POLICY IN BRAZIL

FGV | EBAPE EDITORA

The rights of this edition are reserved to
EDITORA FGV
Rua Jornalista Orlando Dantas, 9
22231-010 | Rio de Janeiro, RJ | Brasil
Tel.: 21-3799-4427
editora@fgv.br | www.editora.fgv.br

Printed in Brazil

1st edition – 2022

Grafic design and layout: Abreu's System
Revision: Katherine Marie Eichhorn
Cover and layout: Estúdio 513

Cataloging-in-Publication data prepared by the
Mario Henrique Simonsen Library/FGV

New studies on civil-military relations and defense policy in Brazil / Octavio Amorim Neto (editor). – Rio de Janeiro : FGV Editora, 2022.
232 p.

Includes bibliography.
ISBN: 978-65-5652-199-2

1. Relações entre civis e militares. 2. Controle civil do poder militar. 3. Brasil – Defesa I. Amorim Neto, Octavio. II. Fundação Getulio Vargas.

CDD – 322.5

Elaborated by Mariane Pantana Alabarce – CRB-7/6992

Summary

Civilian Scholars and the Study of Civil-Military Relations and Defense Policy in Brazil's Unstable Democracy

Octavio Amorim Neto

Introduction

After one of the longest military regimes in Latin America's history, Brazil transitioned to democracy in 1985. It was inevitable that, from then on, the political power of the military would decline. However, the extent to which the country's armed forces would eschew politics was never clear, given the vast role it had always played in domestic affairs since the onset of the republic in 1889. Indeed, after Fernando Collor was sworn in as president on March 15, 1990, the decline began in earnest. After all, Collor had been the country's first directly elected president in 29 years. Even the fact that he was a right-wing politician with intimate links to the now-defunct military regime did not prevent him from downsizing military bureaucracies, cutting down defense budgets, and canceling weapons programs (Hunter, 1997).

But the Collor presidency soon floundered. He was impeached on corruption charges in October 1992. Remarkably, the armed forces remained aloof from the political battles that led to Collor's downfall. His vice-mate, Itamar Franco, was immediately invested as the new chief executive. The beginning of Franco's term was chaotic and very unstable – economically and politically. No wonder he sought support from the barracks (Amorim Neto, 2015:322-323). However, by this time, the armed forces had already accepted a new pattern of civil-military relations, whereby they would refrain from interfering in any political crisis. The counterpart of this new posture on the part of the military was the staunch advocacy of their corporate rights, secured during the negotiations that had led to the end of the military regime (D'Araújo, 2010:109).

In 1994, in the wake of the Real Plan, the Itamar Franco administration managed to quell Brazil's chronic high inflation, and Fernando Henrique Cardoso, the finance minister who had masterminded the plan, was elected president in the first round in October that year. The Cardoso presidency was a turning point in Brazilian history. Under his leadership, for the first time in decades the country began to benefit – simultaneously – from democracy, relative political stability, low inflation, social inclusion, some growth, and poverty alleviation. Not surprisingly, Cardoso was re-elected in 1998.

It was under the rare social-political-economic setting described right above that another turning point took place in Brazilian history, namely, the creation of the Ministry of Defense (henceforth MD) in 1999 and the dissolution of the Ministries of the Army, Navy, and Air Force, that had been exclusively headed by a general officer from each respective service. Albeit reluctantly, the armed forces accepted the new MD (Alsina, 2006; D'Araújo, 2010; Oliveira, 2005).

Then, after three failed attempts, Luis Inácio Lula da Silva, leader of the center-left Workers' Party (PT), was finally elected president in 2002. From humble origins, his rise to the highest office would inevitably be another turning point in Brazil's history, from which civil-military relations would not escape. Under Lula's two terms (2003-2011) and the first half of the first term of his successor (2011-2013), Dilma Rousseff, also affiliated with the PT, the country started to benefit not only from democracy, relative political stability, and low inflation, but also from higher rates of social inclusion, economic growth, poverty alleviation, inequality reduction, and international prestige than under Cardoso.

Despite the political and economic success of the PT-led governments in 2003-2013, there were some episodes of civil-military crises and tensions (Martins Filho, 2010). But all of them were solved in a relatively orderly and constitutional manner. There was also progress in terms of civilian control of the armed forces through the publication of Brazil's *National Strategy of Defense* in 2008, drafted with some civilian input, the enactment of the *New Defense Act* in 2010, which strengthened the role of the defense minister, and the publication of Brazil's first *White Paper on National Defense* in 2012. Civilians made up 66.7% of the authors of this document (Amorim Neto, 2019:4). While most defense policy decisions remained in the hands of the military or were delegated to the latter (Pion-Belin and Martinez, 2017:207), civilians gradually started to get more involved in defense policymaking. This was real progress for a country that throughout most the 20th century had become used to a military monopoly on defense policy.[1]

It was under the above-described political setting that Brazilian civilian scholars began to study defense policy, military and strategic affairs, and international security as they had never done before. Academics and researchers play a key role in what Bruneau (2005) and Pion-Berlin (2005; 2006) call the balance of competence in defense matters. Scholars are particularly well-positioned to produce independent analyses of and information on those subjects. In turn, these analyses and information provide politicians and policymakers with input that is independent of that provided by the armed forces themselves. Though vital for any democracy that cares about its national defense, military input should not be the sole source of defense knowledge and expertise. That is why academic work is so relevant to civilian control of the military. In the 1950s, there was only one teaching and research institution in Brazil focused on national security, the Escola Superior de Guerra (ESG), which was totally controlled by the military. By the late 2000s there were twelve centers, groups or academic think tanks, within the civilian realm focused exclusively on military, strategic, and international security studies (Figueiredo, 2010). By 2022, there were almost fifty exclusively civilian research groups and centers registered with Brazil's National Research Council (CNPq).

The creation and proliferation of the above-mentioned research institutions are compelling evidence of the growing scholarly interest in a research area once dominated by the military. And such institutions created a considerable potential for reducing the asymmetry of information that used to mark the relationship between civilians and the armed forces in Brazil. Moreover, since 2005 the country has had the Brazilian Defense Studies Association (ABED). In 2014, the first issue of the *Revista Brasileira de Estudos de Defesa* (Brazilian Journal of Defense Studies), a journal sponsored by ABED, was published.

In short, in its first three decades Brazil's democratic regime managed to substantially reduce the political power of the armed forces, although the latter kept enjoying a considerable measure of autonomy in many areas (Bruneau and Tollefson, 2014; D'Araújo, 2010:107-123; Pion-Berlin and Martinez, 2017; Zaver-

1 Defense policy is here loosely defined as the combination of the official guidelines on the employment of the armed forces with the actual employment that is given to the latter.

ucha, 2000; 2005). Regarding the balance of competence in defense matters, the civilian academy made notable strides towards reducing civil-military asymmetry.

Surprisingly, for a number of reasons – associated mostly with the economic mistakes and political failings of the Dilma Rousseff administration, particularly in the 2013-2015 period –, starting in a shady area between 2015 and 2018, all the gains made since the 1990s – in terms of civilian control of the military and the removal of the military from the center of the political arena – began to rapidly erode (Akkoyunlu and Lima, 2022; Amorim Neto and Acácio, 2020; Harig, 2021; Hunter and Vega, 2022). Some of the main events that led to this erosion include the following: the appointment, in February 2018 – that is, still under the Michel Temer presidency (2016-2019) – of the first general officer to head the MOD since the creation of the portfolio in 1999; the tweet by the then Army commander, General Eduardo Villas-Bôas, issued in April 2018, putting pressure on the Federal Supreme Court on the eve of the habeas corpus trial filed by former President Luiz Inácio Lula da Silva; the appointment by President Bolsonaro of dozens of active-duty and reserve military personnel to occupy cabinet positions (including the MD) and thousands of officers to civilian sub-cabinet positions in the federal bureaucracy; as president; Jair Bolsonaro began to treat the Armed Forces as a key political pillar of his government (Couto, 2021; Martins Filho, 2021; Passos, 2021); during the pandemic, Bolsonaro appointed an active-duty general, Eduardo Pazuello, to head the Ministry of Health; and from 2020 onwards, Jair Bolsonaro threatened to use the Armed Forces to pressure Congress and the Federal Supreme Court.

According to Serra (2008), the countries that democratized since the onset of the Third Wave of Democracy (which began in 1974 with the Carnations Revolution in Portugal) underwent a "military transition," which occured simultaneously with the political transition to democracy. Military transitions have three stages: (1) to avoid coups d'états; (2) to remove military officers from politics, stripping them of any veto power on government decisions unrelated to national defense and drastically reducing the military's autonomy; and (3) the establishment of civilian supremacy, when civilians effectively direct defense policy (Serra, 2008:48). Until 2015-2016, Brazil was in the second stage and trying to step into the third. Since then, the military transition has been going backward owing to the renewed political power of the military (Amorim Neto and Acácio, 2020).

FGV, EBAPE, CAPES, and the Study of Civil-Military Relations and Defense Policy

In 2008 the Brazilian School of Public and Business Administration (EBAPE) at the Getulio Vargas Foundation (FGV), Rio de Janeiro, received a grant from the *Programa Pro-Defesa* ("Pro-Defense Program") funded by the Coordination for the Improvement of Higher Education Personnel (henceforth CAPES), an agency of Brazil's Ministry of Education. The project that EBAPE would develop under this grant in 2009-2012 focused on defense strategic management. The project's key goals were to create and consolidate a body of scholars who could produce research and expand scientific output on national defense issues associated with management studies, such as public policies and national defense, defense budget and resource management, international security and defense scenarios, and science, technology and innovation in national defense. The book edited by Motta, Schmitt, and Vasconcellos (2016) is representative of the research agenda proposed by EBAPE's *Pro-Defesa*.

In addition, in 2012 EBAPE received a new grant from CAPES, called *Pro-Estratégia*, designed to foster academic research on civil-military relations and the making and implementation of defense policy in Brazil from a comparative perspective. Brazil's High Command and General Staff College (ECEME) would be a partner with EBAPE in carrying out this project. Note that the year in which *Pro-Estratégia* started, 2012, was the peak of the process of strengthening civilian control of the military described above. Note also that CAPES required that, for a civilian institution to be awarded the *Pro-Estratégia* grant, it would have to partner with a military academic institution. The idea was to foster civil-military cooperation in the research of civil-military relations and defense policy. Thus, the EBAPE-ECEME partnership. The goals of EBAPE's *Pro-Estratégia* were in perfect sync with the state of civil-military relations by the early 2010s.

While FGV, through both its School of Social Sciences (CPDOC) and EBAPE, had always been a leading institution in the study of the Brazilian armed forces and military politics, their approach to these topics had been mostly historical and managerial (as evinced by EBAPE's *Pro-Defesa*), EBAPE's *Pro-Estratégia* was meant to adopt a political science approach, with a concern with qualitative and quantitative methods and cross-national comparisons. This is the novelty brought about by this project.

It was with the above-mentioned goals in mind that young scholars were granted MA and PhD fellowships funded by the EBAPE-ECEME *Pro-Estratégia* between 2012 and 2017. EBAPE complemented the *Pro-Estratégia* funds with generous resources, so research assistants could be hired and talks by foreign guests could be organized. With both *Pro-Estratégia* and EBAPE money, international civil-military relations scholars came to EBAPE and ECEME to present their ideas and latest works. Thus, Thomas Bruneau, Aurel Croissant, Olivier France, Richard Goetze, David Pion-Berlin, Jack Riley, and Arturo Sotomayor delivered talks at both institutions between 2014 and 2017.

In 2017 the EBAPE-ECEME *Pro-Estratégia* ended. With the benefit of hindsight, the official end of this CAPES-funded research program would coincide with the demise of a virtuous era in Brazil's civil-military relations.

The Organization of this Volume

This volume contains some of the best scholarly works produced by a new generation of young civilian students funded by the EBAPE-ECEME *Pro-Estratégia* who did their MA or PhD at EBAPE or labored as research assistants at the latter. Moreover, to have their works included in this book, these civilian students also needed to have studied or be studying abroad and to be interacting with EBAPE faculty on a regular basis even after their official time at EBAPE. The latter criterion was adopted because one of EBAPE's main goals is to internationalize its output and networks.

The topics covered in the chapters on this volume are among those most relevant for the study of Brazil's civil-military relations and defense policy. The topics include (1) the role of civilians vis-à-vis that of the military within Brazil's MD, (2) the motivations and consequences of the lengthy Brazil-led United National peacekeeping operation in Haiti (MINUSTAH in 2004-2017), (3) the relations between the military and Brazil's National Organization for Indigenous Affairs (FUNAI) in 1967-2021, (4) the sources of the orientation of national security documents, (5) civil-military relations and transparency, and (6) the motivations and consequences of small powers fighting alongside big powers in major conflicts.

The first three chapters deal with the first three above-mentioned topics and are focused exclusively on the Brazilian case. The remaining chapters are on the latter topics and take a comparative approach. One is cross-national and quantitative and the other two offer well-structured two-case studies comparing Brazil with one Latin American country, namely, Colombia or Mexico.

That said, the first chapter by Pimenta seeks to fill a gap in the literature on civil-military relations. For the author, the scholarly debates over how civilians could or should control the military are still limited. Pimenta focuses on civilian presence in Brazil's MD from its creation to 2021. This chapter seeks to connect the relationship between civilian control, institutional stability, and the quality of democracy. By unifying these three aspects, the chapter highlights the real civilian contribution to defense policy, distinguishing rhetoric from reality in the Brazilian context. Pimenta proposes that extensive civilian presence in the MD does not necessarily guarantee civilian control. Empirically, the author seeks to identify whether there is a civil-military balance in the holding of hierarchical positions within the MD, and check whether civilian officeholder's performance can impact and be impacted by the military within the Ministry. Pimenta's findings indicate that there actually is an imbalance: the military are the MD's main workforce and act to impose barriers on civilian officers. In addition, civilians hold lower hierarchical positions within the Ministry, are absent from the decision-making process, and generally have limited access to information. In addition, civilian terms of office are usually shorter. Finally, monitoring and controlling the military requires a highly trained and skilled workforce, which is challenging to build due to a lack of investment in civilian expertise. These elements coalesce into civilians facing real performance barriers that stem from their relatively lower *status* within the MD and the pattern of their interactions with military officers.

The second chapter by Anselmo asks the following questions: why do states contribute troops to peacekeeping missions? In particular, why would middle powers participate in peace operations? Anselmo seeks to answer these questions by focusing on the motivations and consequences of Brazil's participation in peacekeeping – with particular attention to its prominent role in the UN-led peacekeeping operation in Haiti (Minustah, 2004-2017). More to the point, Anselmo identifies Brazil's objectives in contributing to peacekeeping efforts and what goals were achieved.

According to Anselmo, one of the key assumptions underlying the scholarly literature on peacekeeping is that the countries that benefited from maintaining the international *status quo* were precisely those that dominated UN peacekeeping. The Western middle powers were the main troop-contributing countries in the UN system until the end of the Cold War, after which the number and types of operations increased. As a result, the countries participating in peacekeeping have also changed from the usual middle powers to emerging and small powers.

Moreover, Anselmo highlights an essential change: the consumer countries of the UN security system have become international security providers. These countries do this mainly because they understand that their participation will result in domestic institutional reform, international signaling, and budgetary increment. Thus, peacekeeping operations are part of a strategy to achieve domestic and international objectives. Anselmo's main findings indicate that budget complementation is not a significant factor in the case of Brazil. However, internal reform and international signaling were relevant to the country. Therefore, the peacekeeping operation in Haiti could be turned into a tool to achieve those goals. All told, Brazil ended up not only failing to achieve internal reform and international signaling, but the experience of the Brazilian armed forces in Haiti produced the opposite effect to the ones that had been desired.

As mentioned above, Brazil began to witness the return of the military to important cabinet portfolios during the presidency of Michel Temer. This return also intensified the debate about the links between the military and top positions in the federal bureaucracy. By discussing the appointment of military personnel to civilian positions in Brazil in the past five decades, the chapter by Farias seeks to identify which factors generate different patterns of bureaucratic appointments in the social area. What changes in such patterns did Brazil's new democratic regime effect as compared to the military regime? More to the point, Farias aims to study the determinants of the appointment of non-political experts to social agencies through a longitudinal study of the *Fundação Nacional do Índio* (FUNAI), the Brazilian national agency for indigenous affairs, in 1967-2021.

The chapter by Farias shows that FUNAI has been essentially driven by political preferences over its history. Her analysis of appointment patterns focuses on partisan factors and the professional background of appointees. Her findings indicate that both regime type (military *versus* democratic) and the political ideology of presidents are key explanatory conditions. Under democracy, policy experts (indigenists, sociocultural anthropologists, and career bureaucrats) finally began to be appointed to head FUNAI, whereas under the military regime partisan appointees prevailed. Thus, Farias highlights that democracy created checks on those appointed to run indigenous affairs, thereby increasing the costs of appointing only partisans or loyalists. This is surprising because the ideology of the military regime was essentially technocratic. But even under democracy, right-wing presidents have incentives to appoint partisans to head FUNAI. This is also surprising because right-wing presidents tend to be more technocratically oriented than left-wing chief executives. Finally, Farias's chapter shows the extensive political influence of the Brazilian military over an area that is not directly linked to national defense.

What is the relationship between defense policies and economic development policies? The chapter by Acácio discusses how these policies are linked and mutually reinforcing. The author advances an underexplored research agenda on the association between, on the one hand, the content of democracies' national security or defense policy documents and, on the other, a set of political, economic, and international variables. Empirically, he uses an original dataset of declaratory defense policy documents but also analyzes qualitative evidence from Brazil, India, and South Africa. His findings indicate that countries with low levels of external threats have more developmental content in their defense policy documents. In turn, countries in which civilians control the defense sector have, on average, more developmental content in their defense policy. Unequal countries are also associated with greater developmental content in their national security documents. Moreover, the association between inequality and the developmental content in defense policy is more intense if civilians control the defense sector.

Thus, for Acácio, countries end up putting their resources where their direst needs are, even if the stated goals of defense policy stipulate that guarding against foreign threats is the primary objective. Finally, by relying on econometric analysis, rarely used by students of civil-military relations and defense policy in Brazil, Acácio makes an important methodological contribution to this subfield.

Latin American civilians are generally uninterested in national defense issues. Among the causes of this lack of interest are low expectations of war, the low impact of the defense industry on the job market, and the low saliency of defense issues to attract politicians' and voters' attention. This attention deficit as regards defense policy, to use the expression suggested by Pion-Berlin and

Trinkunas (2007), leads to scarce knowledge of defense issues by civilians. In turn, this scarce knowledge could possibly lead to a low level of accountability of the armed forces, contributing to a low-quality democracy. And one of the key factors in improving democracy and the quality of public policies is precisely transparency. Thus, in her chapter, Rodrigues explains how civil-military relations have transformed and shaped democratic consolidation in Latin America. According to her, there is a fundamental dilemma for transparency in defense policies. On the one hand, there is a consensus that opacity in the public sector can result in corruption and inefficiency, in addition to making it difficult to evaluate and monitor the decisions made and implemented by the armed forces. On the other hand, secrecy may be legitimate due to the sensitivity of defense policies.

Based on her analysis of Brazil and Mexico, Rodrigues argues that access to military records depends on how the relationship between civilians and military personnel is structured. Both countries have strong freedom of information laws. And in both countries, there is a divided pattern of civil-military relations because of the extensive isolation of the military institutions. However, both countries present different levels of separation/integration between civilians and the military, which may have directly influenced the transparency of defense issues. Empirically, Rodrigues analyzes Brazil and Mexico from the outset of democracy (Brazil in 1985 and Mexico in 1994) up to 2012. By using process tracing to understand critical institutional changes, she evaluates civilian access to military records in Brazil and Mexico using historical and legal analysis, along with primary data from semi-structured interviews conducted in both countries. Rodrigues's main finding is that Brazil's model of civil-military relations has produced greater transparency in defense policies than in Mexico, despite Mexico's stronger Freedom of Information (FOI) legislation. This is a very relevant puzzle. For example, Mexico still maintains its main strategic defense document almost fully classified. This is a consequence of the greater integration of civil-military relations in Mexico, which, surprisingly, generates less political confrontation between civilians and the military – therefore leading to lower levels of transparency on defense policy – than in Brazil.

In the last chapter Accorsi addresses the causes and consequences of the participation of minor powers in important conflicts alongside great powers. This author is particularly concerned with the decisions made by Brazil and Colombia to participate (or not) in the Korean War (1950-1953). Brazil refused to participate in this war, despite American pressure, whereas Colombia did join in. Note that Brazil had participated in WWII (Brazil had sent an Army division to Italy to fight alongside the US Fifth Army), whereas Colombia had not. Accorsi argues that a minor power accepts to fight this kind of conflict when its leaders realize that they will be rewarded, and, therefore, demand material benefits from the great power with which they ally. However, even when the leader of a minor power wants to fight alongside a great power, his or her preference can be vetoed or blocked if there is no civilian control over the armed forces. The consequences of these findings reaffirm the autonomy of small powers in the international system and show that they often make consequences-oriented decisions. Furthermore, Accorsi argues that states often use foreign policy to satisfy material domestic preferences, which converge on the findings of Acácio discussed above.

In addition, the cases of Brazil and Colombia show that small powers tend to infer their future gains based on past relationships with major powers. However, when demand for foreign assistance by a minor power is remarkably intense, as was the case with Colombia during the Korean War, a great power can successfully recruit an ally to send troops to a major war, regardless of the great power's past behavior. But this should not be expected to happen often. Finally, Accorsi's work has important policy implications: for smaller powers, knowing the past consequences of their joining a coalition led by a great power can better inform their future decisions on whether to do it or not and how to negotiate their support.

All told, the six chapters of this volume offer novel – theoretical, methodological, and empirical – contributions to the study of classical and fresh issues associated with Brazil's civil-military relations and defense policy by a new generation of Brazilian scholars. The conclusion of the book provides a brief and selective evaluation of defense studies in Brazil and speculates at what such studies will investigate after the Bolsonaro presidency.

Acknowledgments

This book would not have been possible without the unflinching support provided by Professor Carlos Ivan Simonsen Leal, the Dean of FGV, Professor Flavio Vasconcellos, the chair of EBAPE, Professor Eduardo Andrade, the vice-chair of

EBAPE, and Professor Roberto Pimenta, head of EBAPE's Academic Training and Research Center, to research on civil-military relations and defense policy. Due to their strenuous and unwavering efforts, EBAPE has been able to overcome the daunting economic hardships Brazil has been facing in the past seven years and keep thriving as a research and teaching institution. It is the luck of this book's editor to be working at EBAPE since 2011 and to be present at and be a beneficiary of the academic revolution Professors Leal, Vasconcellos, Andrade, and Pimenta have led throughout this period. To the four of them, the gratitude and admiration of the editor of this book.

In the name of EBAPE, this book's editor would like to effusively thank Brazil's Ministry of Education, through its Coordination for the Improvement of Higher Education Personnel (CAPES), for the *Pro-Estratégia* grant and all sorts of support it gave us throughout 2013-2017.

Furthermore, the chapters' authors and the editor are very grateful for all the international scholars who visited EBAPE under the sponsorship of the EBAPE-ECEME *Pro-Estratégia*. Their talks and interaction with the students and faculty were simply key to the development and improvement of EBAPE's research and output on the topics covered by this book. Thomas Bruneau was our most frequent visitor. His wisdom, knowledge, generosity, and unbounded energy have been an inspiration to all of us. Muito obrigado por tudo, Tom!

Finally, the chapters authors and the editor would also like to show their appreciation for the ECEME officers and civilian professors who helped us in so many ways from 2013-2017. Working alongside them was also extremely illuminating to our investigations. Last but not least, we would like to thank Gabriel Bento Madeira for his excellent editorial and research assistance.

References

AKKOYUNLU, Karabekir; LIMA, José Antonio. 2022. Brazil's Stealth Military Intervention. *Journal of Politics in Latin America*, 14(1), p. 31-54.

ALMEIDA, Maria Hermínia Tavares de. *Os anos de ouro:* ensaios sobre a democracia no Brasil. Livros Horizonte, 2019.

ALSINA Jr., João Paulo Soares. *Política externa e política de defesa no Brasil:* síntese imperfeita. Brasília: Câmara dos Deputados, 2006.

AMORIM NETO, Octavio. Democracia e Relações Civis-Militares no Brasil. In: CINTRA, Antonio Octávio; AVELAR, Lúcia Avelar (ed.). *Sistema Político Brasileiro:* uma introdução. Rio de Janeiro: Fundação Konrad Adenauer, 2015, p. 315-330.

________. The Impact of Civilians on Defense Policy in New Democracies: The Case of Brazil. *Latin American Politics and Society*, 61(3), 2019, p. 1-28.

________; ACACIO, Igor. De volta ao centro da Arena: causas e consequências do papel político dos militares sob Bolsonaro. *Journal of Democracy em Português*, 9, p. 1-29.

BRUNEAU, Thomas Charles. Civil-Military Relations in Latin America: The Hedgehog and the Fox Revisited. *Revista Fuerzas Armadas y Sociedad*, 19, 2005, p. 111-131.

________; TOLLEFSON, Scott D. Civil-Military Relations in Brazil: A Reassessment. *Journal of Politics in Latin America*, 6(2), 2014, p. 107-138.

COUTO, Claudio. Do governo-movimento ao pacto militar-fisiológico. In: AVRITZER, Leonardo; KERCHE, Fábio; MARONA, Marjorie (eds.). *Governo Bolsonaro: Retrocesso Democrático e Degradação Política*. Belo Horizonte: Autêntica Editora, 2021, p. 35-49.

D'ARAÚJO, Maria Celina. *Militares, democracia e desenvolvimento: Brasil e América do Sul*. Rio de Janeiro: Editora FGV, 2010.

FIGUEIREDO, Eurico de Lima. Os estudos estratégicos, a Defesa Nacional e a Segurança Internacional. In: LESSA, Renato (ed.). *Horizontes das Ciências Sociais no Brasil:* Ciência Política. São Paulo: Barcarolla, 2010, p. 271-296.

HARIG, Christoph. Militarisation by Popular Demand? Explaining the Politics of Internal Military Roles in Brazil. *Bulletin of Latin American Research*. 2021, Advance on-line publication. Retrieved from https://onlinelibrary.wiley.com/doi/abs/10.1111/blar.13289. February 18, 2022.

HUNTER, Wendy. *Eroding Military Influence in Brazil:* Politicians Against Soldiers. Chapel Hill: University of North Carolina Press, 1997.

________; VEGA, Diego. Populism and the Military: Symbiosis and Tension in Bolsonaro's Brazil. *Democratization*, 29(2), 2022, p. 337-359.

MARTINS FILHO, João Roberto. Tensões militares no governo Lula (2003-2009): a pré-história do acordo com a França. *Revista Brasileira de Ciência Política*, 4, 2010, p. 283-306.

________. Maquiavel, Bolsonaro e os soldados. In: MARTINS FILHO, João Roberto (ed.). *Os militares e a crise brasileira*. São Paulo: Alameda, 2021, p. 71-87.

MOTTA, Paulo Roberto; SCHMITT, Valentina Gomes Haensel; VASCONCELLOS, Carlos Antonio Raposo de (ed.). *Desafios gerenciais de defesa*. Rio de Janeiro: FGV Editora, 2016.

OLIVEIRA, Eliézer Rizzo de. *Democracia e defesa nacional:* a criação do Ministério da Defesa na presidência de FHC. São Paulo: Manole, 2005.

PASSOS, Anaís Medeiros. Militares e política no governo de Jair Bolsonaro. In: AVRITZER, Leonardo; KERCHE, Fábio; MARONA, Marjorie (eds.). *Governo Bolsonaro:* retrocesso democrático e degradação política. Belo Horizonte: Autêntica Editora, 2021, p. 217-225.

PION-BERLIN, David. Political Management of the Military in Latin America. *Military Review*, 85(1), 2005, p. 19-31.

________. The Defense Wisdom Deficit in Latin America: A Reply to Thomas C. Bruneau. *Revista Fuerzas Armadas y Sociedad*, 20, 2006, p. 51-62.

________; MARTINEZ, Rafael. *Soldiers, Politicians, and Civilians:* Reforming Civil-Military Relations in Democratic Latin America. Cambridge: Cambridge University Press, 2017.

________; TRINKUNAS, Harold. X. Attention Deficits: Why Politicians Ignore Defense Policy in Latin America. *Latin American Research Review*, 42(3), 2006, p. 76-100.

SERRA, Narcís. *La Transición Militar:* Reflexiones En Torno a La Reforma Democrática de Las Fuerzas Armadas. Barcelona: Randon House Mondadori, 2008.

ZAVERUCHA, Jorge. *Frágil democracia:* Collor, Itamar, FHC e os militares: (1990-1998). Rio de Janeiro: Editora Record, 2000.

________. *FHC, Forças Armadas e Polícia: entre o autoritarismo e a democracia.* Rio de Janeiro: Record, 2005.

Inching Forward: The Evolution of Civilian Control in Contemporary Brazil's Ministry of Defense

Gabriel Alves Pimenta

Introduction

In 1999, the ministry of defense (MD), a new civilian institution, replaced the war ministry to impose civilian oversight over national defense. Inside the MD, officers and civilians converge, compete, and interact to influence the outcome of its activities (Francis Fukuyama, 2014; Huntington, 1968). As a result of its hierarchical and bureaucratic structure, the distribution of seats and occupation of different hierarchical levels determines which interest group guides the agenda.

In modern democracies, civilians and the military coordinate to develop the mechanisms, policies, and strategies that guide national defense. These distinct actors promote their particular interests through routine strategic interactions. In cases of unaligned interests, the most influential actor will likely change the course of action to suit its interests better.

Civil-military relations (CMR) studies the interaction between civilians and the military to understand its determinants and outcomes. The consensus in the literature is that in a democracy, civilian control over the military is desirable as it works to prevent coups and insubordination.

At this point, I need to highlight what I consider to be the literature's most relevant yet underexplored gap. Focusing frequently on military activities and optimal behavior, the literature widely disregards civilians. Few authors have discussed how civilians could or should control the military. This chapter will pay much-needed attention to how civilians exist in a defense ministry to shed light on their contributions and limitations. It contains an analysis of the civilian presence in Brazil's Ministry of Defense from its inauguration until today, fundamental to understanding civilian control *status* and how to improve it. Many studies, such as David Pion-Berlin's "Defense Organization and Civil-Military Relations in Latin America" (2009), State that civilian control and military effectiveness are codependent phenomena. This research focuses exclusively on Brazil's civilian participation and contribution to control over the military and does not venture into effectiveness.

This chapter begins to cover the literature gap by connecting the relationship between Civilian control (Almeida, 2010; Amorim Neto, 2012; L. Cleary & McConville, 2006; Cohen, 1997; Diamint, 1999), institutional stability (Allison & Zelikow, 1999; Farah, 2011; Nascimento, 1967; Oliveira, 2004; Secchi, 2009; Soares & Mathias, 2002; Souza, 2001; Wahrlich, 2012) and prosperity of democracy (Mainwaring, 1989; Marques, 2003; Newman, 2009; Rezende & Afonso, 2004). By unifying these three aspects, this research will highlight the actual civilian contribution to defense policy, distinguishing rhetoric from reality in the Brazilian context.

The fundamental concern of this chapter is how far civilian control over the military has *de facto* advanced in Brazil. The main research question is: Is the civil presence, as seen in Brazil's Ministry of Defense, sufficient for establishing civilian control over the military?

The central hypothesis tested is that the MD's extensive civilian presence does not ensure Civilian control. Authors that studied the ministry in the past report on the military undertone of the institution contradicting official rhetoric from different administrations that use the extensive civilian presence and leadership as evidence of civilian control. This research addresses the issues of seat occupation balance, hierarchical positions, and performance that may impact and be impacted by the military presence inside the organization.

According to official rhetoric, this research's evidence suggests that civilians rarely occupy more seats than the theory. Civilian control demands a highly trained and knowledgeable professional body, and according to evidence, despite some civilians' academic background, the training inside the institution is still innocuous. Still missing in Brazil, the robust worker's body takes time and investment to build, and without it, civilian control is inherently limited. The civilian workforce needs to understand the field and the tools at their disposal, and they additionally need tenure to perform their jobs with little external pressure. In addition, military presence is ubiquitous and significantly limits civil participation in the institution.

This research's evidence suggests an imbalance in occupation. Primarily, the occupation has a zero-sum nature since it is determined by percentual occupation of seats; therefore, the more extensive military occupation, the more limited civilian occupation[1]. The military occupies the MD as a permanent workforce and acts as gatekeepers to the institution. Military officials impose barriers on incoming workers until they gain their trust. Moreover, another obstacle to civilian control emerged in the evidence; civilians occupy lower hierarchical positions inside the ministry, keeping them away from the decision-making process and filtering their access to information. Another element that emerged during the research is that civilians' tenure is shorter, making their presence in the military a revolving door and reducing the timeframe in which they can develop and apply skills usefully. Furthermore, monitoring and controlling the military requires a heavily trained and capable workforce, which is hard to form due to civilians' lack of investments and expertise. All these elements conflate into civilians face actual performance barriers that stem from their condition inside the institution and their interactions with the military.

This research is organized into four sections, as follows: Literature Review where I present the theoretical basis for the study; Methodology, where I show the data collection methods; Results dedicated to clarifying the findings of the research; and, Conclusion containing final considerations and future research propositions.

Literature Review

Military activity has a dual intimate connection to the State's very existence. The nation-state holds the ever-growing necessity for protection against internal and external threats, making military activity fundamental to State survival; however, the monopoly over the use of force by armed forces with political aspirations presents the biggest threat to the State (Bruneau & Tollefson, 2006; Cohen, 2002). Thus, controlling military activity is essential for the State.

Nation-State's stability depends on a balance between civil society, military institutions, and the international system debated since classic antiquity (Desch,

1 Changes in absolute number of seats do not imply changes in proportions of occupation.

2001; Cohen, 2002). In other words, throughout history, a country's *status quo* depended on a combination of external and internal threats, military capability to respond to those, and how civilians motivated said responses. Another essential factor is how these actors behaved in the past. The current CMR debate understands that history is a significant part of these interactions, and thus civil-military dynamics depend on past interactions and interfere in future configurations.

The modern study of CMR has advanced since Samuel P. Huntington first theorized about the relationship between the soldier and the State (1957). Not much has changed in focus and scope; research primarily focuses on the ideal applications of military capabilities and how to control political inclinations. Many theories deal with different types and forms of control and application. CMR's inaugural theoretical debate brought attention to Huntington's (1957) typology of contrasting types of control, with Huntington favoring *objective* control and Morris Janowitz (1960) favoring *subjective* control. Decades later, Laura Cleary and Teri McConville's (2006) developed a multilevel typology of control – *Democratic, Civilian,* and *Civil* – a more nuanced approach to control that has significantly less traction in the literature.

Over the years, CMR theory has evolved and embraced different subtleties of reality and has successfully comprehended essential parts of the phenomena that emerge from the interaction of such distinct social groups, expanding beyond typologies of control. However, some criticism is due. Mainly normative, the literature on CMR had limited its attention to military behavior and activity, frequently disregarding civil participation, until the late 1990's when the first look at civilians emerged on *Through Corridors of Power* (Pion-Berlin, 1997). CMR theory usually pays attention to the *dos* and *don'ts* of military action and completely forsakes what civilians ought to be doing once the AFs are limited to their mission. So, we know which activities the AFs are not supposed to exert, but we have little idea about who is supposed to do so in their place, let alone how they are supposed to do so.

Civil-military relations makeup part of the interaction between two components of society and influence the country's defense strategic development (Egnell, 2009). Conflicts that stand out in this relationship arise mainly from the interaction between institutions. Directly connected to typologies of control and CMR theory is human nature's struggle for power and control – both intrinsic to CMR and its politics (Vajpeyi & Segell, 2014). This struggle is the primary concern when establishing control mechanisms over the military, as they will resist losing power and autonomy to other groups. Thus, CMR focus on the institutional aspects of this relationship and their interactions with the struggle for control (Cleary and McConville, 2006). To achieve effective control over the military, civilian experts must organize and occupy the defense institutions on the matter (Pion-Berlin, 2009; Barany, 2012; L. Cleary & McConville, 2006; Winnand & Saint-Pierre, 2010). The idea of a strong ministry of defense as vital for the healthy development of CMR and military activity implies that MDs are the central institution responsible for a centralized decision-making process that is not easily forsaken or circumvented by military authority (Pion-Berlin, 2009).

The ways of war and military activity are a complex aggregation of nuances, cultural values, *modi operandi,* and sensitive activities that require a lifelong dedication to learn. As such, it is not possible for an outsider to fully understand the ways of the force without complete immersion and risk of cultural contamination. The fundamental principles of military culture are discipline and hierarchy, and all military activity will necessarily abide by those. Thus, a civilian who embeds into the military culture will begin to value and adhere to these core values; it is hard for a civilian to learn it without accepting some of its cultural idiosyncrasies and turning into a "soldier." On the other hand, it is fundamental for the military body to present values shared with society (Serra & Bush, 2010). On the civilian side, civilians will follow social and democratic principles where hierarchy and discipline, though present, are not the main elements. While analyzing republics, where the public interest is critical, civil servants will adhere to values such as legality, transparency, and morality before concerning themselves with hierarchy and discipline.

A primordial example of culture conflict emerges from the handling of information; the nature of military activity requires discretion and privy, meanwhile by principle, civilian activity has to remain public, and all decisions have to be publicized before turning into action, in a hybrid environment such as the MD this cultural difference may turn irreconcilable. These and many other cultural clashes influence civilian and military interactions and act as obstacles to common ground in decision-making.

Another defining point within defense ministries, the highly-trained military body has difficulty dealing with the newly introduced civilian elements that lack training and preparation, usually leading to civilians being ignored and circumvented by the military. Military officers, who have dedicated their lives preparing for their work, are reticent of civilians' adequacy to deal with defense issues. Consequently, civilian integration happens by creating and imposing new institutions and reporting structures on the military, compounding the distrust of their adequacy to the task and whether civilians are on their side. These conditions may result in the military ignoring and excluding civilians from the process (Pimenta, 2014; Cortinhas & Vitelli, 2021).

Defense ministries limit the military's autonomy, which generates discomfort and discontent; civil institutions assume bureaucratic hierarchies to facilitate the transition, apparently simplifying the military understanding of this new structure (Cleary and McConville, 2006). This simplification is a double-edged sword, as the military may abuse their knowledge of the bureaucratic structure to prevent civilians from taking complete control. For example, in Brazil today, the military performs most of the planning and implementation of missions and projects independently, as pointed out by Amorim Neto and Acacio (2021).

When observing the ministry of defense in contrast with the armed forces, we have a disproportionate match, similar to the dichotomy proposed by Huntington (1957). The current arrangement has specialized professionals (Military) placed under the control of individuals with limited knowledge and far less training but with much higher bureaucratic power inside the organization. From this difference in capabilities, conflicts and distrust arise. This disparity also causes communication glitches, disrupts project development, generates sub-optimal results, and negatively affects institutional relations (Cleary & McConville, 2006). Furthermore, in scenarios where the military manages to grasp significant power positions inside the organization, they can circumvent civilians making their contribution to policy formulation and projects nearly irrelevant.

Narcis Serra and Peter Bush (2010) presented a fundamental point, the self-regulation issue. As most of the literature tends to oversee, Civil and Military bodies must work together to achieve control and effectiveness. A fully centralized decision-making process in the hands of civilians alone is as ineffective to the national interest as fully autonomous armed forces. The two defense actors need to coordinate and cooperate to achieve a higher-quality outcome. Cooperation and coordination rely on mutual understanding and respect, a problematic point between Brazil's distrusting soldiers and civilian newcomers.

To facilitate cooperation and coordination *occupying* the country's defense institution with qualified personnel is a prime concern. However, it takes time to carry out this occupation ideally, and the urgency of issues related to defense requires filling the structure without time to train public officials. Countries may then choose to use the military as a quick solution to occupation, which opens the institution for military capture. Some alternatives allow dealing with this flaw to avoid the possible negative impact of military occupation over civilian control. According to David Chuter and Laura Cleary (2006), the options are Civilianization, Relocation, and Outsourcing, these options in detail work like this:

- Civilianization: bringing in military personnel, either active or retired, as civilians, without their rankings, allowing them to, in theory, operate outside of the constraints of the military agenda and values;
- Relocation: transferring between units of the government civil servants whose specialty may prove valuable;
- Outsourcing: means hiring specialists under temporary contracts to fill specific requirements in the organization.

It is worth noting that all occupation options must accompany an effort to mold a permanent professional staff responsible for acting on the MD. This professional body must present specific characteristics to minimize and possibly eliminate disputes (Cleary & McConville, 2006).

Several authors stress the vital importance of creating a civilian labor body to act in the National Defense. Barany (2012) highlights the need for civilian experts to formulate defense policies, as they can collaborate and understand the military in developing these. Cleary and McConville (2006) point to the permanent civil body as a critical element of civilian control. Bruneau and Tollefson (2006) emphasize the need for civilian professionals capable of supporting the military effort, highlighting tasks related to the field of defense which require civil expertise. Furthermore, the civilians must be able to interact with the military, as pointed out by Serra & Bush (2010), for whom "Civilian control must involve military themselves as much as is possible."

About Brazil

In Brazil, Defense issues are inauspicious in academia and politics, a legacy of the 21 dictatorial years; thus, attention paid to CMR is limited (Brustolin, 2014; Winnand & Saint-Pierre, 2010). In this context, the constitutional prerogative of Civilian control receives scant attention, disregarding its significance for national defense (Amorim Neto & Acacio, 2021). Brazil's 1990s Defense policy inherited from the dictatorship period featured full military autonomy, completely disregarding coordination between the three forces and political guidance (Marques, 2003; Jenne & Martinez, 2021; Lima et al., 2021). Consequently, the defense agenda was frequently and widely divergent from national political interests, hindering the international insertion process and forcing, in 1999, the creation of the MD, a civil institution responsible for implementing mechanisms of control over the Military (Oliveira, 2004; Zaverucha, 2006).

Zaverucha (2006) states that the choice of General Benedito Onofre Leonel to carry out the task of structuring the MD showed that, despite being an instance of civil power, the ministry would have military shading in a process "neither clear and linear nor without contradictions" (Fuccille, 2006).

In Brazil, institutional relations changes, particularly hierarchical ones, happen slowly. The MD's military structural presence and nature are evidence of said slowness, an institution supposedly responsible for civilian supremacy retaining a militarized structure and demeanor. Other pieces of evidence are the differential treatment met by the armed forces, such as retirement policy, special military tribunals, distinguished academic institutions, and constantly expanding spending, all remnants of the transition to democracy (Castro & D'Araújo, 2000; Martínez et al., 2013; Oliveira, 2004; Zaverucha & Rezende, 2009; Zaverucha, 2006).

Though democracy in Brazil can still be considered a recent phenomenon, the country seems to have established democratic control (L. Cleary & McConville, 2006). Brazilian democracy is part of the third wave of democratization (Huntington, 1991). The re-democratization process was completed in 1989 and has been stable for 32 years.

Increasing interest over defense is expressed in the National Defense Strategy (Brasil, 2012a) and associated with Brazil's growth on a global level; still, civilians' lack of preparation and interest in the subject is a constant source of conflict with the AFs. While this shows a transformation in national planning (Martínez, D'Araújo, Rial, & Salomón, 2013), it does not reflect reality. Although promising, Brazil still suffers from timid and limited legislative activity regarding defense and many relegated issues (Amorim Neto, 2010). The limited attention given to defense concentrates on one crucial area, the budget. Budgetary control represents the primary mechanism used by the parliament to control the agenda, delegating everything else to the AFs.

The peaceful history of Brazil in Latin America is a crucial point of analysis on the low political incentive to discuss issues related to national defense. Classified by Thomas Bruneau (2013) and Pion-Berlin (2005), though fragile and endowed with little attention, the debate on defense has expanded and gathered strength in the Latin American academic circles. In Brazil, we have evidence of increasing academic interest in the subject, and we can, by analyzing the MD servants, verify that we already have academic experts on defense-related subjects working in the area.

Also important to note is that despite the growing interest, the training of experts, as described by Zoltan Barany (2012), depends on key elements still missing in their institutional training. Although the eyes of the academia have already turned to the debate (Bruneau & Tollefson, 2014) and professionals specialized in the subject have emerged, an institutional effort from the MD is still necessary. It needs to train and absorb these professionals more adequately.

Brazil still figures in the list of countries identified by Pion-Berlin and Trinkunas (2007) as countries with "Attention Deficit" to national defense. Despite the effort to establish the MD and increasing institutionalization of elements, such as the National Strategy (Brasil, 2012a), the National Policy (Brasil, 2011), and the White Book of Defense (Brasil, 2012b), Brazil still fails to produce knowledge and interest about its defense system. In addition, the management of defense in Brazil undergoes differential treatment regarding parliamentary control. Defense is a foreign environment for National Congress's control mechanisms (Zaverucha & Rezende, 2009).

Civil-military relations makeup part of the interaction between two components of society and influence the country's Defense folder strategic development (Egnell, 2009). However, conflicts that stand out in this relationship mainly arise from the interaction between institutions. Thus, CMR focuses on institutionalizing this relationship (Cleary and McConville, 2006).

In Brazil, institutional relations changes, particularly hierarchical ones, happen slowly. Another critical point, the highly-trained military body has difficulty dealing with the newly introduced civilian elements. Military officers, which have dedicated their lives preparing for their work, are reticent of civilians' adequacy to deal with defense issues. Civilian integration happens by creating and imposing new institutions and reporting structures on the military, compounding the distrust of their adequacy to the task and whether civilians are on their side. Furthermore, there is little incentive in and out of military academies to prepare professionals to operate in these new conditions, both civilians and military alike (Winnand & Saint-Pierre, 2010).

Different questions regarding the creation and occupation of the ministry emerge. However, the MD plays a crucial role in reducing the armed forces' autonomy and political influence. In addition, the timid parliamentary concern and relative failure to discuss and manage the agenda intensifies military skepticism of civil servants' occupation and training (Lima et al., 2021; Cortinhas & Vitelli, 2021; Pimenta, 2014).

The defense ministry limits the military's autonomy, which generates discomfort and discontent; civil institutions assume bureaucratic hierarchies to facilitate the transition, apparently simplifying the military understanding of this new structure (Cleary and McConville, 2006). This simplification is a double-edged sword, as the military may abuse their knowledge of the bureaucratic structure to prevent civilians from taking complete control. Today, the military performs most missions and projects independently, as Amorim Neto and Acacio (2021) pointed out. In Brazil, we have the new institutions seeking the ideal means of operation and adapting their tools to the agenda's needs interacting with the already established armed forces, which have *modi operandi* and *habitus* well-defined, and highly qualified components to operate within these parameters.

In Brazil, the occupation of the MD suffers from a combination of harmful factors. Latin America remains a mostly peaceful region, and the primarily idle military is constantly trusted to perform other security-related tasks and many unrelated tasks such as infrastructure and social service provisions (Pion-berlin, 2005; Jenne & Martinez, 2021; Lima et al., 2021). One of these tasks is the occupation of the ministry seats that go beyond the exclusively military seats (Cortinhas & Vitelli, 2021). This occupation tendency limits the MD's capacity to perform its objectives of imposing civilian control and reducing disputes between the forces (Winnand & Saint-Pierre, 2010). Many authors understand that these conditions inside the MD only ensure budgetary control over the military, as the armed forces retain widespread autonomy and are a crucial influence in policymaking (Amorim Neto & Acacio, 2021). For many authors, these conditions keep the military as a constant threat to democracy in Brazil (Jenne & Martinez, 2021; Cortinhas & Vitelli, 2021).

To overcome these challenges, the professional body of the Ministry of Defense demands features typical of the other ministries and some distinctive elements. This professional body must fit the Weberian bureaucratic administration in Brazil, following five core principles: legality, impersonality, morality, publicity, formality, impartiality, and efficiency[2], ensuring public administration characteristics that frequently conflict with military activity. Other features, such as training and stability (tenure), are core elements as they lower the civil servant's susceptibility to political pressures.

A few notions have influenced all public administration in Brazil since its origins (Motta, 2007; Nunes, 1997). They are corporatism, clientelism, personalism, bureaucratic insulation, and procedures universalism. The Ministry of Defense, susceptible to the influence of these principles, is a constant target of reforms to modernize its bureaucratic structure (Lustosa, 2008), and its professional body must mature to deal with these elements daily.

Corporatism is the natural tendency interest groups have to control resources and procedures for self-benefit. Inside the State, this tendency translates into structural capture interest groups that occupy key positions inside the organization to determine the dynamics for resource usage (Nunes, 1997). Inside the MD, it represents the control of resources by the military, familiar with the field and with the structure they occupy seats that guarantee more extensive autonomy and control.

Clientelism uses resources to generate a dependency relationship created by exchanging resources and services (Nunes, 1997). In the case of public service, it influences the dynamics between interest groups, those who control resources vs. those who need them. For the defense ministry, interest groups, particularly the military ones, may manage resources and use them to make other interest groups unable to perform independently.

2 As defined by article 37 of the Brazilian constitution.

Personalism happens when professional decisions follow personal interests. Inside public administration, this phenomenon overcomes the public interest and frequently legality to favor personal connections between servants (Nunes, 1997). In the MD, personalism emerges in the occupation and appointment of individuals, especially former military, to occupy DAS seats.

Bureaucratic insulation is a characteristic of highly technical services (Nunes, 1997; Subirats, 2006). The high skill and knowledge of the workers make them less susceptible to influence from other interest groups who lack such skills, making the institution opaque. This phenomenon prevents political influence and oversight from external institutions, such as congress. In the case of the MD, it goes further since the military workers may use their technical skills and field advantage to difficult the understanding and oversight of other servants inside the ministry.

Procedure's universalism determines that interactions inside public institutions are understood and replicable by any individual or interest group, as their legal-rational norms are formal and public (Nunes, 1997). This characteristic goes against corporatism, as the formal norms are explicit and available to all actors. Inside the MD, procedures universalism seems to benefit the pre-established workforce. Newcomers, mainly civilians, have difficulty adjusting to the routine, and military understanding of procedures makes their presence circumventable.

Building a career that meets the MD's needs is a struggle with low-interest levels, lack of familiarity with society and rulers, limited knowledge on the subject, and few professionals prepared to work in the defense field (Pion-Berlin, 2005a). Permeated with unique features, this field needs officials prepared for such an exercise. The first necessary step is creating interest and producing knowledge about defense (L. Cleary & McConville, 2006; Pion-Berlin, 2009). Literature has concluded that effective control mechanisms over the military beyond budget restrictions require greater social and governmental interest (Bruneau, Matei, & Sakoda, 2009; Pion-Berlin, 2009). If society and the government are not familiar or have a shallow comprehension of a topic, their interest will remain limited. Thus, more knowledge about defense must be available to increase the understanding and deepen social and governmental interest.

Methodology

This research employs a combination of different qualitative tools both in data collection and analysis. Two primary data sources were available, given the target of contrasting official rhetoric and field reality. The first source was archives and official documents that reflected the official rhetoric, including statements from armed forces and government representatives. The second source was *in loco* interviews with the ministry's civil servants, which was crucial to outline the reality of the field perceived by those in it.

Through archival and literature research, I identified the fundamental concepts about the field: effectiveness, relevance, presence, occupation, interaction, integration, and coordination. The analysis allowed me to construct the inquisitive framework with which I would approach the research object.

The official data collected details servers' distribution inside the ministry's structure. According to positions, education, and age, initial comparisons between military and civilians allow theorization regarding responsibilities' distribution in the MD that contradicts official rhetoric and encourages the search for qualitative information over field reality.

Encouraged by the initial contradiction, I conducted preliminary interviews with military officers and political appointees of the MD, which led to reformulated parameters, then consolidated in a script with open questions. The literature widely portrays the vision and military perceptions about reality, and the preliminary round reinforced that assessment; thus, interviews following the revised parameters had exclusively civilian participation. The modified parameters are training, capacity building, co-existence, and participation. I applied the script in semi-structured interviews with civil servants occupying DAS positions in the MD selected by accessibility (Flick, Kardoff, & Steinke, 2004).

The initial analysis followed the themes addressed by the short script; subsequent analysis then used empirical saturation to identify and isolate issues arising throughout the interview process (Bardin, 1979; Vergara, 2006). The interviews followed the general conditions defined by Thiry-Cherques (2009):

1. Interviews were conducted secluded and privately;

2. The participants did not know each other's answers;
3. The questions adhered to consistent domain knowledge.

Bellow, I discuss the research results and the conclusions they lead.

Discussion

Evidence gathered during the interviews shows how civilians perceive themselves in the MD, while quantitative evidence allowed to describe the ministry's workforce in numerical terms, comparing the number of civilians and military who work in the ministry, according to official reports. Since the MD's inauguration in 1999, the official rhetoric promoted by several administrations places high confidence in civilian control over the military. Many politicians and military officials assert that the Brazilian military works with the government to promote Brazil's best interest and that civilians control the decision-making process in the government and inside the ministry[3].

The political and institutional movements observed since the establishment of the ministry until Michel Temer's administration increased, on paper, civilian powers[4]. Several instances and progressive changes reinforced the belief that Brazil moved towards a fully consolidated civilian control over the military. Notably, the longstanding tenure of minister Nelson Jobim, from 2007 to 2011, represented at the time the stable presence of an experienced civilian in the office. Jobim also represented an active voice in favor of civilian control, often mediating and controlling conflicts and criticisms targeting the MD[5].

Other examples of the perceived progress of civilian control: 1) the establishment of the joint staff of the armed forces, perceived as a conflict suppressor

---

3 Barros, Alexandre. Saudades de Itamar e Hargreaves. *O Estado de São Paulo*. Disponível em: https://advance.lexis.com/api/document?collection=news&id=urn:contentItem:7X91-WXT0-YC5N-315G-00000-00&context=1516831. September 15, 2009.

4 Monteiro, Tânia. Governo Lula quer dar poder de polícia às Forças Armadas. *O Estado de São Paulo*. https://advance.lexis.com/api/document?collection=news&id=urn:contentItem:7X91-WY60-YC5N-310C-00000-00&context=1516831. November 6, 2009.

5 Jobim chama de "ridículas" críticas a Lula. *O Globo* (Brazil). https://advance.lexis.com/api/document?collection=news&id=urn:contentItem:51WV-NBW1-JD87-S01J-00000-00&context=1516831. January 8, 2011.

between the forces[6]; 2) legislative efforts to regulate internal subsidiary missions of the armed forces[7]; 3) the establishment of formal civil oversight over military ranking promotions[8]; 4) Celso Amorim nomination as a minister in 2011. These and many other examples were used in interviews, in the ministry corridors, and in different instances to reinforce the notion that civilian control was established over the military. Several politicians and political analysts praised the nomination of Celso Amorim as a particular signal that civilians were in control over the military in Brazil[9]. In conversations and interviews with high-ranking military officers inside the Army Command and General Staff School (ECEME) becomes clear that the rhetoric is embedded and present; generals, colonels, and lieutenant-colonels alike assert that the armed forces are subservient and under civilian control[10].

However, the data gathered beyond the rhetoric analysis casts doubt over those statements given the significantly smaller presence of civilians and how much influence the civilians have in that process. The MD is a component of the Federal Executive branch of government. It was created in1999 and represented a fundamental part in developing and implementing projects of national interest. (Oliveira, 2004; Zaverucha, 2006). It centralizes decision-making processes of the Defense agenda, previously divided among four military ministries: Air Force, Army, Navy, and Military House. The restructuring of National Defense aimed to equalize the interest of the military and civilians (de Oliveira, 2004). The military government's repression of opposing sectors built a scenario of mistrust and misunderstandings between the military and political sectors. That did not prevent their active participation in the development of MD, even defining its outlines (Fuccille, 2006; Zaverucha, 2006). Figure 1 evidences the military outlines described by Zaverucha (2006).

---

6 Defesa reforçada. *O Globo* (Brazil). https://advance.lexis.com/api/document?collection=news&id=urn:contentItem:7WPG-FSY1-2S4G-M02S-00000-00&context=1516831. September 12, 2009.

7 O emprego das Forças Armadas. *O Estado de São Paulo*. https://advance.lexis.com/api/document?collection=news&id=urn:contentItem:7X91-WYW1-2SPK-C1CN-00000-00&context=1516831. November 11, 2009.

8 Monteiro, Tânia. Militares aceitam maior presença do poder civil nas Forças Armadas. *O Estado de São Paulo*. https://advance.lexis.com/api/document?collection=news&id=urn:contentItem:7X91-WY60-YC5N-3216-00000-00&context=1516831. November 7, 2009.

9 Lula elogia nomeação de Celso Amorim e diz que ele é um "homem de Estado". *Correio Braziliense*. https://www.correiobraziliense.com.br/app/noticia/politica/2011/08/06/interna_politica,264299/lula-elogia-nomeacao-de-celso-amorim-e-diz-que-ele-e-um-homem-de-estado.shtml. 6 ago. 2011.

10 Interviews conducted in 2013 during the Operational Strategic Planning Exercise (EPEO).

Figure 1
Organizational Chart (2021)

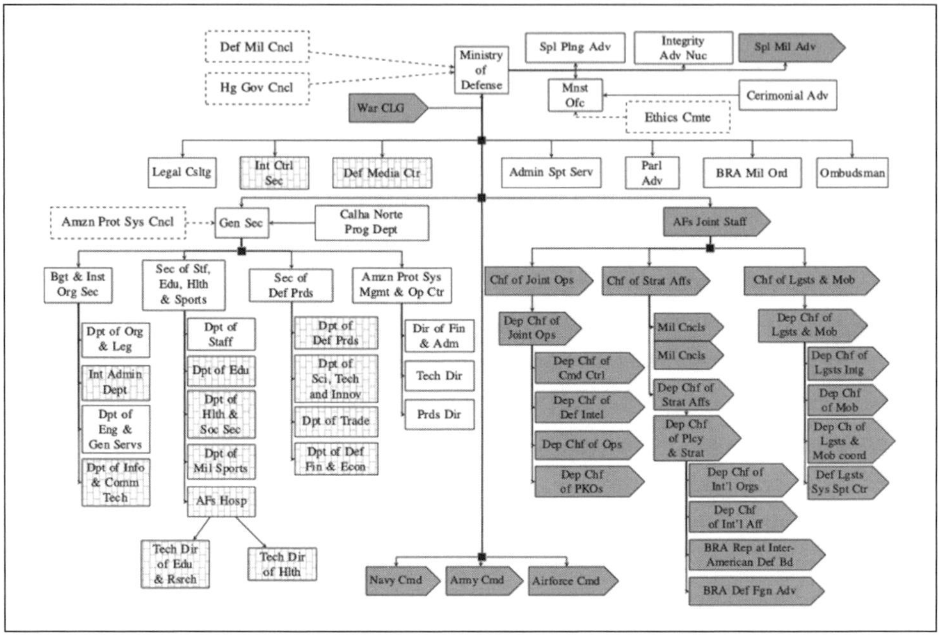

Source: Simplified representation elaborated by the author based on <https://www.gov.br/estrutura/file/organograma>.

This image shows the updated division of the MD's subunits, emphasizing the origins of the unit's leader through shape and fill; this allows for a deeper understanding of power distribution in the organization. Cells' colors and vertical and horizontal placement indicate leadership, civilian or military nature, and proximity to policy decision-making or implementation.

The structure is color-coded: white cells are civilian-led, gray and brick-patterned are military. It stems from the minister's cabinet at the top and connects directly to the commands reflecting the intention behind the organization to submit the military to civilian control and oversight. The chart branches display an intended division on two sides civilians on the left headed by the General Secretary and military on the right under the armed forces joint staff. The rectangular nodes are civilian in nature, meaning that the attributions and roles of that unit are related to public administration rather than military activity and in theory should be performed by civil servants. The arrow-like nodes are military in nature, meaning that their activities are directly connected to routine military activity such as resource and troop management, and thus should be performed by the military.

Another relevant aspect of the chart is that the cell's position indicates how close each unit is to policymaking, cells located higher on the chart are closer to political decision-making, and those closer to the bottom are consequently more involved with implementation. Given this structure, it is possible for interest groups that are not part of policymaking to still hold significant influence over implementation.

Organizational chart analysis shows that military officials occupy leadership positions more frequently than civilians. Some cells are naturally occupied by the military, especially on the right side of the chart, as they are part of the military side of the organization; however, the military occupies their posts and occupy seats that civilians should occupy. Departments that would allow for direct civilian oversight over budget, innovation, technology, education, and trade are currently occupied by the military. Furthermore, retired military officers appear as civilians on the chart, reducing the *de facto* civilian occupation (Pimenta, 2014; Cortinhas & Vitelli, 2021). Thus, when we observe the significant presence of the military in the lower cells of the chart, including the bottom left, we understand that the military has a strong influence over the policy implementation process. This form of institutional capture gives the false impression that civilians have complete control over military policy since they hold the leading positions closer to decision-making but allow for the implementation according to the military's wishes.

Figure 2 shows the occupation of seats in the MD between 2011 and 2021. The top line (•) represents the total number of units, the second line (▲) shows the number of units run by active military, the third (■) shows units labeled as run by civilians, and the fourth (♦) shows units occupied by *de facto* civilians.

The data shows two attention-grabbing trends in the period. First, the MD structure has grown 32.6%, from 46 in 2011 to 61 seats in 2021. The growth on paper makes this structure more robust. Second, though labeled civilian occupation fluctuates between 41% in 2011 and 37% in 2021 of available seats, the civilian *de facto* occupation has decreased from 39% in 2011 to only 27% in 2021. The number of retired military officers acting as civilians, which increased from 5.5% at the beginning of the period to 26% of civilian seats by the end, explains this trend.

These occupation trends are particularly significant in the MD. As friction between civilian and military and within military groups permeates the ministry's daily routine balancing its actors' interests and practices is a fundamental institutional challenge (Fuccille, 2006; de Oliveira, 2004; Zaverucha, 2006).

Figure 2 – Unit Leadership Occupation in Absolute Numbers (2011-2021)

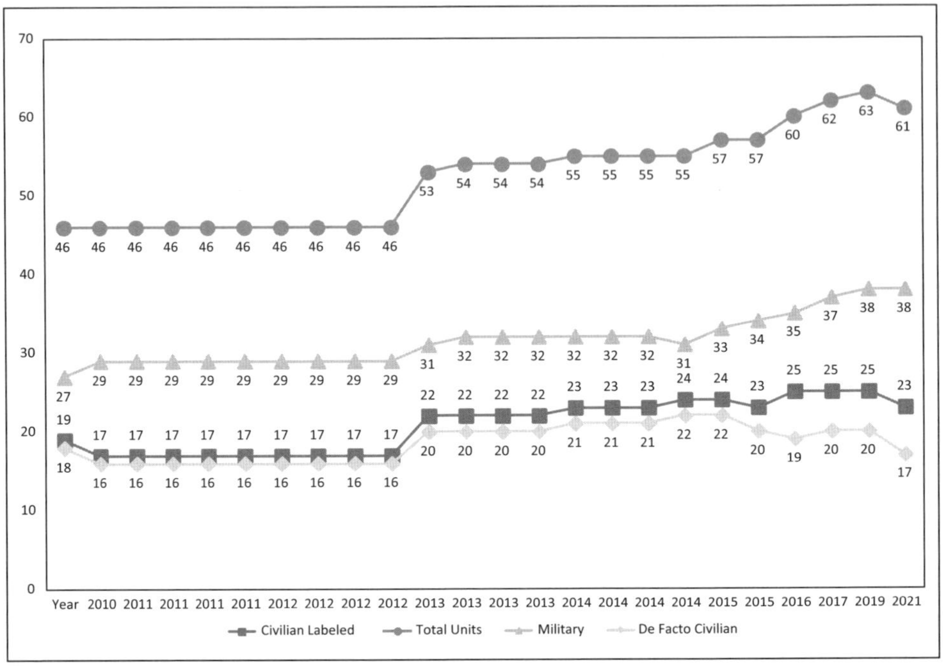

Source: Elaborate by the author based on decrees 7.476, 7.974, 8.978, 9.570, and 2011-2021 Organizational charts available on < https://www.portaltransparencia.gov.br>.

Seats' distribution influences resource disputes and may reflect prestige within the political sector. For example, in 2013, a reform of the structure of the MD increased by seven the number of units[11], out of which four were controlled by *de facto* civilians, which marked the administration's effort to reinforce the civilian aspect of the institution. Thus, today's dwindling numbers of *de facto* civilian seats may reflect further decreasing attention to defense from politicians and a weakening civilian control over the military.

Attention deficit to defense is a characteristic common to most, if not all, political parties in Brazil (Pion-Berlin 2005; Winnand & Saint-Pierre, 2010; Cortinhas & Vitelli, 2021). However, the decrease in *de facto* civilian occupation in the MD began to further decrease in 2017 with the appointment of the first

11 The units created by the April 1st, 2013, decree 7.476 were 1) Ombudsman, 2) Logistics Deputy, 3) General Secretariat, 4) Calha Norte Program Department, 5) Personnel, 6) Information Technology, and 7) Pandiá Calógeras Institute.

military defense minister, Gen. Joaquim Silva e Luna. The declining tendency intensified in 2018 consequence of a political strategy implemented by Pres. Jair Bolsonaro, a former army captain, increased military participation in the government well beyond defense[12] (Amorim Neto & Pimenta, 2020).

It is essential to comment that the subunits' independence characterizes the holding structure adopted in the ministry. This structure favors the integration and dissemination of knowledge between subunits while allowing and amplifying cultural clashes (Azeredo, 2012). Particularly in the MD, Priscilla Azeredo (2012) points out that public administration's conflict of interest and political influence remains significant due to the holding structure. Combined with the seat occupation trend, these characteristics paint a concerning picture. More military officers occupying units further expand military culture in the institution. Given the amplified nature of cultural disputes in this setting, it may negatively impact the institution's civilian control and cooperation.

The installed structure restricts external interference, and the budget becomes the primary tool for external control. Featuring currently a total of R$82 Billion – approximately US$14.5 Billion – the MD budget is among the seven most significant in the country. Figure 3 shows how expenditures make up this amount: management 59.7%, social security 24%, projects 13.73%, foreign debt 1.68%, and disaster relief fund 1.11%. It is possible to observe that management and social security costs take over 83.7% of the budget.

In the context of government expenditure, the defense budget figures are among the top 10 largest budgets[13] of the country, but the military frequently complains about budget constraints in developing its projects. A closer analysis reveals that 92.05% (●) of management expenditure goes to military expenditure, divided into 47.9% to personnel (✚) and 44.15% retirees/pensioners (▲), making AFs employees, retirees, and beneficiaries the most significant ministry expenditure, while civilians make up for less than 1% of this budget (■). Figure 4 details the increasing military personnel cost, reaching amounts higher than 45 billion Reais annually in 2021, and compares it to the civilian cost.

---

12 Bolsonaro uses the military as jacks of all trades, placing them in many different government seats in other areas, and putting into high gear the distancing of the military from their primary missions, identified by Pion-Berlin (2005).

13 According to government data defense budget usually starts the budget planning process (PLO) as the fifth largest but after cuts commonly figures as the seventh or eighth largest.

Figure 3
Budget Distribution 2021

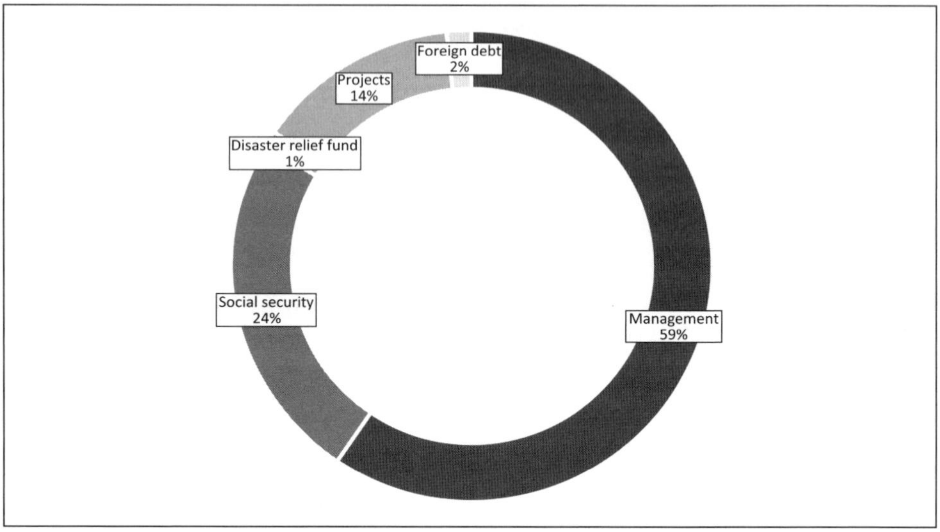

Source: Elaborated by the author based on data available at Portal da Transparência. <https://www.portaltransparencia.gov.br>

Figure 4
Personnel Expenditure in R$ Billions (2008-2021)

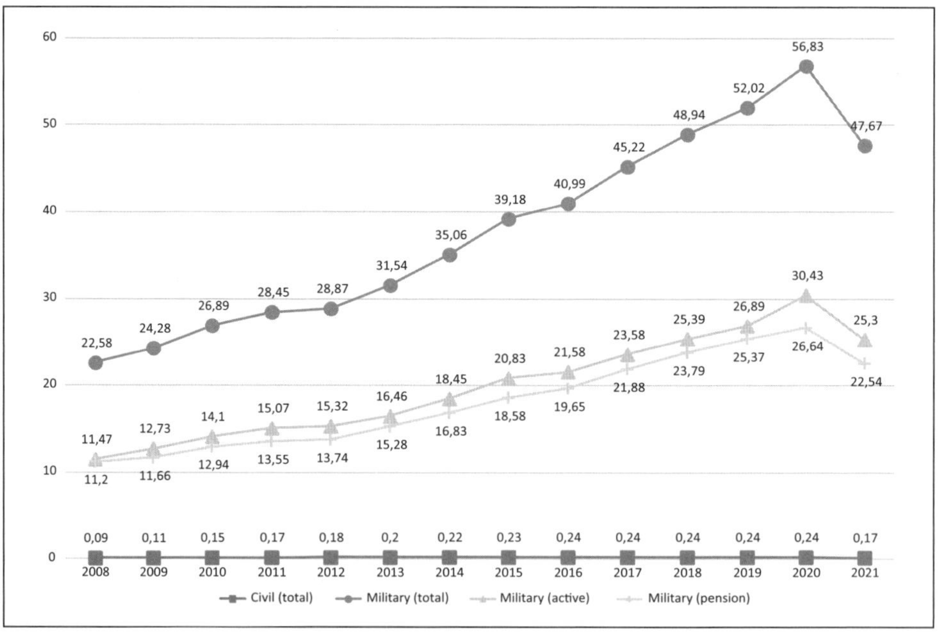

Source: Elaborated by the author based on Portal da Transparência. <https://www.portaltransparencia.gov.br>

The graph details the trends in personnel expenditures; there is a significant imbalance between civilian and military costs – the stark difference in absolute amounts echoes in the cost increase trends. While civilian spending has remained stable since 2008, military personnel increased by 111% in the same period. The personnel cost includes the military occupying seats inside the ministry.

The functions within the ministry, from technical to policy formulation and legislative proposals, are the responsibility of officials composing the workforce, consisting of civilian and military officials, outsourced contractors, and trainees. Remarkably, the representatives of the armed forces occupy 62.3% of positions, while civil servants account for only 37.7% of them[14]. The existence of exclusively military positions, especially in advisory bodies, explains, in part, the military superiority over civilians in the MD. Furthermore, active and retired military personnel frequently occupy civilian seats. Data about this occupation is difficult to gather; however, it is safe to assume that it follows the trend observed in figure 2, as military leaders frequently invite retired colleagues to work in their units.

Figure 5
Personnel Distribution (2008-2021)

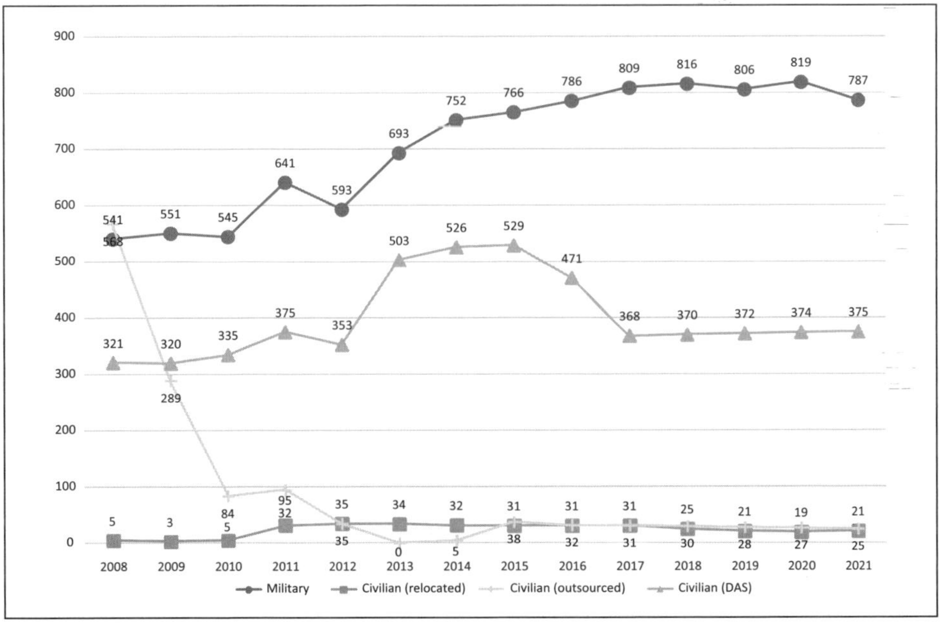

Source: Elaborated by the author based on data from Portal da Transparência. <https://www.portaltransparencia.gov.br>

14 Detailed on figure 2.

Among agencies of the Executive branch, the MD presents an exception. Throughout 15 years of existence, no servers' public procurement took place. Therefore, the workforce, thus, consists of requested military, relocated civilian servants, and outsourced personnel that fit the distribution of seats in figure 2[15].

On figure 5, we observe the number of individuals employed inside the MD. The top line (•) represents the military employees. The second line represents the civilians hired for management and advisory seats (▲). The third and fourth lines reflect outsourced (✚) and relocated (■) civilians.

Analyzing workforce distribution helps to understand each group's influence in the MD. Another relevant component of the MD's workforce is the senior management and advisory (DAS) positions. These commissioned positions comprise most of the top ministerial administration, divided into six levels (level 1 being the lowest). Figure 5 shows that DAS positions make up nearly 90% of the civilian workforce; the remaining workers are public employees relocated from other ministries or outsourced with short-term contracts.

According to official reports and evidence gathered during the research, the civilian presence in the MD is extensive and spreads through the ministerial structure. However, evidence suggests this presence does not form a long-term work body, mainly containing public employees not permanently linked to the ministry. Simply put, civilian positions' occupation occurs through the mechanisms described in the literature as *civilianization, relocation,* and *outsourcing.* These mechanisms are viable options for the Defense institution that still needs time to build a permanent professional body, but they do not ensure civilian control. These occupation options are fundamentally limited in reach and effectiveness, bringing different advantages and challenges.

Civilianization is naturally the simplest yet most controversial option for civilian control; it brings reserve and retired military to occupy civilian seats. These are heavily trained and efficient workers who understand the institution's needs. However, due to their background and training, they are adept and replicate military culture, weakening civilian control.

Relocation is one option that brings in seasoned bureaucrats capable of efficiently maintaining and replicating procedures without expanding the insti-

15 Requested military may occupy, and appear as civilians in the charts, relocated and outsourced personnel are civilians and show as such on figures.

tution's military dominance. However, the lack of understanding of the field's requirements causes constant friction with the military officers and limits their capacity to oversee activities unique to defense, limiting civilian control over these.

On the other hand, outsourcing specialists bring in workers that comprehend the field and do not expand military culture. These workers, however, face some severe limitations inside the ministry stemming from their contracts' temporary nature. Their training on defense matters does not reflect direct knowledge of the internal processes of the ministry, making their adaptation slow. Combined with their high turnover, they form an unfamiliar group whose military counterparts do not trust and tend to exclude from decision-making processes until otherwise. The limited interactions with the military reduce the opportunities and overall quality of their contribution and dramatically impacts their capacity to oversee the military.

According to the evidence found in the interviews[16], the perceived presence of civilians in MD is extensive. Nonetheless, civilians themselves identify problems in that presence and recognize the need to create a Defense analyst career as part of the solution to these problems. The main problem identified was the presence of military reserve officers occupying DAS positions that civilians should occupy. While not degrading t he quality of the work, this presence delays the establishment of civilian control and strengthens the reproduction of a military logic within the institution.

According to the evidence, civil participation in the MD is constant. Despite not forming a permanent civil servant body, civilians have a voice and significant activity in developing guidelines and ministry projects. Two aspects negatively affect civil participation and control: the non-characterizing of a permanent body and the vast presence of the military. The fact that civilians do not form a permanent body limits their access to central planning elements and core activities of the MD, which affects the establishment of the control in the institution. At the same time, the presence of the military in positions that ought to be occupied by civilians generates friction coming from the clash of cultures of civil and military. Due to their more extensive numbers, the military ensures that their culture holds the upper hand, even if the environment permits establishing civilian control.

16 Interviews and technical visits conducted at the Ministry of Defense in August 2014.

Nonetheless, civil and military established cooperation. Despite the identified friction between cultures, decision-making and project participation exclude neither civilians nor military. Evidence points to a situation described in the literature, the Civil-Military Relations in the Ministry of Defense reached the point where both parties fulfill complementary roles. However, the military still performs civilian functions. There is no consensus among the servers on the existence of training programs offered by MD. While this fact alone demonstrates an inappropriate setting for establishing civilian control, this phenomenon begs further consideration.

All respondents have higher education degrees, and most have graduate degrees, which shows that a qualified workforce exists through individual effort. However, when questioned about the offer and the quality of training programs for matters related to national defense in the MD, servers tend to say that the courses offered are unsatisfactory and feature superficial content. That is when the training opportunities even appear. Most servers stated that training results from an individual push and the employee interested in preparing to perform better in the field has few incentives and support from the MD and ought to do it by themselves. All this analysis is done based on interviews conducted during the second Rousseff mandate; thus, we need to highlight that the situation has changed.

Since Michel Temer's administration, the military openly regained control over areas that had been, at least on paper, under civilian authority. In interviews conducted in 2021[17], former civil servants from the ministry expressed similar concerns present in the interviews conducted in 2014. Evidence shows that the military is even more present than in 2014, and civilians are mostly isolated in their units.

According to the 2021 interviews, it is common to see units divided between civilian and military groups that barely interact daily, an ominous sign of the deteriorating conditions inside the ministry. It was explained that the integration of both workgroups is possible if spearheaded by military authority, but civilians have a hard time introducing themselves in their units. According to one of the interviews, the initial communication between civilian newcomers and their

---

17 Interviews conducted online with five civilians who worked with and inside the ministry between 2017 and 2018.

military counterparts requires the intervention of higher-ups. If not instructed to do otherwise by superiors, military officers frequently ignore civilians' presence, e-mails, and calls in their units. This situation was not explicitly mentioned in any of the interviews in 2014.

No representatives of the Bolsonaro administration agreed to participate in interviews. However, looking at the civilian occupation's negative trends since the beginning of the administration – portrayed in figures 2 and 5 – it is safe to assume that civilians are losing ground. This trend is observable not only in the MD but in all areas of the government where the presence of military officers in civilian seats has increased exponentially[18][19].

Conclusion

Confronting evidence from the field with the official rhetoric and academic theories proved a fruitful exercise that highlighted several inconsistencies. The official discourse, supported by quantitative data reports, gives us the impression that Brazil has reached an advanced stage of civilian control and is slowly regressing. The military primarily acts as a national interest development tool but has slowly regained autonomy and political influence based on official rhetoric and data.

However, when we compare these elements with the empirical evidence obtained by visiting the MD, we observe the formation of a structure that allows civilian control over the Defense folder. This process is at an intermediate moment, the military does not have all of its previous prerogatives, but its autonomy has yet to reduce to ideal levels. By continuing to move forward in this process, Brazil will climb the ladder from *democratic control* to *civilian control* and, finally, to *civil control.*

As said before, Brazilian democracy is now 25 years old. Its consolidation process is, in some areas, still well underway. A crucial step in the democratic

18 Presença de militares em cargos civis mais que dobrou no governo Bolsonaro. *O Globo*. https://oglobo.globo.com/politica/presenca-de-militares-em-cargos-civis-mais-que-dobrou-no-governo-bolsonaro-25079165. June 27, 2021.

19 Marchesini, Lucas. Em 70 órgãos, militares ocupam 18,3% dos 14,6 mil cargos comissionados no governo Bolsonaro. Metrópoles. https://www.metropoles.com/brasil/em-70-orgaos-militares-ocupam-183-dos-146-mil-cargos-comissionados-no-governo-bolsonaro. August 1, 2021.

establishment process was the creation of MD in 1999, which partially established civilian control by extinguishing four military institutions and centering control of the folder in one institution with a civilian personality. However, looking beyond the macrostructure, we observe that the absence of the institution by a civilian bureaucratic body limits the reach of said control. When comparing the rhetoric adopted since 1999 by politicians and the military with the empirical evidence obtained by visiting the MD in 2014 and reinforced in 2021 by interviewing servants, we observe an apparent inconsistency. Though the structure that should promote civilian control over the military exists, it fails to do so. Civilian occupation is limited to suboptimal levels, and it is also restricted to less relevant units, frequently being kept out of hierarchically relevant positions and excluded from operationally pertinent units.

The discourse publicized and repeated in the corridors of the MD claims that having a civilian ministry and large civilian worker basis grants the institution civilian control. Since 2016, three generals have occupied the seat subsequently, but the rhetoric did not change. In a closer analysis, we observe that military individuals permeate the civilian structure and reproduce the logic they embraced and nourished from their academy days onwards; the respect of these officers for the institution is unquestionable, as is their ability to work inside it. It is necessary to differentiate control effectiveness from work effectiveness. Evidence of military presence puts civilian control in question. However, the quality of work performed by these officers is high, and their technical expertise is highlighted several times by their civilian counterparts.

When we analyze the *habitus*[20] of the field, military logic takes over. There are apparent attempts to repeat military practices on MD's routine and several adaptations of the structure to match military logic. We can identify this adaptation by observing the existence of Ministry insignias – pins with multicolored letters MD –, which identify the levels of positions held, which is a logical repetition of military stars, immediately identifying individual hierarchy.

Despite the evident hierarchical logic, the MD environment was at some point cooperative and allowed the free exchange of ideas between civil and military officials, but this seems to have been lost recently. The most significant limitation in this area is the restricted debate between military individuals since they must

20 Bourdieu, Pierre. *Outline of a Theory of Practice*. Cambridge University Press, 1977.

follow the hierarchical path. Their extensive presence in the formal structure, the strict adherence to hierarchy, and the protection of military interests set the corporatist tone frequent in Brazilian public administration (Nunes, 1997), curbing civil contribution to the field without openly marginalizing it.

Two other features of public administration that alter the field are bureaucratic insulation and procedures' universalism. The insulation, in defense, is justified by the specific nature of the subject and the demand for specific technical knowledge. It also impacts the budget control and development of projects, given that the MD disputes resources with other areas of the federal executive branch. The peculiar defense issues wrapped in mechanisms and procedures that address equitably different agendas within the federal administration reflect on procedures universalism. This equalitarian treatment halts the Defense analyst's career creation, claiming that specific scope public competitions are not related to the State's objective.

After carefully observing empirical data, this chapter points out that civilian control has advanced in Brazil until 2016 but has partially regressed since then. Problems such as the dispute between forces, military culture, and civilian disinterest remain since before MD's inauguration; others, like culture clashes, emerge from the close interactions inside the MD.

Considering the holding structure described by Azeredo (2012), which favors the autonomy of the subsidiary bodies, then civilian control still needs other mechanisms to advance further and settle.

The MD as an institution fulfills clear objectives, mainly signaling the country's commitment to democracy internationally. Despite being subject to harmful elements of public administration and the dynamism of the political landscape, the MD has an undeniable contribution to the democratic balance, demonstrating institutional resilience, which is critical to the continuity of this phenomenon.

Returning to the initial objective of this work, we have that civilian presence in MD plays a limited role in Brazil. This article aimed to clarify the civilian perception of their participation in the MD, analyzing it from the perspective of the occupation, hierarchy positioning, and performance. The search for control over the National Defense agenda has advanced significantly until 2016, contributing to the country's development goals and international integration. This process has unquestionable institutional and democratic stability, fundamental points of agreement in the literature, and elements that can contribute to establishing effective and stable, civilian control. However, the limited reach observed in all aspects and the recent regressions caused by the Bolsonaro policies place Brazil further from that goal.

In contact with the literature, this evidence allows discussion of topics pointed by David Pion-Berlin (2007; 2005), as the little attention given to Defense in Latin America. There is still a low level of interest in Brazil given to the theme, as highlighted by Amorim Neto (2010). However, in this study, it was observed that there are efforts to change this, and the topic has begun to occupy a prominent place in the national political debate. There is a growing interest in the case, with the creation and expansion of graduate programs and research support on issues related to defense nationwide. We can say that there is a constant reduction in the attention deficit described and debated by Bruneau (2005) and Pion-Berlin (2007; 2005a). This growing interest in the topic has led to new specialists likely composing the body of leading experts described by Barany (2012) and Cleary and McConville (2006). It is fitting to emphasize that the training of civil servants is *necessary* but not *sufficient* to establish civilian control.

This chapter points out that the establishment of civilian control processes observed in Brazil has different elements that influence the development of the ministry. As described in this research, the establishment of civilian control still needs to resume its advance. To prevent the reversion of critical milestones reached in political disputes and divergences of interests between civilian and military, leading authors such as Bruneau and Tollefson (2014) and D'Araújo and Castro (2000) consider the Brazilian democracy as consolidated.

In Brazil, we have evidence of increasing scholarly interest in the subject, and we can, by analyzing the MD servants, verify that we already have academic experts on defense-related topics working in the area.

This research has shown that civilians inside the ministry are crucial. However, there are ongoing civil professional body civilians who represent active roles in their respective agencies. This presence tends mainly to dissolve the military monopoly on the Defense folder, reducing, even if slowly, their influence. The constant reduction in the percentage of GDP allocated to military spending illustrated that fact, as pointed out by Amorim Neto (2014).

The civilian presence and other initiatives, such as the White Book of National Defense, that once showed the executive and legislature's increasing attention to the topic (Bruneau & Tollefson, 2014) have been steadily subverted by increasing opacity of the defense agenda and expanded presence of the military. Changes that have occurred in Brazilian defense that ruled out the military as a threat to the institutions of the democratic regime (Amorim Neto, 2014) have been frequently challenged. The MD has demonstrated a resilient presence while constant anti-democratic pressure keeps the military in line with the regime.

This research approaches National Defense optimistically, seen as a process heading towards establishing civilian control and cooperation between civil and military. I believe that a steady increase in interest in the topic in the country, going in the opposite direction observed by Bruneau (2005) and approaching the depiction of Pion-Berlin (2005) and Bruneau and Tollefson (2014).

We can see that the Ministry of Defense as an institution has partially advanced its civilian control-building process and encouraged the defense debate in Brazil. The MD needs to become more robust, and many advances still need to occur. In contrast with Chile, whose ministry is vastly occupied by civilians, a lot still needs to be done. However, in contrast with some of its other neighbors, it made significant progress. Brazil's MD is the youngest Defense institution in LA, thirty-four years younger than the Colombian MD, built in 1965 (Donadio & Tibiletti, 2014). Thus, it is natural that many adjustments still need to happen.

Finally, despite the insipient training and the reproduction of military logic, the civilian presence and contribution to defense were active and participatory for a long time. Furthermore, the defense agenda's national relevance has expanded. Such conditions tend to encourage the strengthening and adaptation of the civilian control process the country's needs.

References

ALLISON, G. T.; ZELIKOW, P. *Essence of Decision:* Explaining the Cuban Missile Crisis. Boston: Little, Brown, 2nd ed., New York: Longman, 1999.

ALMEIDA, P. de. Estratégia Nacional de Defesa: comentários dissidentes. *Boletim Meridiano 47*. 2010. Retrieved from http://www.ecsbdefesa.com.br/defesa/fts/ENDCD.pdf.

AMORIM NETO, O. O papel do Congresso nas questões de defesa: entre a abdicação e o comprometimento. In: JOBIM, N.; ETCHEGOYEN, S. W.;

ALSINA JÚNIOR, J. P. S. (eds.), *Segurança internacional:* perspectivas brasileiras. Rio de Janeiro: FGV Editora, 2010.

________. Democracy, Civil-Military Relations and Defense Policy in Brazil. *APSA 2012 Annual Meeting Paper*. 2012. Retrieved from http://papers.ssrn.com/sol3/papers.cfm?abstract_id=2110718.

________. Democracia e relações civis-militares no Brasil. In: AVELAR, L.; CINTRA, A. O. (eds.), *Sistema Político Brasileiro:* uma introdução. 3rd ed., 2014, p. 315-30. Rio de Janeiro: Fundação Konrad Adenauer. Retrieved from http://www.encontroabcp2014.cienciapolitica.org.br/resources/anais/14/1409780251_ARQUIVO_AmorimNeto-DemocracyandCivil-MilitaryRelationsinBrazil-ABCP2014.pdf.

________; ACACIO, I. P. *One Step Forward, One Step Back:* The Impact of the Defense Ministry on Defense Policymaking in Brazil (1999-2020). LASA. 2021.

________; PIMENTA, G. A. The First Year of Bolsonaro in Office: Same Old Story, Same Old Song? *Revista de Ciência Política*, 40(2), 2020, p. 187-213.

AZEREDO, P. G. de. *Vantagens e desvantagens da estrutura de holding na administração pública: um estudo de caso do Ministério da Defesa*. Fundação Getulio Vargas, 2012.

BARANY, Z. *The Soldier and the Changing State: Building Democratic Armies in Africa, Asia, Europe and the Americas.* 1st ed., Princeton: Princeton University Press. 2012.

BARDIN, L. *Análise de conteúdo*. (LA Reto & A. Pinheiro, trad.). São Paulo: Edições 70, 1979.

BARROS, Alexandre. Saudades de Itamar e Hargreaves. *O Estado de São Paulo*. Retrieved from https://advance.lexis.com/api/document?collection=news&id=urn:contentItem:7X91-WXT0-YC5N-315G-00000-00&context=1516831. September 15, 2009.

BOURDIEU, Pierre. *Outline of a Theory of Practice*. Cambridge University Press, 1977.

BRASIL. *Política Nacional de Defesa*. 1st ed., Brasília: Ministério da Defesa.

________. *Estratégia Nacional de Defesa*. 1st ed., Brasília: Ministério da Defesa, 2012a.

________. *Livro Branco de Defesa Nacional*. 1st ed., Brasília: Ministério da Defesa, 2012b.

________. Ministério da Defesa, despesas do órgão: execução orçamentária e financeira. 2021. Retrieved from https://www.portaltransparencia.gov.br/orgaos-superiores/52000-ministerio-da-defesa.

BRUNEAU, T. C. Civil-Military Relations in Latin America: The Hedgehog and the Fox Revisited. *Fuerzas Armadas Y Sociedad*, 19(1-2), 2005, p. 111-131.

________. Policy Issues Civilians and the Military in Latin America: The Absence of Incentives. *Latin American Politics and Society*, 55(4), 2013, p. 143-160. Doi:10.1111/j.1548-2456.2013.00216.x.

________; MATEI, F. C.; SAKODA, S. National Security Councils: Their Potential Functions in Democratic Civil-Military Relations. *Defense & Security Analysis*, 25(3), 2009, p. 255-269. Doi:10.1080/14751790903201406.

________; & TOLLEFSON, S. D. (eds.). *Who Guards the Guardians and How Democratic Civil Military Relations*. 1st ed., Austin: University of Texas Press, 2006.

________. Civil-Military Relations in Brasil: A Reassessment. *Journal of Politics in Latin America*, 2, 2014, p. 107-138.

BRUSTOLIN, V. M. Dimensões e aplicacões do Orçamento de Defesa do Brasil/Dimensions and executions of the Defense Budget of Brazil. *Mural Internacional*, 5(1), 2014, p. 38-45. Doi:10.12957/rmi.2013.8372.

CASTRO, C.; D'ARAÚJO, M. *Democracia e forças armadas no Cone Sul*. Rio de Janeiro: Fundação Getulio Vargas. 2000. Retrieved from http://bibliotecadigital.fgv.br/dspace/handle/10438/6730.

CLEARY, L.; MCCONVILLE, T. (eds.). *Managing Defence in a Democracy*. 1st ed., London & New York: Routledge, 2006. Retrieved from http://books.google.com/books?hl=en&lr=&id=X6gA5CxcvcIC&oi=fnd&pg=PT5&dq=Managing+Defence+in+a+Democracy&ots=7OKL57rMZJ&sig=o-jEX2WW1LIuZWEdw_ig2wci5UoQ.

COHEN, E. A. Civil-military Relations. *Orbis*, 41(2), 1997, p. 177-186. Doi:10.1016/S0030-4387(97)90061-2.

________. *Supreme Command*. 1st ed., New York: Ancho Books, 2002.

Constituição da República Federativa do Brasil de 1988. Brasília, 1988. Recovered March 20th, 2022.

CORTINHAS, J. S.; VITELLI, M. G. Limitações das reformas para o controle civil sobre as forças armadas nos governos do PT (2003-2016). *Revista Brasileira de Estudos de Defesa*, 7(2), 2020.

Defesa reforçada. *O Globo* (Brazil). Retrieved from https://advance.lexis.com/api/document?collection=news&id=urn:contentItem:7W-PG-FSY1-2S4G-M02S-00000-00&context=1516831. September 12, 2009.

DESCH, M. C. *Civilian Control of the Military:* The Changing Security Environment. 1st ed., Baltimore: Johns Hopkins University Press, 2001.

DIAMINT, R. C. *Control Civil Y Fuerzas Armadas En Las Nuevas Democracias Latinoamericanas.* 1st ed., Buenos Aires: Grupo Editor Latinoamericano S.R.L. 1999. Retrieved from http://books.google.com/books?id=W-cAOAAAAYAAJ&pgis=1.

DONADIO, M.; TIBILETTI, M. de la P. *Atlas Comparativo de la Defensa en América Latina y Caribe.* 1st ed., Ciudad Autónoma de Buenos Aires: RESDAL, 2014.

EGNELL, R. *Complex Peace Operations and Civil-Military Relations.* 1st ed., New York: Routledge. 2009.

FARAH, M. F. S. Administração pública e políticas públicas. *Revista de Administração Pública*, 45(7), 2011, p. 813-836. Retrieved from http://www.scielo.br/pdf/rap/v45n3/11.pdf.

FLICK, U.; KARDOFF, E. von; STEINKE, I. *A companion to qualitative research.* London: Sage. 2004. Retrieved from http://scholar.google.com/scholar?hl=en&btnG=Search&q=intitle:A+Companion+to+Qualitative+Research#0.

FUCCILE, L. *Democracia e questão militar:* a criação do Ministério da Defesa no Brasil. Universidade Estadual de Campinas, 2006. Retrieved from http://www.bibliotecadigital.unicamp.br/document/?code=vtls000378085&opt=1.

FUKUYAMA, F. *Political Order and Political Decay:* From the Industrial Revolution to the Globalization of Democracy. Macmillan, 2014.

HUNTINGTON, S. P. *The Soldier and the State:* The Theory and Politics of Civil-military Relations. Cambridge: Harvard University Press. 1957.

________. *Political Order in Changing Societies.* 1968.

________. Democracy's Third Wave. *Journal of Democracy*, 2(2), 1991, p. 12-34. Doi:10.1353/jod.1991.0016.

JANOWITZ, M. *The Professional Soldier:* A Social and Political Portrait. Simon and Schuster, 1960.

JENNE, N.; MARTINEZ, R. Domestic Military Missions in Latin America: Civil-military Relations and the Perpetuation of Democratic Deficits. *European Journal of International Security*, 2021, p. 1-26.

Jobim chama de "ridículas" críticas a Lula. *O Globo* (Brazil). Retrieved from https://advance.lexis.com/api/document?collection=news&id=urn:contentItem:51WV-NBW1-JD87-S01J-00000-00&context=1516831. January 8, 2011.

LIMA, R. C.; SILVA, P. F.; RUDZIT, G. No Power Vacuum: National Security Neglect and the Defence Sector in Brazil. *Defence Studies*, 21(1), 2021, p. 84-106.

MARCHESINI, Lucas. Em 70 órgãos, militares ocupam 18,3% dos 14,6 mil cargos comissionados no governo Bolsonaro. *Metrópoles*. Retrieved from https://www.metropoles.com/brasil/em-70-orgaos-militares-ocupam-183-dos-146-mil-cargos-comissionados-no-governo-bolsonaro. January 8, 2021.

Lula elogia nomeação de Celso Amorim e diz que ele é um "homem de Estado". *Correio Braziliense*. August 6, 2011.

LUSTOSA, F. Brasil: 200 anos de Estado; 200 anos de administração pública; 200 anos de reformas. *Revista de Administração Pública*, 42(5), 2008, p. 829-874.

MAINWARING, S. *Transitions to democracy and democratic consolidation: theoretical and comparative issues*. Vol. 1985. 1989. Retrieved from http://www.undp.org.eg/portals/0/int forum/democratic consolidation_mainwaring.pdf.

MARQUES, A. Concepções estratégicas brasileiras no contexto internacional do pós-Guerra Fria. *Revista de Sociologia e Política*. 2003, p. 69-85. Retrieved from http://www.scielo.br/pdf/rsocp/n20/n20a7.pdf.

MARTÍNEZ, R.; D'ARAÚJO, M. C.; RIAL, J.; SALOMÓN, L. Las Relaciones Civiles-Militares en Sociedades en Tranformación: América Latina. *Documentos CIDOB América Latina*, 36, 2013, p. 1-36.

MONTEIRO, Tânia. Militares aceitam maior presença do poder civil nas Forças Armadas. *O Estado de São Paulo*. Retrieved from https://advance.lexis.com/api/document?collection=news&id=urn:contentItem:7X91-WY60-YC5N-3216-00000-00&context=1516831. November 7, 2009.

MOTTA, P. R. A modernização da administração pública brasileira nos últimos 40 anos. *Revista de Administração Pública*, 2007, p. 87-96.

NASCIMENTO, K. Reflexões sobre estratégia de reforma administrativa: a experiência federal brasileira. *Revista de Administração Pública*, 1(1), 1967, p. 12-50.

NEWMAN, E. Failed States and International Order: Constructing a Post-Westphalian World. *Contemporary Security Policy*, 30(3), 2009, p. 421-443. Doi:10.1080/13523260903326479.

NUNES, E. *A Gramática Política no Brasil:* clientelismo e insulamento burocrático. Rio de Janeiro: Jorge Zahar, 3rd ed., Brasília: Jorge Zahar Editora, 1997. Retrieved from http://copyfight.me/Acervo/livros/NUNES, Edson – A grama%CC%81tica poli%CC%81tica do Brasil.pdf.

O emprego das Forças Armadas. *O Estado de São Paulo*. Retrieved from https://advance.lexis.com/api/document?collection=news&id=urn:contentItem:7X91-WYW1-2SPK-C1CN-00000-00&context=1516831. November 11, 2009.

OLIVEIRA, E. R. de. *Democracia e defesa nacional:* a criação do Ministério da Defesa na presidência de FHC. 1st ed., Barueri: Manole, 2004. Retrieved from http://books.google.com/books?id=WFUC5QqnSbAC&pgis=1.

PIMENTA, G. A. *Defesa e controle:* uma análise da presença civil no Ministério da Defesa brasileiro (Master's dissertation), 2014.

PION-BERLIN, D. The Defense Wisdom Deficit in Latin America: A Reply to Thomas C. Bruneau. *Revista Fuerzas Armadas Y Sociedad*, 20(1), 2005, p. 51-62. Retrieved from http://www.fasoc.cl/files/articulo/ART45a4f392d-6f6a.pdf.

________. Defense Organization and Civil-Military Relations in Latin America. *Armed Forces & Society*, 35(3), 2009, p. 562-586. Doi:10.1177/0095327X08322565.

________; Trinkunas, H. Attention Deficits: Why Politicians Ignore Defense Policy in Latin America (Falta De Atención:? Por Qué Los Políticos Ignoran Las Políticas de Defensa en América Latina?). *Latin American Research Review*, 2007, p. 76-100.

Presença de militares em cargos civis mais que dobrou no governo Bolsonaro. *O Globo*. Retrieved from https://oglobo.globo.com/politica/presenca-de-militares-em-cargos-civis-mais-que-dobrou-no-governo-bolsonaro-25079165. https://www.correiobraziliense.com.br/app/noticia/politica/2011/08/06/interna_politica,264299/lula-elogia-nomeacao-de-celso-amorim-e-diz-que-ele-e-um-homem-de-estado.shtml. June 27, 2021.

REZENDE, F.; AFONSO, J. A federação brasileira: fatos, desafios e perspectivas. *Desafios para o Mercosul*. 2004, p. 1-71. Retrieved from http://joserobertoafonso.ecn.br/attachments/article/1250/Bird2002.pdf.

SECCHI, L. Modelos organizacionais e reformas da administração pública. *Revista de Administração Pública*, 43(2), 2009, p. 347-369. Doi:10.1590/S0034-76122009000200004.

SERRA, N.; BUSH, P. *The Military Transition:* Democratic Reform of the Armed Forces. P. Bush (ed.), Cambridge University Press, 2010.

SOARES, S.; Mathias, S. Forças armadas, orçamento e autonomia militar. *Perspectivas: Revista de Ciências Sociais*, 24(25), 2002, p. 85-113. Retrieved from http://200.145.78.103/index.php/perspectivas/article/view/403.

SOUZA, C. Federalismo e descentralização na Constituição de 1988: processo decisório, conflitos e alianças. *Dados*, 44, 2001, p. 513-560. Retrieved from http://www.scielo.br/pdf/dados/v44n3/a03v44n3.pdf.

SUBIRATS, J. *Coletânea de políticas públicas*: volume 2: el papel de la burocracia en el proceso de determinación e implementación de las políticas publicas. 2006.

THIRY-CHERQUES, H. R. Saturação em pesquisa qualitativa: estimativa empírica de dimensionamento. *Revista PMKT*, 3, 2009, p. 20-27. Retrieved from http://scholar.google.com/scholar?hl=en&btnG=Search&q=intitle:-Saturação+em+pesquisa+qualitativa:+estimativa+empírica+de+dimensionamento#0.

VAJPEYI, D. K.; SEGELL, G. (eds.). *Civil-Military Relationships in Developing Countries*. 1st ed., Lanham: Lexington Books, 2014.

VERGARA, S. C. *Métodos de pesquisa em administração*. Atlas. 2012.

WAHRLICH, B. Reforma administrativa federal brasileira: passado e presente. *Revista de Administração Pública*. 2012. Retrieved from http://bibliotecadigital.fgv.br/ojs/index.php/rap/article/viewArticle/5965.

WINAND, É.; SAINT-PIERRE, H. L. A fragilidade da condução política da defesa no Brasil. *História* (São Paulo), 29, 2010, p. 3-29.

ZAVERUCHA, J. The fragility of the Brazilian Defense Ministry. *Revista de Sociologia e Política*, 2(25), 2006, p. 107-121.

________; REZENDE, F. da C. How the Military Competes for Expenditure in Brazilian Democracy: Arguments for an Outlier. *International Political Science Review*, 30(4), 2009, p. 407-429. Doi:10.1177/0192512109342689.

Peacekeeping and Brazilian strategy in the early 21st century: missed opportunities

André Anselmo

Introduction

Why do states contribute to peacekeeping? The question is not new, and as the last decades saw a resurgence of the practice of peacekeeping, explanations abound. A most interesting point of view comes from Neack (1995), who claimed that the countries whose interests benefit the most by maintaining the international *status quo* were precisely the ones dominating UN peacekeeping, perhaps as a means to keep it that way.

For decades, Western middle powers were the primary troop-contributing countries in the UN system. That changed with the end of the Cold War (Kathman, 2013). The number and character of the operations increased. The countries contributing to peacekeeping also changed, from the usual middle powers, such as Canada, Norway, or Sweden, to emerging and small powers, such as Bangladesh, India, and Pakistan.

A new question arises, then. Why did these newcomers, until then consumers in the UN security system, become international security providers instead? From the several possible reasons for such behavior, Sotomayor (2010; 2013) distills three general explanations for why new democracies contribute to peace operations: domestic institutional reform, international signaling, and budget supplementation. Peacekeeping is part of a state's (grand) strategy, one of the possible instruments used to attain domestic and international objectives.

This chapter focuses on the reasons for and consequences of Brazil's participation in peacekeeping – with particular attention to its prominent role in the UN-led peace operation in Haiti (MINUSTAH, 2004-2017). It seeks to answer two questions: what were Brazil's objectives contributing to peacekeeping efforts? Did the country achieve its objectives? I start with Sotomayor's framework and delve further into Brazilian strategic goals to answer these questions[1].

The results show that the budget supplement is not a significant factor for Brazil. However, official defense documents show that domestic reform and international signaling were the country's interests, and peacekeeping was one of the tools used to achieve these ends. Ultimately, the country failed to reach its goals. In particular, the armed force's experience in Haiti brought to bear the opposite of the desired effect.

The chapter proceeds as follows: first, I review the literature and data on peacekeeping participation, focusing on Brazil's experience. Second, I discuss the methodology employed. Third, I discuss the results of the analysis. A brief conclusion closes the chapter.

Peacekeeping and Brazil's place in it

Peacekeeping: a brief overview

As a framework for the UN's approach to establishing peace and security, peacekeeping went through several waves or phases of increase and decline of interest in and deployment of operations (Gowan, 2018). For simplicity's sake, we can divide the history of peacekeeping into two moments: from post-WWII, its inception, to the end of the Cold War, and from the 1990s to now. The first moment is one of *traditional* peacekeeping. The UN would deploy troops, mostly from western middle powers, to establish and maintain ceasefires (as was the case in Suez) or isolate belligerents (as occurred in Cyprus). The second moment, after the 1990s, is one of *robust* or *complex* peace operations. Operations under the UN aegis still deployed troops but increasingly included civilian components engaged in actions falling under the umbrella of *peacebuilding* or *state-building*. The military component of the operations secured the terrain while the civilian component engaged in rebuilding institutions and governments, facilitating elections.

1 This chapter's goal is not to explore the intricacies of Brazil's strategy. For in depth discussions that also inform this chapter, see Spektor, 2021; Brands, 2011; 2010; Milani and Nery, 2019; Milani, Pinheiro, and de Lima, 2017.

At the end of World War II, Canada began a campaign to gain special *status* for itself and other middle powers, claiming they could responsibly use their "powers" to maintain world peace. Canada kickstarted the idea but had support from other middle powers at the time (Wood, 1988:31). In theory, these were powers that had sufficient economic and military capacity to be seen as effective agents in promoting peace and stability but which were limited enough not to be influenced in their role by their geopolitical ambitions as great powers. The proposal was not successful, but it became an essential component in the deliberations that led to the resolution of the Suez Crisis in 1956, which led to the first formal implementation of a UN Peacekeeping Operation (Neack, 1995). Until the late 1980s, *traditional peacekeeping* remained a "prerogative" of the middle powers (MacKay, 2017).

By the 1990s, the situation started to change. A new cycle of peace operations emerged, in no small part due to the end of the Cold War. However, a series of operational design mistakes and lack of foresight halted the ambitious expansion of the 1990s; the disasters in Rwanda, Yugoslavia, and Serbia tarnished the UN's reputation. In 1993, the UN had over 77,000 troops and police stationed at various operations. By 1999, this number fell to 12,000 (Gowan, 2018). The 2000s saw a new surge in peace operations around the globe but primarily focused on Africa. The UN rebranded peacekeeping as a "global enterprise" in response to the retreat of the US and other middle powers from peacekeeping, which led to a scarcity of personnel and material and financial resources. This vacuum was soon filled by developing and emerging powers (Kenkel, 2013; Velázquez, 2010). As one of the emerging powers in the 2000s, Brazil took advantage of this opportunity, sending troops, police, and experts to operations around the globe and fully committing a large contingent to MINUSTAH from 2004 onwards.

Brazil and peacekeeping

Brazilian participation in peacekeeping began in 1957, with the deployment of international troops to guarantee an armistice between the Egyptian and Israeli armies, called (First) United Nations Emergency Force – UNEF I. For ten years, until the end of the mission, Brazil deployed an infantry battalion of approximately 600 men. In addition, the country provided the operation's military commander of UNEF on two occasions: brigade generals Carlos Carlos F. Paiva Chaves (from January to August 1964) and Syseno Sarmento (from January 1965 to January 1966).

Between 1962 and 1963, the UN maintained a Security Force (UNSF) in West New Guinea (also known as West Papua) to monitor and ensure the ceasefire and broker agreements between the Netherlands and Indonesia. Brazil contributed two military observers to the operation. In 1965, the UN Secretary-General sent a Permanent Mission to the Dominican Republic (DOMREP – which, despite its name, lasted only a year). The mission consisted of two military observers, and Brazil provided one of them.

Also, in 1965, Brazil contributed ten military observers to the UNMOGIP (United Nations Observation Mission in India and Pakistan) for a year. The mission is one of the oldest still in operation, but it no longer counts with Brazilian personnel.

As mentioned before – the 1964 military coup radically affected Brazilian participation in the international system and, consequently, in UN peace operations. With the return of the troops from UNMOGIP in 1966, there were no new deployments in UN service. Only after the country's democratization in 1985 was the sending of personnel to peace operations resumed.

In 1988 the UN established the (First) Verification Mission in Angola – UNAVEM. Brazil contributed eight military observers and medical units throughout the mission's mandate, which ended in 1991. To this day, UNAVEM I is known as an example of success and capability among other peace operations. In subsequent years, three more operations were established in Angola, always with Brazilian participation. From 1991 to 1995, the country provided eight military observers, nine military police, and a medical unit to UNAVEM II.

Moreover, in 1995, UNAVEM III was established, responsible for observing the ceasefire between the Angolan government and UNITA forces. This time the Brazilian presence was more significant, with an infantry battalion (about eight hundred men), an engineering company (about two hundred men), two medical units (about forty doctors), fourteen observers, and eleven military police. Brazil was the largest troop contributor to a peacekeeping mission for the first time. Finally, between 1997 and 1998, the United Nations Observation Mission in Angola – MONUA was established. Brazil deployed four military observers, twenty police officers, and two officers who made up the General Staff of MONUA.

Also, in 1989, Brazil provided 21 military observers to the United Nations Observation Group in America – ONUCA, which aimed to demobilize paramilitary forces in Central America. The mission gave rise to two others later: ONUSAL and MARMINCA.

The United Nations Observer Mission in El Salvador – ONUSAL was created in 1991, and Brazil's contingent had approximately seventy military observers, 15 police officers, and a medical unit.

The Mission to Aid Demining in Central America – MARMINCA, in turn, was a mission created by the Organization of American States – OAS, to promote the removal of landmines and the training of personnel for this purpose in several countries in Central America. Brazil contributed with military engineers specialized in this function. In 1992, the United Nations Mission to Mozambique – ONUMOZ, was established to guarantee the fulfillment of the peace agreements signed between the government and the Mozambican National Resistance – RENAMO. Brazil contributed an infantry company (about one hundred and seventy men) and about thirty military observers, seventy police officers, and a medical unit between 1993 and 1994.

During the conflict between Uganda and Rwanda, a United Nations Observer Mission – UNAMIR was established to help implement the Arusha Accords, ending the civil war. Brazil provided ten military observers and a medical team between 1993 and 1994. As mentioned previously, this was one of the lowest points of UN peacekeeping in the 1990s.

The conflicts in the Balkans led to several missions to which Brazil sent troops. The United Nations Peacekeeping Force – UNPF was a mission in itself, to which sixteen military observers were sent in 1996. However, it also covered and directed other missions operating in the region. For the United Nations Protection Force in Former Yugoslavia – UNPROFOR, between 1992 and 1995, approximately thirty military observers and ten police were sent. For the United Nations Prevention Force – UNPREDEP, two observers were sent between 1995 and 1999. For the United Nations Mission in Prevlaka – UNMOP, one observer was sent between 1996 and 2001. For the Confidence Restoration Operation in Croatia – UNCRO, in 1995, 3 police and 17 observers were sent. For UNMIBH, the Mission in Bosnia and Herzegovina, fifty observers and the same number of police were sent in 1996.

Figure 1
Average number of Brazilian personnel engaged in UN Peace operations per year (1990-2018)

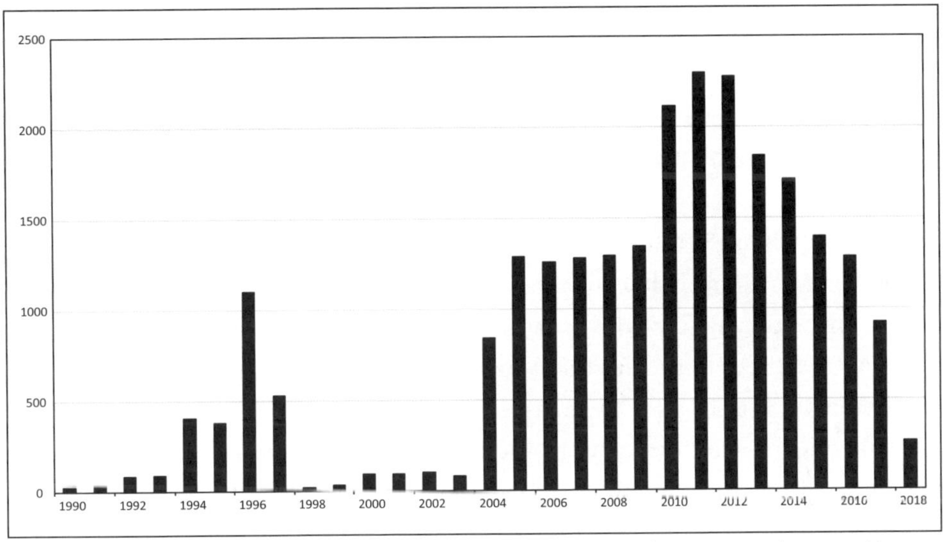

Source: Peacekeeping Database, International Peace Institute. The UN provides monthly contribution numbers. The data presented in this graph consists of annual averages of all Brazilian personnel in peace operations (police, troops, and experts).

The figure above shows three surges of Brazilian participation in UN peacekeeping. The first, during the 1990s, reflects the three UNAVEM missions in Angola, a Portuguese-speaking country in Africa with many ties to Brazil. The second and third are MINUSTAH. Between 2005 and 2009, Brazil deployed on average, 1.400 men to Haiti. Every six months, a new batch of volunteers would come to start a new tour. The third spike is the aftermath of the 2010 earthquake further destroyed Haiti. From 2010 to 2012, Brazilian personnel in Haiti averaged over 2.000 troops. From 2014 onwards, there has been steady decrease in troop contribution due to Brazil's economic troubles at home and in part due to a change in foreign policy priorities. MINUSTAH officially ended in October 2017, and MINUJUSTH[2], a smaller operation without a military component, was put in place. Two years later, in October 2019, MINUJUSTH's mandate ended. The United Nation's Integrated Office in Haiti (BINUH) was put in place to coordinate Haiti's remaining UN programs and funds.

2 United Nations Mission for Justice Support in Haiti.

The numbers alone show the relevance of MINUSTAH to Brazil. However, why would an emerging power with a history of token contributions to peacekeeping heavily invest in a specific mission in a country with so few affinities to it? In the following sections, I will try to answer that.

Other Brazilian military engagements

Brazil is usually seen as a peaceful country and with good reason. Since its independence, most military engagements were internal – separatist movements and open revolts against the central government. The challenge to keep the integrity of the territory kept the Armed forces occupied for most of the 1800s, and domestic politics were the focus in the 20th century.

Its first significant military engagement was the Paraguay War (1864-1870), involving Argentina, Brazil, Uruguay, and Paraguay. It was a turning point in Brazilian military history. After the war, Brazil's armed forces assumed a central role in the public sphere and accelerated the fall of the empire and the beginning of the Republic – in a coup led by the military.

Brazil hoped to stay neutral in World War I, but after German attacks on Brazilian merchant ships, the country joined the Triple Entente's war effort at the end of 1917. Most of the country's participation was in the Atlantic naval campaign. When World War II started, Brazil tried to stay neutral again but joined the Allies in 1942 after German aggression on Brazil's coast. The Brazilian Expeditionary Force, consisting of 25 thousand men and women, fought in the Italian theater.

Since then, Brazil did not engage in any large-scale armed conflicts. Brazil's role in MINUSTAH is the country's most extensive military operation since WWII.

Why participate in peacekeeping?

Sotomayor (2010) analyzed the peacekeeping troop contribution trends of Argentina, Brazil, and Mexico. He determined that previous models that explained contributions to traditional peace operations could not fully explain the commitment of these countries – and, by extension, of other emerging powers – to peace operations. In his 2013 book, *The Myth of the Democratic Peacekeeper: Civil-Military Relations and the United Nations*, he proposed a new model to explain why newcomers invest so much in peace operations.

The model describes three main reasons for that: domestic institutional reform, budget supplementation, and international signaling. In sum, states engage in peacekeeping under the UN to prove themselves to the international community. Each variable is, in turn, composed of three indicators. It is essential to understand that each variable represents a reason to contribute, and each indicator represents a possible effect of participating in the UN security system. Not all reasons are advantageous to all contributors. The indicators are just the same.

Domestic reform

Peace operations are also an excellent opportunity to engage in domestic reform. These reforms are usually costly, not only in financial but also in political resources. By sending troops abroad, it is expected that contact with other (supposedly more professional and advanced) military cultures will decrease these costs. This socialization process encourages the troops to change their self-image, moving them closer to Moskos' image of the soldier-diplomat (1976).

It also helps to change the mindset of the armed forces. An internally oriented mindset makes the military engage mainly in domestic activities and acts of low professional quality (such as Brazil's GLO operations[3]). An externally oriented mindset encourages the armed forces to focus on national defense against external threats. Externally oriented forces will also be less prone to meddling in domestic politics, making this a strategic move for politicians engaged in reforming military institutions and privileges (Stepan and Wolfson, 1988).

Finally, engaging in peace operations can be seen as an invaluable opportunity to coordinate defense and foreign policies, a challenging but vital enterprise (Amorim Neto, 2019).

3 *Garantia da Lei e da Ordem*, or GLOs are operations in which a detachment of military personnel is mobilized by request of the civilian authorities to act in a myriad of civilian roles, such as policing (elections, the 2014 World Cup, the 2016 Olympics), disease control, disaster relief and so on.

The three indicators that comprise this variable are i) transformation of the role and orientation of the armed forces; ii) international socialization of the armed forces; and iii) integration of defense and foreign policies.

Supplementation to the defense budget

Aside from its main budget, the UN has a special budget to pay for its operations. Today, it amounts to around 6.4 billion dollars. According to the UN's Department of Peacekeeping Operations (DPKO), it is roughly equal to 0.3% of the world's total defense budget – a much cheaper alternative to international security. Member states elect to contribute to this special budget; some pay for UN staff costs, and the rest goes to the troop and materiel-contributing countries.

To middle and great powers, the amount certainly is not much. To a developing nation, such as those contributing today, it can represent a significant boost to the defense budget. In essence, peacekeeping may be a possible solution to the old guns *versus* butter dilemma (Mintz and Huang, 1991)[4].

Three indicators comprise this variable: i) a complement to military salaries; ii) sustain or complement operational costs of acquiring new equipment; and iii) attract young people to military service.

International Signaling

Peace operations are also an opportunity to show the international community a change in national identity and state practices. It should be imperative for countries with an authoritarian history. To these countries, participating in peacekeeping can also display the adoption of humanitarian values.

Like the domestic reform, the main argument is somewhat naïve: sending troops to UN peace operations will (at the very least, help to) show the international community that the country is ready to engage in international affairs more seriously, becoming a provider of international security, rather than a consumer.

[4] For a more in-depth look at the economic incentives for troop contributing countries, see Lundgren, 2018; Lundgren, Oksamytna, and Coleman, 2021; 2021; Coleman and Nyblade, 2018; Gaibulloev et al., 2015.

Also, like the other two variables, three indicators make up signaling: i) showing the intent to commit to international order, ii) showing the adoption of a new national identity, and iii) showing the adoption of progressive politics.

Methodology

This qualitative case study applies Sotomayor's (2013) framework to the evidence available to understand Brazil's participation in peacekeeping in the early 21st century and whether it helped the country achieve its objectives.

Data comes from interviews, official UN and Brazil's national data, and the International Peace Institute's (IPI) Peacekeeping Database. Additional data on military expenditure comes from the Stockholm International Peace Research Institute (SIPRI).

The IPI PK Database is an invaluable dataset[5] comprising UN peacekeeping information from November 1990 to 2018. Official UN budgetary and peacekeeping data can be found on the UN website.

Eight semi-structured interviews supplement the analysis[6]. Of the interviewees, six are mid to high-ranking officers (captain to lieutenant colonel) in the Brazilian army. All six served in peace operations as observers/experts and regular troops, including MINUSTAH. The last two interviewees are civilian experts with knowledge of Brazilian defense and foreign policy, particularly MINUSTAH.

The analysis here is restricted to a short period, from 2000 to 2018. Brazil's efforts in peacekeeping are part of a consistent foreign policy established in the 1990s under President Cardoso that evolved in the 2000s under the Worker's Party administrations. The 2016 caretaker government and the 2018 presidential election mark a profound change in Brazilian defense and foreign policy.

Before conducting the analysis, I propose an adjustment to the framework.

5 The datasets and all related information can be found at https://www.ipinst.org/providing-for-peacekeeping-database. Last accessed in February 2022.

6 A table with Interviewee profiles is in Appendix I.

Critique of the framework

Two notes on Sotomayor's framework are necessary. First, its focus is on new democracies engaging with the UN security system. Therefore, it cannot explain the behavior of non-democracies, some of which are among the UN's top troop-contributing countries (like China, Egypt, and Pakistan). Other works seek to understand peacekeeping contribution in general, including by non-democracies. Interestingly, Kathman's (2013; 2017) findings are similar to Sotomayor's: states participate in peacekeeping as a function of domestic imperatives (in non-democracies, reducing the military's domestic reach and its ability to attempt a coup), international imperatives (threat perception and regional rivalries) and budgetary concerns. In sum, very similar to what Sotomayor posits and what I use in this chapter.

Second, the framework assumes that the states under analysis are newcomers to peacekeeping, adopting this practice as part of their strategy *after democratization*. This would be true of Brazil in the 1990s but not so much in the 2000s (ironically, this type of signaling might be necessary again soon).

In fairness, it must be said that the democratization in Brazil is not fully complete. Zaverucha argues that militarization of the police forces (2000; 2008) and the fragility of the Ministry of Defense (2006) are the main obstacles to Brazil becoming a fully realized democracy. Similarly, Denise Garcia (2014) states that the lack of constitutional provisions granting civilian authorities more control over the armed forces and almost nonexistent participation of civil society, media, and academia in military issues keep Brazil from developing as a democracy.

Amorim Neto (2013) paints a better picture. In the last decade, civilians have taken an interest in defense issues, demonstrated by the growth of academic programs about them, both graduate and undergraduate. Furthermore, the three official defense documents – the National Defense Policy, the National Defense Strategy, and the White Paper on National Defense were written with extensive civilian participation (Amorim Neto, 2019).

Nevertheless, incomplete democracy or not, Brazil's intentions by engaging with peacekeeping in the 21st century can hardly be equated with that of a new democracy. This was the work of the 1990s. Moreover, Brazil is not a newcomer to peacekeeping. Brazil is an old hand in traditional and complex peace operations. By the 2000s, it was an emerging (if young) democracy ready to take a more significant role on the international stage.

I suggest a change to the *international signaling* explanation. The challenge then is to establish the country's goals in terms of signaling, if not those of a new democracy. The following section describes selecting three new indicators of international signaling.

New goals

Brazil is a middle power, but throughout the 20th century, it has tried to rise above this standing several times. While ultimately unsuccessful, Brazil has followed a coherent line in all of them, trying to influence the international order through soft rather than hard power and staunchly defending the principle of sovereign equality (Mares and Trinkunas, 2016). But how to identify its goals? Furthermore, how to identify if participating in MINUSTAH was a step towards achieving them? Brazil's official defense documents are a good starting point.

In 2012 Brazil finally released two critical defense documents that can help to answer these questions: the Defense White Paper (2012b) and the National Strategy of Defense (2012a).

The White Paper on National Defense lists the Brazilian defense goals as to:

1. Guarantee sovereignty, national patrimony, and territorial integrity;
2. To defend national interests and Brazilian people, assets, and resources abroad;
3. Contribute to regional stability;
4. Contribute to the preservation of national cohesion and unity;
5. Contribute to the maintenance of international peace and security;
6. To intensify the projection of Brazil in the concert of nations and its insertion in international decision-making processes;
7. To maintain modern armed forces, integrated, trained and balanced, and with increasing professionalism, operating together and adequately deployed in the national territory;
8. To make Brazilian society aware of the importance of the country's defense affairs;
9. Develop the Industrial Defense Base, aimed at obtaining autonomy in indispensable technologies;

10. To structure the Armed forces around capabilities, equipping them with personnel and material compatible with strategic and operational planning; and
11. Develop the potential of defense logistics and national mobilization.

It is an extensive list, and it is an acknowledgment of the lack of attention defense matters have suffered in Brazil (and Latin America as a whole) in the last decades (Pion-Berlin and Trinkunas, 2007).

The National Strategy of Defense, on the other hand, looks outward and states the country's intention to engage in peace operations – either UN-led or sponsored by other organisms. It also states the Brazilian intent to enhance its participation in some areas. Summing it up:

1. Relevant international decision-making processes;
2. Decision processes on the Antarctic region;
3. Actions promoting the country's international projection and its commitment to the defense of peace and cooperation among peoples;
4. International forums related to strategic issues, prioritizing regional organizations such as the South American Defense Council (CDS) of the Union of South American Nations (UNASUR);
5. In the intensification of cooperation and trade with African, Central American, and Caribbean countries, including the Community of Latin American and Caribbean States (CELAC); and
6. Consolidation of the South Atlantic Peace and Cooperation Zone and the increase in interregional interaction, such as with the Community of Portuguese Speaking Countries (CPLP), the South American-Africa (ASA) Summit, and the Dialogue Forum India-Brazil-South Africa (IBAS).

From these myriad objectives, it is possible to distill some common points regarding international goals. And they are:

1. Regional integration and stability;
2. Enhancing the presence in the Brazilian influence sphere; and
3. Enhancing Brazilian participation in international decision-making bodies.

Based on the White Paper and the National Strategy of Defense, it is clear that Brazil considers its strategic environment and areas of national interest South America, the Caribbean, the Southern Atlantic, Antarctica, Africa, and the member-states of CPLP.

In the next section, I analyze MINUSTAH and its effects regarding the reassessed model.

MINUSTAH and Brazil's interests

International Signaling

Regional integration and stability

The level of regional cooperation in Haiti was unprecedented, especially when it comes to Argentina, Brazil and Chile, the Latin-American countries most involved in the operation (Braga, 2010). Perales (2011) postulates that much of the recent international activism and political choices of the Latin-American countries can be explained by their cooperation in MINUSTAH. Cooperation in Haiti became part of a regional pattern of cooperation and that impacted how security was discussed in South America (Herz, 2013). Likewise, Jenne (2019) argues that the Latin American experience in peace operations is a result of foreign policy goals that explicitly focus on regional cooperation rather than an interest in peacekeeping *per se*.

Twenty countries contributed to the MINUSTAH military component. Most of the personnel are Brazilian, with an average of about 1,400 soldiers sent per year. Since the beginning of the operation in 2004, the Force Commander appointed to the role was a Brazilian general, which is extremely atypical.

Other troop-contributing countries are Argentina, Bolivia, Canada, Chile, Ecuador, El Salvador, France, Guatemala, Honduras, Indonesia, Jordan, Nepal, Paraguay, Peru, the Phillippines, South Korea, Sri Lanka, the United States and Uruguay.

Roughly half the troops in Haiti are South American, even though the stabilization of Haiti would be more of a concern for its Central American and Caribbean neighbors, such as Mexico and the Dominican Republic. One possible explanation for this regional commitment is that the increased participation of these countries in peace operations since the 1990s generated more specific know-how than the other candidates.

Another noteworthy issue is the shift in their position on humanitarian intervention since the late 1990s in Kosovo. The countries of the region came to agree that sovereignty could be contingent on humanitarian grounds (Chandler, 2002; Perales, 2011).

One possible effect of the cooperation between the South American states in Haiti was Unasur, a project of regional organism that has, among its basic principles, the exchange of information and experience in matters of defense (Villa and Viana, 2010). It also had a South American Defense Council, and one of its missions was to enhance cooperation and regional consensus in conflict resolution (Fett, 2014).

The number of defense-related projects being developed regionally also grew at the time. The highlight is the KC-390 cargo airship, made by a joint venture between Argentina, Brazil and Chile, with some Portuguese and Czech inputs.

Several factors influenced the new prospects for regional integration and cooperation in South America, and there is credible evidence that the cooperation developed in Haiti was part of it (Abdenur et al., 2018:105).

Enhanced presence in Brazil's sphere of influence

The Caribbean, and consequently Haiti, is inside Brazil's intended sphere of influence. Therefore, leading successful stabilization operations in the region could certainly represent reputational gains. There is a reasonably positive evaluation of Brazil's performance in MINUSTAH (Biato, 2011).

But Haiti is one such case. At this point, it is interesting to see if this presence is a new trend or if it is actually part of longstanding political practice.

Between 1990-1997, Brazil was part of three missions in Central America, five missions in Europe and eight missions in Africa. Between 1998-2004, Brazil was part of one mission in Central America, one in the Caribbean; two in Europe; three in Africa; and one in Asia. Between 2004-2014, Brazil was part of four missions in Asia, one in the Caribbean, eleven in Africa, two in Europe and three in the Middle East.

There is a clear trend here. Brazil has mainly contributed to operations in Africa. It has also been a part of every operation in East Timor, a CPLP member since the end of the 1990s. There is no mention of the Middle East in official defense documents, but Brazil's presence there could be seen as an attempt to actively expand the country's sphere of influence by means of peace operations.

Enhancing Brazil's participation in international decision-making bodies

It is hard to pinpoint if MINUSTAH helped Brazil enhance its profile in international decision-making bodies. The country's visibility in the last decade largely resulted from the 2000s' commodity boom and what then foreign minister Celso Amorim called a "proud and active foreign policy." MINUSTAH was certainly a part of it, and was seen as a great opportunity to show expertise in leadership, governance and international security (Perales, 2011).

In 2005 the UN created a *Peacebuilding Committee* to pool resources, formulate plans and advise other organs. The committee is made up of 31 Member States and Brazil was one of the seven elected by the UNGA to be part of it.

A possible way to look at this issue is by analyzing the UN budgets. There are two of special relevance in this case: the ordinary budget and the peace operations budget. Both budgets take into consideration the economic wealth of the contributing members, among other things[7]. The ordinary budget is voted on bi-annually, and the peace operations budget, is annual.

In the 1990s, Brazil's quotas were around 17 million dollars biannually to the ordinary budget. In 2013, it reached 82 million dollars. This amounts to approximately 3% of the total budget. As a comparison, Germany, and Japan, who also vie for a permanent seat in the Security Council, contribute with 7% and 10% of the budget bi-annually.

In the peace operations budget, this figure is even worse. The five members of the Security Council provide almost half of the 7 billion dollars budget. Again, Japan and Germany contribute 7% and 10% approximately. Brazil's quota, on the other hand, only amounts to 0,5% of the total budget.

Therefore, it cannot be said that Brazil has had much improvement in this aspect.

---

7 The budget follows a very complex formula. More on it can be seen in the Committee on Contributions website: https://www.un.org/en/ga/contributions/budget.shtml. Last accessed in February 2022.

Domestic reform

Transformation of the role and orientation of the armed forces

Training can change the orientation of an army. Pion-Berlin (2000) argues that soldiers preparing for international missions tend to interfere less in internal politics. It is common belief that peace operations provide good opportunities to implement this transition, all through interacting with other, more advanced military.

On the other hand, there is no UN-established training or doctrine for peacekeeping. The requirements are that only English-speaking and volunteer soldiers are sent. The UN does not train its peacekeepers; the troop-contributing countries do.

In Brazil, the Brazilian Joint Center on Peace Operations (CCOPAB) is responsible for such training. The Army and Navy had their own peace operations training centers, created in 2005 and 2007, respectively. Only in 2010 they were united in one center responsible for the training of all civilian and military personnel sent to peace operations. An important fact is that many of the center's instructions have direct experience in these operations. Some of them have two or more tours. All interviewees praised both the training programs and the center's facilities.

Nevertheless, training and orientation are far from sufficient. Most troops in Haiti engaged in urban guerrilla and policing tactics. All interviewees compared MINUSTAH to the pacification and policing operation in Rio de Janeiro's *favelas* and most troops engaged in the former were also used in the latter. The very defense documents that preach an international orientation explicitly provide for the use of the armed forces in domestic law and order operations. The constant use of the armed forces in large-scale police operations using tactics learned and refined in Haiti became commonplace in Brazil (Harig, 2019).

In fact, participation in MINUSTAH led to the opposite effect: an increased involvement of the armed forces in public security and high-profile domestic operations, such as providing security during the 2014 World Cup and 2016 Olympic Games and a more prominent role in domestic politics (Harig, 2015). In 2018, General Villas Bôas, then the Army Commander, used his Twitter account to pressure the Brazilian Supreme Court during a trial that could potentially release former President Lula da Silva, arrested under corruption charges, from prison.

Villas Bôas had the full support of the army's high command in this initiative (*O Globo*, 2021). I discuss this further in the next section and in the conclusion.

International socialization of the armed forces

Another common belief is that troops in peace operations socialize with other national troops and civilians, becoming, in time, more democratic and welcoming to civilian control (Passmore, 2020). By nature, modern peace operations are complex (Egnell, 2009) and soldiers effectively depend on civilians, like diplomats, local authorities and NGOs, to accomplish their missions.

Again, training may be an important part of socialization. The presence of civilians in training arguably helps this process. In the Brazilian training center, this presence is very common, as civilians teach languages, international relations, human rights, and international humanitarian law.

In Haiti, Brazil's troops were usually the poster boys for socialization, both on patrol and in other activities that required contact with civilians. The interviewees also recalled their experience with NGOs in Haiti as particularly good (it's noteworthy that one of the most active NGOs in Haiti was the Brazilian *Viva Rio*).

However, it is difficult to ascertain whether this is an effect of training for peace operations and the experience gained in Haiti or a reflection of the so-called "Brazilian style" (Biato, 2011; Sotomayor, 2013). Research into socialization often shows that the opposite effect is produced: the experience militaries gain is often used to support domestic repression (Levin, MacKay, and Nasirzadeh, 2016), produce regime instability (Dwyer, 2015), and is internalized in military training as infantry and police work (Sion, 2006; Jenne, 2020). The latter is most likely true in the case of Brazil, as the tactics learned in MINUSTAH were soon used in public security operations at home, and the military's growing influence in domestic politics soon tested and sometimes overstepped the limits of civilian control[8].

---

8 The most prominent example being the occasion in which the Army Commander threatened the Supreme Court using Twitter. The case is mentioned further on.

Integration of defense and foreign policies

Brazil has a very poor record when it comes to the integration of defense and foreign policies. How these policies are integrated into MINUSTAH is subject to debate. Some point to an unprecedented degree of coordination during the operation.

The second civilian interviewee, a Brazilian diplomat, emphasizes that the relationship between officers and diplomats is very poor. He cites the absolute alienation of Brazil's politicians regarding the operation and the predominant influence of the president in the decision to go to Haiti.

But this is common in Brazil, and the decision-making process for sending troops to peacekeeping is very haphazard. Usually, the UN Department of Peacekeeping Operations sends a communiqué to Brazil's Permanent Mission at the UN about contributing to an operation. The mission sends it to the Foreign Ministry, which consults the president, the Ministries of Defense, Planning and Economy about the availability of troops and money. Then they send a document to Congress, where it is usually approved, and the president gives the final order to send the troops. This system, called byzantine (Kenkel, 2010), is at the mercy of the personality of the president and its ministers (Kenkel 2008).

As a counterpoint, the first civilian interviewee, a scholar who was in Haiti, argued that there was a high degree of coordination, but mainly *because* of the mission. This is supported by Sotomayor (2013), who adds that this could be a product of the activism of the military in the foreign policy debate.

As already mentioned, Amorim Neto (2013) registered an increasing involvement of civilians in defense issues, including the foreign policy community. This was clearly visible in the 2010s when the new defense documents mentioned earlier were written with ample participation from academics, diplomats and politicians (Amorim Neto, 2019). It is likely that cooperation in Haiti influenced, to some degree, the more successful efforts to integrate defense and foreign policy at home.

In any event, most agree that MINUSTAH was a remarkable case that showed a concerted effort from the military, wanting to prove their worth by leading an international operation, the foreign ministry, and President Lula da Silva, keenly intending to capitalize on the mission to help the country's rising profile.

Supplementation to the defense budget

A complement to military salaries

Depending on the relative economic wealth of a nation's military, peacekeeping can be a profitable option. Some poorer countries contribute with troops because the UN will help pay for them.

Data on this is very opaque. The UN only reveals that it reimburses troop-contributing countries with a little over one thousand dollars per soldier per month. This sum is sent to each country, which in turn, pays as much as it wants to each soldier (and some do not).

The military interviewees, all high-ranking officers, downplayed the financial incentives as relevant to volunteering for peacekeeping. In fact, they claim that peacekeeping has very little influence and brings almost no benefits to their careers in the military. They count "personal growth" and "experiencing a ***real*** operation," i.e., field experience, as their actual incentives.

Sustain or complement operational costs of acquiring new equipment

Budgetary concerns are also one important driver of participation in peacekeeping. Through its peacekeeping budget, the UN will also reimburse, to a point, countries for the equipment (personnel gear, vehicles, and so forth) they use.

Brazil's contributions to the UN's ordinary and peacekeeping budgets do not amount to much – the country currently is responsible for around 2% of the general budget[9]. On the other hand, Brazil's military expenditure peaked at around 25 billion dollars in 2010 and remained reasonably stable until 2018. These numbers and Brazilian officials' recurrent comments in international forums indicate that monetary incentives did not affect Brazilian calculations on contributing to peacekeeping (Avezov 2013).

---

9 Exactly 2.013% of the budget, with a net contribution of 57.8 million dollars for the year 2022. For reference, the total budget of the United Nations for the year 2022 is roughly 3 billion dollars. Source: Assessment of Member State's advances to the Working Capital Fund for 2022 contributions to the United Nations regular budget for 2022, available at: https://undocs.org/en/ST/ADM/SER.B/1038. Last accessed in February 2022.

Figure 2
Brazilian military expenditure in billions of dollars (constant 2019 USD, 1990-2018)

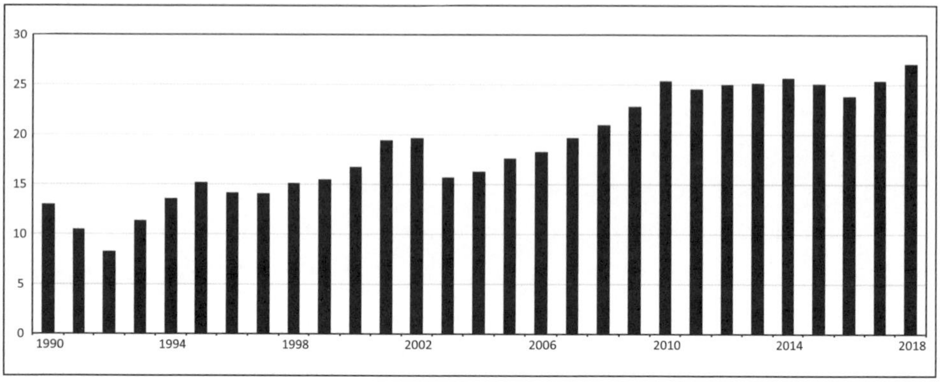

Source: Stockholm International Peace Institute (SIPRI). The data represents Brazilian military expenditure in billions of US$, at constant 2019 prices and exchange rates (i.e., adjusted for inflation), according to the SIPRI methodology. More information can be found at https://www.sipri.org/databases/milex. Last accessed in February 2022.

Attracting young people to the military service

Finally, the prospect of serving abroad and earning money in a foreign currency could help in attracting young people to military service. This can be interesting to countries with professional armed forces, which is not the case in Brazil.

Brazil adopted conscription in 1906 and every regime, civilian or military, since then has kept it so. However, Kuhlmann (2001) claims that in practice, Brazil has a voluntary force. All 18 years old males must report for military service, but only those who want to stay are incorporated into active service.

Nevertheless, the mere fact that conscription is in force makes the point of attracting recruits through the old "join the army, see the world" strategy moot.

Brazil's domestic politics and the legacy of MINUSTAH

So far, this chapter has avoided addressing any developments after 2017, the official end of MINUSTAH. The main reason is that the Brazilian strategy, as analyzed here, has changed substantially since then. Lula da Silva's successor,

Dilma Rousseff (2011-2016), was less engaged in presidential diplomacy than him, and her public security platform relied heavily on the military (Mathias, Zague, and Santos, 2019), which inevitably led to the armed force's increased participation in the domestic arena. In 2016 Rousseff was impeached after a months-long, tumultuous process. Michel Temer, Rousseff's vice president, took office and relied on the military to help his government display a semblance of stability: for the first time since its creation, the Ministry of Defense was headed by a general (albeit a retired one), and several officers were among of the president's closest councilors (Poder 360, 2018).

Further cementing the downgrade in Brazil's peacekeeping profile, the country declined the UN's invitation to deploy troops and participate in MINUSCA and MONUSCO, two UN-led operations in the Central African Republic and in the Democratic Republic of the Congo, respectively. Among the factors that influenced this decision were the 2018 federal intervention in Rio de Janeiro, with almost 30,000 troops deployed, and the emergency humanitarian operations on the border with Venezuela during the refugee crisis (Andrade, Hamann, and Soares, 2021).

Two years later, the election of Jair Bolsonaro, a far-right former army captain explicitly backed by sectors of the armed forces further increased the military's participation in domestic politics. Bolsonaro abandoned Brazil's longstanding foreign policy goals in favor of alignment with the United States (de Sá Guimarães, and de Oliveira e Silva, 2021). The increased profile of the armed forces in domestic politics was reflected in Bolsonaro's government – the military occupied 50% of his cabinet, with thousands of officers also occupying positions in public administration posts completely unrelated to defense (Scharpf 2020) – the biggest example being General Pazuelo's disastrous handling of the COVID-19 pandemic during his tenure as health minister. Under Bolsonaro, Brazil's contributions to peace operations reached their lowest levels (Brant and Machado, 2020).

The legacy of MINUSTAH for Brazil is puzzling, indeed. Perhaps the most profoundly ironic effect of Brazil's prominent role in the operation is the rise of a cadre of officers who occupied command positions in Haiti and since 2018 formed the backbone of Bolsonaro's government. Called the "Haitian generals," this group includes former force commanders (leading the mission's whole military component) and other high-ranking officers[10]. They were sent to Haiti, arguably, because they were the best Brazil's armed forces had to offer. And it is hard to say they became involved in politics *because* they went to Haiti, but one can wonder how much the notion of fixing Haiti is reflected in their belief that they can fix Brazil. One can also wonder if, in the future, Brazilian leaders committed to democracy will be reluctant to deploy troops to expansive peace operations such as MINUSTAH, fearing once more the rise of a group of officers that see themselves as capable of governing Brazil.

Conclusion

As Alsina (2017) concludes, the role of peacekeeping in Brazil's strategy is modest, but not irrelevant. This chapter aimed to understand if by contributing to peace operations, and MINUSTAH especially, Brazil managed to get closer to achieving its strategic goals.

For that, I reassessed a model developed by Sotomayor (2014). It analyses the participation of new major contributors to UN peacekeeping by means of three variables: domestic reform, financial incentives and international signaling. I proposed a small adjustment to the model. By examining Brazilian defense documents, I established a new pattern for international signaling to reflect an emergent power's attempt to expand its international influence and rise to a greater standing in the international community.

The new analysis shows that MINUSTAH brought some if few, good things for Brazil.

There seem to be no financial incentives at all for Brazil to engage in peacekeeping. Alsina (2017) warned that further deterioration of the armed forces' capabilities might change this situation and make peacekeeping an inviting way to supplement the defense budget. With a renewed hand in domestic politics, it remains to be seen if such deterioration will indeed lead to a renewed interest in peacekeeping.

10 See Castro and Marques recent book (2019) containing lenghty interviews with the surviving force commanders. Most franly agree that MINUSTAH was a very positive experience for the armed forces, but not so much for Haiti and Brazil's politics.

As for signaling, there were certain advances in regional cooperation and Brazil has kept its historical trend to operate within its intended sphere of influence: Latin America, Africa and Portuguese-speaking countries. However, increased participation in peace operations hosted by African states does indicate an expansion of said sphere.

On the domestic reform front, some depict MINUSTAH as shining case of cooperation between defense and diplomacy. Military and diplomats worked in concert to make it work with emphatic support from President Lula da Silva. But whatever gains in cooperation that occurred in MINUSTAH seem to extend little further. As the second civilian interviewee stated, communication and cooperation between the Ministry of Defense and the Foreign Affairs Ministry outside of the operation were very poor. A highlight of healthy civil-military relations in the late 2000s and early 2010s is the production a new Defense Strategy and the White Book of National Defense, written by mixed committees of civilians (academics, diplomats, politicians) and members of the armed forces. Such was not the case when the defense documents were reviewed in 2020.

The only lasting institutional effect of Brazil's participation in MINUSTAH is something that many thought unexpected: the increased role of the armed forces in domestic politics. The policing model used by the military in the slums of Port-au-Prince was easily translated to Brazilian *favelas*. The enhanced profile of the armed forces as tools in the public security realm led to more and more deployments: from fighting drug lords to policing big events, like the 2014 World Cup and the 2016 Olympic Games, to finally taking over public security during a federal intervention in the State of Rio de Janeiro in 2018 (with, at best, lackluster results). This, in turn, increased the military's influence in the public security domain (Harig, 2019; 2015) and, later, in domestic politics at large. Several Brazilian officers who served in Haiti, both as force commanders and in other functions, openly participated in the presidential elections in 2016 supporting Jair Bolsonaro, and many eventually joined his administration. When it comes to domestic reforms, peacekeeping might have given Brazil the opposite of the expected results and the worst unintended consequence: once more legitimizing the armed forces as political actors with an ever-increasing role in government and domestic politics.

References

ABDENUR, Adriana Erthal; KUELE, Giovana; FOLLY, Maiara; MACEDO, Gustavo. Brazil and MINUSTAH: lessons from academic literature. In *Brazil's participation in MINUSTAH (2004-2017):* perceptions, lessons and practices for future missions. Rio de Janeiro: Igarapé Institute and CCOP-AB, 2018, p. 101-111. Retrieved from https://igarape.org.br/wp-content/uploads/2018/03/Brazils-Participation-in-MINUSTAH-2004-2017.pdf.

ALSINA, João Paulo S. Grand Strategy and Peace Operations: The Brazilian Case. *Revista Brasileira de Política Internacional*, 60, November 2017. Retrieved from https://doi.org/10.1590/0034-7329201700204.

AMORIM NETO, Octavio. Democracia e relações civis-militares no Brasil. In AVELAR, Lúcia; CINTRA, Antônio Octávio (eds.). *Sistema Político Brasileiro:* uma introdução. Rio de Janeiro: Fundação Konrad Adenauer, 3nd ed., 2013, p. 315-330.

________. The Impact of Civilians on Defense Policy in New Democracies: The Case of Brazil. *Latin American Politics and Society* 61(3), 2019, p. 1-28. Retrieved from https://doi.org/10.1017/lap.2019.3.

ANDRADE, Israel de Oliveira; EDUARDA, Passarelli Hamann; SOARES, Matheus Augusto. Brazil's Participation in United Nations Peacekeeping Operations: Evolution, Challenges, and Opportunities. *Discussion Paper*, January 2021, p. 1-40. Retrieved from https://doi.org/10.38116/dp254.

ARTURO, C. Sotomayor. *The Myth of the Democratic Peacekeeper:* Civil-Military Relations and the United Nations. Baltimore: Johns Hopkins University Press, 2014.

AVEZOV, Xenia. The New Geopolitics of Peace Operations: A Dialogue with Emerging Powers: South America Regional Dialogue. *Journal of International Peacekeeping*, 17(1-2), 2013, p. 162-170. Retrieved from https://doi.org/10.1163/18754112-1702006.

BIATO, Marcel. Brazil's Mission in Haiti. In HEINE, Jorge; THOMPSON, Andrew Stuart (eds.). *Fixing Haiti:* MINUSTAH and Beyond. Tokyo: United Nations University Press, 2011, p. 191-203.

BRAGA, Carlos Chagas Vianna. MINUSTAH and the Security Environment in Haiti: Brazil and South American Cooperation in the Field. *International Peacekeeping*, 17(5), 2010, p. 711-22. Retrieved from https://doi.org/10.1080/13533312.2010.516979.

BRANDS, Hal. *Dilemmas of Brazilian Grand Strategy*. Stategic Studies Institute. 2020. Retrieved from https://doi.org/10.21236/ADA528802.

________. Evaluating Brazilian Grand Strategy under Lula. *Comparative Strategy*, 30(1), 2011, p. 28-49. Retrieved from https://doi.org/10.1080/01495933.2011.545686.

BRANT, Danielle; MACHADO, Renato. Sob Bolsonaro, verba para missões de paz atinge mínima histórica. *Folha de S. Paulo*, September 19, 2020, sec. Mundo. Retrieved from https://www1.folha.uol.com.br/mundo/2020/09/sob-bolsonaro-verba-para-missoes-de-paz-atinge-minima-historica.shtml.

BRASIL. *Estratégia nacional de defesa*. Brasília: Ministério da Defesa, 2012a.

________. *Livro Branco de Defesa Nacional*. 1ª Brasília: Ministério da Defesa, 2012b.

CASTRO, Celso; MARQUES, Adriana A. (eds.). *Missão Haiti:* a visão dos Force Commanders. 1st ed. Rio de Janeiro, RJ, Brasil: FGV Editora, 2019.

CHANDLER, David. *From Kosovo To Kabul:* Human Rights and International Intervention. London: Pluto Press, 2002.

COLEMAN, Katharina P.; NYBLADE, Benjamin. Peacekeeping for Profit? The Scope and Limits of "Mercenary" UN Peacekeeping. *Journal of Peace Research*, 55(6), 2018, p. 726-741. Retrieved from https://doi.org/10.1177/0022343318775784.

DE SÁ GUIMARÃES, Feliciano; DE OLIVEIRA E SILVA, Irma Dutra. Far-Right Populism and Foreign Policy Identity: Jair Bolsonaro's Ultra-Conservatism and the New Politics of Alignment. *International Affairs*, 97(2), 2021, p. 345-363. Retrieved from https://doi.org/10.1093/ia/iiaa220.

DWYER, Maggie. Peacekeeping Abroad, Trouble Making at Home: Mutinies in West Africa. *African Affairs*, 114(455), 2015, p. 206-225. Retrieved from https://doi.org/10.1093/afraf/adv004.

EGNELL, R. *Complex Peace Operations and Civil-Military Relations:* Winning the Peace. Routledge, 2009.

FETT, Priscila. Missões de paz e o multilateralismo brasileiro. *Universitas – Relações Internacionais* 12(1), 2014, p. 137-49. Retrieved from https://doi.org/10.5102/uri.v12i1.249.

GAIBULLOEV, Khusrav; GEORGE, Justin; SANDLER, Todd; SHIMIZU, Hirofumi. Personnel Contributions to UN and Non-UN Peacekeeping Missions: A Public Goods Approach. *Journal of Peace Research*, 52(6), 2015, p. 727-42. Retrieved from https://doi.org/10.1177/0022343315579245.

GOWAN, Richard. Peace Operations. In WEISS, Thomas G.; DAWS, Sam. (eds.). *The Oxford Handbook on the United Nations*. 2nd ed., New York: Oxford University Press, 2018. Retrieved from https://doi.org/10.1093/oxfordhb/9780198803164.013.23.

HARIG, Christoph. Synergy Effects between MINUSTAH and Public Security in Brazil. *Brasiliana-Journal for Brazilian Studies*, 3(2), 2015, p. 142-168. Retrieved from https://doi.org/10.25160/v3.i2/d6.

________. Learning to Fight in UN Peacekeeping. *Defence Studies*, 20(1), 2019, p. 39-60. Retrieved from https://doi.org/10.1080/14702436.2019.1704177.

HERZ, Monica. Assumptions on Intervention and Security in South America. In KENDEL, Kai Michael (ed.). *South America and Peace Operations:* Coming of Age. Routledge, 0 ed., 2013, p. 25-44. Retrieved from https://doi.org/10.4324/9780203071502.

JENNE, Nicole. Peacekeeping, Latin America and the UN Charter's Chapter VIII: Past Initiatives and Future Prospects. *International Peacekeeping*, 26(3), 2019, p. 327-353. Retrieved from https://doi.org/10.1080/13533312.2019.1588729.

________. Civilianizing the Armed Forces? Peacekeeping, a Traditional Mission for the Military. *Defence Studies*, 20(2), 2020, p. 105-122. Retrieved from https://doi.org/10.1080/14702436.2020.1726741.

KATHMAN, Jacob D. United Nations Peacekeeping Personnel Commitments, 1990-2011. *Conflict Management and Peace Science*, 30(5), 2013, p. 532-549. Retrieved from https://doi.org/10.1177/0738894213491180.

KATHMAN, Jacob D.; MELIN, Molly M. Who Keeps the Peace? Understanding State Contributions to UN Peacekeeping Operations. *International Studies Quarterly*, 61(1), 2017, p. 150-162. Retrieved from https://doi.org/10.1093/isq/sqw041.

KENKEL, Kai Michael. Out of South America to the Globe: Brazil's Growing Stake in Peace Operations. In *South America and Peace Operations*. London: Routledge, 2013.

________. Global Player Ou Espectador Nas Margens? A "responsabilidade de proteger": definição e implicações para o Brasil. *Revista da Escola de Guerra Naval*, 12, 2008, p. 6-57.

________. South America's Emerging Power: Brazil as Peacekeeper. *International Peacekeeping*, 17(5), 2010, p. 644-661. Retrieved from https://doi.org/10.1080/13533312.2010.516958.

KUHLMANN, Paulo Roberto Loyola. *O serviço militar, democracia e defesa nacional:* razões da permanência do modelo de recrutamento no Brasil. USP, 2001.

LEVIN, Jamie; MACKAY, Joseph; NASIRZADEH, Abouzar. Selectorate Theory and the Democratic Peacekeeping Hypothesis: Evidence from Fiji and Bangladesh. *International Peacekeeping*, 23(1), 2016, p. 107-132. Retrieved from https://doi.org/10.1080/13533312.2015.1108845.

LUDGREN, Magnus. Backdoor Peacekeeping: Does Participation in UN Peacekeeping Reduce Coups at Home? *Journal of Peace Research*, 55(4), 2018, p. 508-523. Retrieved from https://doi.org/10.1177/0022343317747668.

________; OKSAMYTNA, Kseniya; COLEMAN, Katharina P. Only as Fast as Its Troop Contributors: Incentives, Capabilities, and Constraints in the UN's Peacekeeping Response. *Journal of Peace Research*, 58(4), 2021, p. 671-686. Retrieved from https://doi.org/10.1177/0022343320940763.

MACKAY, R. A. The Canadian Doctrine of the Middle Powers. In *Empire and Nations:* Essays in Honour of Frederic H. Soward. Heritage. Toronto: University of Toronto Press, 2017, p. 133-143. Retrieved from https://doi.org/10.3138/9781442654075-012.

MARES, David R.; TRINKUNAS, Harold A. *Aspirational Power:* Brazil on the Long Road to Global Influence. Brookings Institution Press, 2016.

MATHIAS, Suzeley Kalil; ZAGUE, Jose Augusto; SANTOS, Leandro Fernandes Sampaio. A política militar brasileira no governo Dilma Rousseff: o discurso e a ação. *Opinião Pública*, 25(1), 2019, p. 136-168. Retrieved from https://doi.org/10.1590/1807-01912019251136.

MILANI, Carlos R. S.; NERY, Tiago. Brazil. In *Comparative Grand Strategy*. Oxford: Oxford University Press, 2019. Retrieved from https://doi.org/10.1093/oso/9780198840848.003.0007.

________; PINHEIRO, Leticia; DE LIMA, Maria Regina Soares. Brazil's Foreign Policy and the "Graduation Dilemma". *International Affairs*, 93(3), 2017, p. 585-605. Retreived from https://doi.org/10.1093/ia/iix078.

MINTZ, Alex; HUANG, Chi. Guns *versus* Butter: The Indirect Link. *American Journal of Political Science*, 35(3), 1991, p. 738-757. Retrieved from https://doi.org/10.2307/2111564.

MOSKOS, Charles C. *Peace Soldiers:* The Sociology of a United Nations Military Force. Chicago: University of Chicago Press, 1976.

NEACK, Laura. UN Peace-Keeping: In the Interest of Community or Self? *Journal of Peace Research*, 32(2), 1995, p. 181-196.

O GLOBO. Tuíte de Villas Bôas em 2018 passou pelo Alto Comando. *Valor Econômico*, October 2, 2021, sec. Política. Retrieved from https://valor.globo.com/politica/noticia/2021/02/11/tuite-de-villas-boas-em-2018-passou-pelo-alto-comando.ghtml.

PASSMORE, Timothy J. A. Democratization and Troop Contributions to United Nations Peacekeeping. *Armed Forces & Society*. November 2020 . Retrieved from 0095327X20968197. https://doi.org/10.1177/0095327X20968197.

PERALES, José Raúl. Haiti and the Regional Dynamics of International Co-operation. In HEINE, Jorge; THOMPSON, Andrew Stuart. (eds.). *Fixing Haiti:* MINUSTAH and Beyond. Tokyo: United Nations University Press, 2011, p. 175-190.

PION-BERKIN, D. Decision-Makers or Decision-Takers? Military Missions and Civilian Control in Democratic South America. *Armed Forces & Society* 26(3), 2000, p. 413-436. Retrieved from https://doi.org/10.1177/0095327X0002600304.

________; TRINKUNAS, Harold. Attention Deficits: Why Politicians Ignore Defense Policy in Latin America. *Latin American Research Review* 42(3), 2007, p. 76-100.

PODER 360. Sob Temer, Forças Armadas têm o maior prestígio desde o fim da ditadura. *Poder 360*, February 26, 2018. Retrieved from https://www.poder360.com.br/governo/sob-temer-forcas-armadas-tem-o-maior-prestigio-desde-o-fim-da-ditadura/.

SCHARPF, Adam. Dangerous Alliances: Populists and the Military. *Giga Focus Latin America*, 1, February 2020, p. 13.

SION, Liora. "Too Sweet and Innocent for Wa"?: Dutch Peacekeepers and the Use of Violence. *Armed Forces & Society*, 32(3), 2006, p. 454-474. Retrieved from https://doi.org/10.1177/0095327X05281453.

SOTOMAYOR, Arturo C. Why Some States Participate in UN Peace Missions While Others Do Not: An Analysis of Civil-Military Relations and Its Effects on Latin America's Contributions to Peacekeeping Operations. *Security Studies*, 19(1), 2010, p. 160-195. Retrieved from https://doi.org/10.1080/09636410903546822.

________. *The Myth of the Democratic Peacekeeper:* Civil-Military Relations and the United Nations. Baltimore: Johns Hopkins University Press, 2013.

SPEKTOR, Matias. Strategies of Rising Brazil: Postmortem Review, Looking Forward. *Contemporary Politics*, August 2021, p. 1-18. Retrieved from https://doi.org/10.1080/13569775.2021.1961452.

STEPAN, Alfred; WOLFSON, Leandro. Las Prerrogativas de Los Militares em Los Nuevos Regímenes Democráticos. *Desarrollo Económico*, 27(108), 1988, p. 479-504. Retrieved from https://doi.org/papers2://publication/uuid/A9848D20-B35F-4F38-B458-6DCB11297E5D.

VELÁZQUEZ, Arturo C. Sotomayor. Why Some States Participate in UN Peace Missions While Others Do Not: An Analysis of Civil-Military Relations and Its Effects on Latin America's Contributions to Peacekeeping Operations. *Security Studies*, 19(1), 2010, p. 160-195. Retrieved from https://doi.org/10.1080/09636410903546822.

VILLA, Rafael Antonio Duarte; VIANA, Manuela Trindade. Security Issues during Lula's Administration: From the Reactive to the Assertive Approach. *Revista Brasileira de Política Internacional*, 53, 2010, p. 91-114.

WOOD, Bernard. *The Middle Powers and the General Interest*. Toronto: North-South Institute, 1988.

ZAVERUCHA, Jorge. Fragile Democracy and the Militarization of Public Safety in Brazil. *Latin American Perspectives*, 27(3), 2000, p. 8-31. Retrieved from https://doi.org/10.1177/0094582X0002700302.

________. The Fragility of the Brazilian Defense Ministry. *Revista de Sociologia e Política*, 2(25), 2006, p. 107-121.

________. La Militarización de La Seguridad Pública em México, 1994-1998. *Nueva Sociedad*, 213, 2008, p. 128-146.

Websites and databases referenced

International Peace Institute, Peacekeeping Database: https://www.ipinst.org/providing-for-peacekeeping-database.

Stockholm International Peace Research Institute (SIPRI), Military Expenditure Database: https://www.sipri.org/databases/milex.

United Nations General Assembly, Administrative and Budgetary Committee (5th Committee): https://www.un.org/en/ga/contributions/budget.shtml.

United Nations General Assembly, Assessment of Member State's advances to the Working Capital Fund for 2022 contributions to the United Nations regular budget for 2022: https://undocs.org/en/ST/ADM/SER.B/1038.
United Nations Peacekeeping Data: https://peacekeeping.un.org/en/data.

Appendix I – Interviewee profiles

In 2013 I conducted 8 semi-structured interviews with two civilians and six army officers with previous experience in peacekeeping operations. Most interviewees also had direct experience with MINUSTAH. The length of the conversation varied greatly in length, but the average interview time was about one hour.

To protect the identity of the interviewees, at their request, I use numbers to refer to each one. I provide only their rank (occupation, in the case of the civilians), to which operation they were sent and in which capacity.

Interviewee nº	Rank/Occupation	PKO experience
1	Civilian academic, specializing in civil--military relations and peacekeeping.	MINUSTAH, after the 2010 earthquake
2	Brazilian diplomat and academic, specializing in defense and foreign policy	–
3	Army Colonel	ONUMOZ – observer[1]; MINUSTAH – regular troop.
4	Army Lt. Colonel	MARMINCA – observer; UNMIT – observer.
5	Army Major	MINUSTAH – regular troop; CCOPAB – instructor;
6	Army Major	UNIMIS – observer; UNAMID – observer.
7	Army Major	MINUSTAH – regular troop; CCOPAB[2] – instructor.
8	Army Captain	MINUSTAH – regular troop.

Notes: 1) Observers are now called "experts on mission." 2) Brazilian Joint Center on Peace Operations, the center all Brazilian personnel participating in peacekeeping must attend. It provides instruction to the military contingents, civilian media, academics etc.

The civil-military politics of indigenous affairs in Brazil (1967-2021)[1]

Camila Scheidegger Farias

Introduction

After the end of the military regime in Brazil, a series of reforms aimed to turn the bureaucracy into a more meritocratic one. Moreover, the 1988 constitution has taken the Brazilian state to new levels of professionalism. However, some discretionary power related to appointments was kept to the Executive (D'Araújo, 2007, 2009).

Politicians can use political appointments as patronage opportunities, channels to bring specific skills to the bureaucracy, or influence policymaking (e.g., Dargent, 2014; Geddes, 1994). Political groups have been battling over the control of these valuable posts, especially in bureaucratic areas that are less insulated, i.e., agriculture and social policy agencies (Praça and Lopez, 2018).

The military is a central agent of the state *apparatus,* having considerable influence on the country's politics over the years, even after the democratization process in Brazil (see Amorim Neto, 2015; Stepan, 1988). Nevertheless, in post-democratization, public demand for greater civil society control over the military seems to have reduced their participation in official governmental and high-level bureaucratic positions at civilian agencies.

Recently Brazil saw a return of military officers from cabinet positions to the chair of bureaucratic agencies during the presidency of Michel Temer (Aug/2016-Dec/2017). This return has also heightened the debate about the ties between the military and high-level positions in the bureaucracy.

So here the question is: what factors drive the different patterns of appointments of bureaucracies in the social arena? Have these dynamics shifted after

1 This paper is a version of Camila Scheidegger Farias' master thesis defended at the Getulio Vargas Foundation in 2018, advised by Octavio Amorim Neto.

the democratization process in Brazil? To address this question, I will study the factors that lead to the appointment of non-policy experts to social agencies through the longitudinal study of the National Indian Foundation (henceforth FUNAI), the Brazilian national organization for indigenous affairs (1967-2021).

FUNAI has long been driven by political preferences, with many of its surrounding agents disputing posts over its history. However, the agency and Brazilian indigenous politics remain largely overseen by the political science literature[2] to which this chapter intends to contribute.

Despite FUNAI's institutional vulnerability, for some periods it has been headed by indigenists (e.g., the administrations of anthropologists Márcio Meira, Mar/7-Apr/12 and Marta Maria Azevedo, Jun/12-Apr/13), that is, personnel with considerable experience or training in indigenous affairs.

However, it is noteworthy that the concept of experts to FUNAI – i.e., what expertise is needed to take meaningful leadership roles at the agency? – is still examined between sociocultural anthropologists, the traditional scholarly field that has studied indigenous affairs. The lack of consensus among scholar is seen in the writings of sociocultural anthropologist Antônio Carlos de Souza Lima (1994, 2012).[3]

In line with the work of D'Araujo and Petek (2018) and Praça and Lopez (2018), a recent strand of the literature focuses more on the nuance that lies in between the polarization seen in public administration than the dichotomy of appointing politicians *versus* bureaucrats. So, moving past their potential partisanship, I aim to advance the political appointees to agencies in the social area by focusing on the professional background of those candidates. Moreover, in this study, I conceptualize agency expertise as discussed by Barberia and Praça (2014:6): training or practical experience in central policies formulated and implemented by the bureaucratic agency.

The following sections of this chapter discuss the political and institutional context of political appointments to FUNAI – starting with its predecessor, SPI.

---

2 See Soares 2020 for more on the field of indigenous politics in Brazil.

3 Recently the President of the American Anthropological Association has emitted an apology on their website. He stated that while the field has "often assigned themselves as experts over the cultural narratives and social histories of the first cultures of the America [...] many have neither respected Indigenous knowledge systems and community contributions nor addressed the intended and unintended impacts of anthropological research on those communities". So, this an on-going debate not only in Brazil but in the world.

Finally, I present the hypothesized causal conditions for selecting policy experts to FUNAI, my methodological strategy, and finally present the results found here.

The military and the first governmental indigenous affairs agency in Brazil

Before FUNAI, there was the Indian Protection and Localization of National Workers Service (SPILT). Created in 1910 officially, the mission of the SPILT was to "assist and protect the Indians in their integration into national society (Vieira and Quack 2016, 389), including land tenure affairs. The creation of the agency was linked to the programmatic line of work of the Ministry of Agriculture, Industry and Commerce (MAIC) to increase the presence of national workers (rather than European settlers) in areas of remote access and limited economic development (Oliveira, 2014) Only after 1918 dealt exclusively with issues related to indigenous affairs, being renamed to Indian Protection Service (SPI) (Bigio, 2007).

The military had a defining role in the creation and leadership of that agency. Appointed by the then Minister of Agriculture, Industry and Commerce, the first to direct the agency was Colonel Cândido Mariano da Silva Rondon. Rondon was a positivist military officer who gained notoriety with his work in the installation of telegraph networks in the interior of the country – the so-called *Comissão de Linhas Telegráficas* – with a "non-violent" approach towards the contacted indigenous communities (Bigio, 2007).

Using the technique of contact spread by Rondon, members of the SPI crew tried to contact indigenous peoples and conduct a "pacification" process, i.e., to establish a peace accord to cease violence between indigenous peoples and "civilians." This practice was conducted by *sertanistas*, a formal position in FUNAI, but also considered an ideological tradition of explorer who worked in the interiors of the country with indigenous peolpes (p. 89).

Moreover, Rondon and his generation of military intellectuals are also credited with delineating the guiding principles of the early work of the agency with concepts and presuppositions of the positivist tradition, such as the rational and scientific principles or the general perspective of humanity's progress (Oliveira and Souza Lima, 1981:277).

Rondon established the so-called integration policy. The indigeneity was seen as a transient phase, and the state's role was to help incorporate indigenous populations into what they called "civilization." Policies included coordinating programs to teach non-indigenous agricultural methods to the contacted or – "pacified" – communities and relocating populations from their land to indigenous posts.

Additionally, the 1916 civil code officially instituted the tutorship of autochthonous peoples by the Brazilian government. According to the civil code – modified in 2001 – individuals from indigenous communities were deemed by the state as relatively incapable of certain acts of civil life along with other Brazilians over the age of 16 and under 21 years of age, for instance (Araújo et al., 2006:162). Their imposed legal disability was only retracted under the 1988 constitution.

Then in 1939, the National Council for the Protection of the Indians (henceforth CNPI) was established to act as an institution that would formulate and advise Brazilian indigenist policies.[4] From the early 1960s, in the final period of existence of the SPI, the CNPI was the instance in which the presence of sociocultural anthropologists and indigenists more dedicated and concerned with the cultural aspects of indigenous affairs were concentrated (CPDOC, n.d).

According to (Bigio, 2007), Rondon was not able to develop successors in SPI, and after 1963, the SPI's public image was very worn out due to the irregularities investigated during a Parliamentary Inquiry Commission (CPI) set up in the Chamber of Deputies.

Hence, it was amidst (national and international) public turmoil over the allegations of omission and complicity in the corruption and deaths of indigenous peoples involving the SPI that the military administration of General Costa e Silva created the National Foundation of the Indian (FUNAI) (Albert, 1991). FUNAI came to substitute the CNPI and the SPI, which were extinct. Next, an overview of FUNAI's political and administrative context across its 54 years of existence is covered.

---

[4] CNPI or *Conselho Nacional de Política Indigenista* in Portuguese.

The military, the Amazon region and the National Foundation of the Indian (FUNAI)

Since colonial times, Brazil's history of indigenous affairs has been marked by great contradictions between the state and indigenous populations. It alternates phases of direct conflict and exploitation of labor and resources to the tutelage of the state and paternalistic policies.

In the '90s, along with other decentralization reforms in Brazil by former right-wing President Fernando Collor de Melo, FUNAI had its service portfolio significantly reduced. Several presidential decrees from February 4, 1991, delegated FUNAI's activities in the sectors of health, education, rural development and environmental protection to the Ministries of Health, Education, Agrarian Development and Environment, respectively (Souza Lima, 2015).

For instance, health service provision for indigenous peoples is currently an attribution of the Special Secretariat for Indigenous Health – after being under the National Health Foundation, Funasa, from the late '90s until 2010 – an arm of the Ministry of Health. To add to the complexity of the policy arena, the execution of many of the public services to indigenous populations have been outsourced to mostly non-indigenous organizations, including NGOs (Shankland and Athias, 2007).

While FUNAI is not the main provider of basic public services anymore, FUNAI still has the role of overseeing access to those by indigenous communities. Indigenous peoples in Brazil account for 0.5% of the population, while its increasing income gap compared to non-indigenous peoples suggests that this is an important attribution of the state.[5] (IBGE, 2010).

Other roles of FUNAI include the indigenous land demarcation process, i.e., "the administrative process of identifying and signaling the limits of the territory traditionally occupied by indigenous peoples (FUNAI, 2021)." This is an important step in the attainment of the constitutional right to indigenous land tenure for these original communities. FUNAI is also responsible for the protection of isolated or recently contacted peoples, as well as overseeing indigenous peoples' constitutional rights.

5 The poverty gap between indigenous and non-indigenous people has increased by an alarming 99 percent in Brazil in only a decade (from the early 2000s to the late 2000s), according to The World Bank (2015).

So, while some activities related to indigenous affairs have been delegated to other ministries or even outsourced to NGOs, the overall welfare access to indigenous peoples is still one of the main attributions of FUNAI according to its statute (Brazil, 2017). Because the scope of FUNAI's work is more flexible than more structured bureaucracies, like regulatory agencies, the organization's top political appointees carry extensive policymaking power. The president of FUNAI can change the structure of FUNAI, including its departments and attributions, that is, what kind of work. Because of their institutional mandate, they are also accountable for the state's overall approach toward indigenous affairs.

However, social agents' policy interests – i.e., the enforcement of the constitutional rights that social movements helped to write – also often translate into the pressure to take part in appointment decisions. As an example, in October 2021, the current president of the National Indian Foundation (FUNAI), Marcelo Augusto Xavier da Silva, was the subject of a request for removal from office for administrative impropriety by the NGO Articulation of Indigenous Peoples of Brazil (Apib) to the Federal Court. According to the request, Xavier's administration makes the demarcation of indigenous lands unfeasible, facilitates irregular use and takeover of indigenous land and fails to defend indigenous rights in court (*Congresso em Foco*, 2021).

However, Xavier's policy direction is in line with Brazil's congressional conservative coalition and President Bolsonaro. The Brazilian 2020 public budget, the first under Bolsonaro's rule, shrunk the amount of funding for FUNAI's main programs by 40% compared to the previous year. And Bolsonaro has already been publicly vocal about wanting to stop indigenous land tenure processes wanting to turn mining legal in indigenous land (*Exame*, 2019). To justify, he returned to old critical speeches on Brazilian indigenous affairs, which argued that the ratio of indigenous groups to reserve is too high and would hinder the agricultural development of the country and that mining would be beneficial to indigenous people's economic development.

The Executive's policy interest vs. politics link in FUNAI is also evident in the extent that coalition members take part in the appointment process. For instance, under Temer and Bolsonaro's leaderships, the congressional farm lobby, which represents the country's powerful agribusiness sector, and the evangelicals, have had a major influence in suggesting names to FUNAI and also removing in case of discontentment with the appointees' work (Potter, 2020).

So, while the extent of the administrative power of FUNAI's leaders to implement targeted policies is great, the extent they can diverge significantly from powerful principals has been demonstrated to be usually low, as shown in the high turnover rates of the position (ISA, 2021b). FUNAI's top position is highly disputed by different groups (e.g., social movements, Conservative coalitions, etc.). One of the reasons that understanding who gets appointed to the head of FUNAI matters is that these patterns show significant clues on the policy direction intended for the indigenous affairs area.

The approach that FUNAI's leaders take towards indigenous populations can deepen socioeconomic disparities and even mortality rates due to health crises or land conflicts. The president, as the main leader of the institution, is responsible for deploying appropriate resources to the well-being of indigenous groups, FUNAI's primary objective. This includes coordinating with other public agencies so that the appropriate resources get to indigenous peoples, including food or medicine, and providing security for communities and their land (i.e., from illegal loggers or land expropriators). Leaders' purposeful non-responsiveness or disastrous policies have led to the killings of indigenous as well as non-indigenous people over the years and, thus, the relevance of the position.

Furthermore, during the organization's trajectory, whenever indigenous groups faced critical land disputes or other important claims, indigenous leaders demanded responses from the President of FUNAI himself. The power to alleviate (or aggravate) tension between activists, governmental agents, indigenous groups, landowners, and others involved in another critical attribute of the position.

FUNAI itself is a complex organization. First, there is not only one but many indigenous communities and ethnicities, each with its own leadership. Furthermore, those involved in indigenous affairs face severe disagreements over the moral, cultural and legal aspects of indigenist policies, resulting in great contradictions. Inside the bureau, more than one vision for the agency has coexisted (Trinidad, 2016).

FUNAI faces controversy, not only with outside agents but with insiders, which increases the complexity of running the agency. Pozzobon (1999), for instance, has described that inner politics has greatly influenced political appointments. Many presidents have left office due to disagreements over the use of other high-level political positions of FUNAI in regional posts by the ministers and the Executive. Also, the author claims that clientelistic "factions" have always run

FUNAI.[6] Hence even when conflict with outside actors does not break, FUNAI leadership must deal with the multiple groups and opinions inside FUNAI.

According to Garfield (2000:546), during the military regime, the military interest in FUNAI can be explained by the fact that "FUNAI embodied the growing hegemony of the state over the Amazonian frontier (and the countryside in general), and its efforts to foster capitalist growth and social consensus through bureaucratic administration."

Comparatively to the SPI, the military promoted a vigorous push towards the professionalization of FUNAI's cadre, following the efforts of their agenda in Brazil of forming a technocrat public administration. For instance, from 1970 until 1985, ten formation courses for indigenist technicians were organized first by FUNAI, then by the University of Brasilia, and finally by the National School of Public Administration (ENAP) (Bigio, 2007).

The military presence during the military regime diverges from those early years of the SPI: the military chairs of FUNAI had no previous experience with indigenous affairs and lacked the "humanist" principles advocated by Rondon and his followers. Also, the military presence represented a consequence of the regime, as it was spread across different realms of the government (Oliveira, 1988 *apud* Bigio, 2007).

While military pressure to direct FUNAI's goals has received praise from some sectors of society which claimed that the eminent military undertakings – especially in the Amazon – have brought better access to governmental services and infrastructure to remote populations, the period also fostered social mobilization that opposed the military developmental policies in FUNAI.

Furthermore, the military has remained influential in the politics of the Brazilian Amazon region after the democratization process. According to (Castro, 2006), the Amazon region became increasingly important to Brazilian National defense in the first couple of decades after the democratization process.

The resource-rich dense Amazon rainforest, which divides the Brazilian territory with several of its South American neighbors, is an important region for national defense policymaking. However, beyond practical defense objectives, Castro (2006) argues that the army involvement in the area is also geopolitical.

6 For example, sertanistas, Apoena Meireles, Nov/1985-May/1986 and Sydney Possuelo, Jun/1991-May/1993 and more recently General Franklimberg Freitas, May/2017-Apr/2018).

For instance, arguments used by the military to justify intervention in the region included the protection of international greed in the area and the necessity of urbanizing and occupying the region for not being populated enough. However, 23% of the territory is indigenous lands (ISA, 2021a). So, conflicting views over control of the Brazilian territory and land seem to account for some of the reasons why the military in Brazil is still involved in political clashes with indigenous groups or pro-indigenous social movements. However, ideological views also seem to account for it this conflict between social movements and the military. Across recent Brazilian history, there seems to be an alignment between the military and right-wing politicians and voters in Brazil since the military regime was also a conservative movement.

So, it is noteworthy that besides the military, another pivotal group to the politics of indigenous affairs in Brazil and thus to FUNAI are social movements. The latter is composed mainly of societal agents (national and international NGOs, indigenous groups, intellectuals, partisans from left-wing parties, and civil servants, among others) who act through different channels to bring notoriety to the pro-indigenous cause, often clashing with the government and with the military.

Drawing from Dargent (2014), I argue that in social agencies, the influence of key agents is vital to the decision of whom to appoint. This is especially true since the sector has been argued as more vulnerable to political interference than others (D'Araujo and Petek, 2018; Dargent, 2014). My hypothesis is also aligned with the traditional strand of Political Science that argues that political agents have a significant role in shaping bureaucratic structure (Moe, 1989).

For my case study, I conducted a comparative historical analysis to verify which contextual factors drove the presence (and absence) of policy experts in the country's official indigenous agency, the National Indian Foundation (FUNAI). Here I focus particularly on the top position of FUNAI, the presidency, as it is a centerpiece in Brazilian official indigenous affairs.

Dialoguing with the literature on political appointments that recently has shifted from the dichotomy of appointing partisans and technicians to the attributes and background of leaders, the focus here is not to investigate expertise separately from partisanship. Instead, the goal is to differentiate complete strangers to indigenous affairs from those acknowledged as well-trained or experienced leaders, regardless of their partisan ties. The focus on technical expertise, regardless of partisan ties, is supported by the findings from Lewis

(2007) that suggest that the background of agents occupying bureaucratic positions impacts agency performance.

Moreover, political and technical criteria are not necessarily contradicting. For instance, Márcio José Brando Santilli (Sep/95-Mar/96), chosen by Fernando Henrique Cardoso (PSDB), was both a former state representative from the PMDB party (1982-1986) and an experienced indigenist. While in Congress, Santilli was one of the leaders of the commission on indigenous affairs and an active representative of indigenous peoples in the constitutional process (1987-1988). He was also the founder of a pro-indigenous NGO, Núcleo de Direitos Indígenas (NDI), the predecessor of Instituto Socioambiental (ISA) (CPDOC/FGV, n.d.)

Hence, the first condition I analyze is the influence of two important groups on the politics of the agency. More specifically, whether the strength of social movements and military influence over the incumbent influence the appointment patterns to FUNAI. Due to a closer alignment between social movements and *indigenistas* (i.e., FUNAI careeristis and socialcultural anthropologists) over the years, I theorize that, if social mobilization had an influence on politicarl appointments to the agency, the former group would push for the appointment of leadership from this *indigenista* background.

For this study, I use a broad definition of social movements, which argues that they can be expressed through various channels (i.e., protests, riots, judicial action, lobbying government) and by multiple agents (i.e., national and international NGOs, indigenous groups, intellectuals, partisans from left-wing parties, civil servants). Also, like Vieira and Quack (2016), I consider that pro-indigenous social mobilization manifests itself through international linkages or networks, and therefore, the impact of national from international pressure cannot be fully separated.

As for the military presence in FUNAI, due to the strategic interest in FUNAI, I hypothesize that army men would have fewer incentives to delegate to these professionals traditionally associated with indigenous affairs. So, through its link with the Executive, they would push for the appointment of loyalists that address their national security agenda.

However, while it is important to analyze the influence of interest groups, the agenda and preferences of the Brazilian president are important factors since high-level appointments of the agency, such as the head of FUNAI, are attributions of the Executive. Since 2003 the responsibility of these appointments has been delegated from presidents to the presidential chief of staff. While it cannot be disregarded that appointments can be handed over to other actors (e.g., the ministry under which FUNAI resides) and allies – as many posts are in coalitional governments – here for academic purposes, the main political agent under study are presidents, representing his cabinet and other parts of his government.

Moreover, Presidents do not act only based on electoral goals but also to maximize policy preferences (Amorim Neto, 2006). In areas that have a more strategic interest in having positive outcomes, it is plausible that the concern of being blamed for bad decisions might provide incentives to delegate power to policy experts. By doing so, they can both legitimize their agenda (signaling to voters their concern with the subject) and guarantee that no bad consequence will arise in that area that they can be accounted for.

Based on Amorim Neto (2006a), I adopt the definition that the ideology of a president is that of his or her party. Therefore, presidents with a party that identifies as conservative are considered right-wing. Here I argue that non-right-wing incumbents – centrists or leftists – will contribute to the appointment of experts to public agencies like FUNAI, as their agenda is more bound to social policies than right-wing politicians. Nevertheless, in less strategic areas to the president, there is more room to use positions as political tools. For center-right or full right-wing politicians, it becomes less costly to have an agent as the head of the public institution to implement their agenda or to use it as a "political resource" and delegate the decision to others.

Hence, through a comparative historical analysis, I verify the role of those political and societal agents in the appointments to the leadership position at FUNAI across its 54 years of existence, including a regime transition. Moreover, I will analyze if the establishment of a democratic regime has changed two pivotal groups' power dynamics and influence. Below I summarize my arguments, and in the next section, I further detail the empirical design of my qualitative analysis.

- Hypothesis 1: International and national social mobilization contributed to the appointment of experts to FUNAI.
- Hypothesis 2: Military influence over presidents did not contribute to the appointment of experts to FUNAI.
- Hypothesis 3: Non-rightist presidents in office appointed experts to FUNAI.

Empirical strategy and data

I conduct a within-case assessment of the case of FUNAI, that is, the variations of patterns of appointments across time. The comparative historical case study by nature is limited in external validity, that is, the ability to generate explanations that can cover other cases (e.g., in other countries or even different periods); it allows for capturing details that are context-specific, which is the goal of the present analysis (George and Bennett, 2005). The contextual analysis of FUNAI is especially relevant, as patterns of appointments in Brazil were found to differ according to the nature of the agency and the resources dealt with (Dargent, 2014; Lopez and Praça, 2015; Praça and Lopez, 2018).

As aforementioned, I adopt the concept of policy expertise from Barberia and Praça (2014:6), which is the "background in main policies formulated and implemented by a certain agency." So, both on-the-job training (e.g., FUNAI employees), as well as formal educational training (e.g., sociocultural anthropology, linguistics, etc.) are considered forms of expertise in my analysis. The engagement on indigenous rights causes as "indigenists" is also considered practical experience with indigenous affairs (e.g., engaging in NGOs and other civil society organizations).

For the case selection, it comprises all FUNAI's presidents from its creation in December of 1967 until April 2021 that stayed in office more than 100 days,[7] resulting in 37 (i.e., two have been in office twice) in total, from the universe of 41. The presidents of FUNAI are also the unity of analysis.

Non-experts to FUNAI were considered those who were appointed to the leadership of FUNAI without training or expertise in the field, e.g., FUNAI's first President, José de Queirós Campos (Dec/67-Jun/70). Also, those that have only very little experience in the bureaucracy related to FUNAI or indigenous affairs were here considered non-experts. E.g., the retired sergeant and accountant Gerson da Silva Alves (Apr/85–Sept/85) worked at bureaucratic functions at FUNAI.

Experience in peripheral areas or a relatively strong background in indigenous affairs was considered here experts, e.g., Júlio Gaiger (Mar/96-Jul/97), a lawyer, his background in indigenous affairs started in 1977. It included positions at

---

7 The presidents not included in the analysis are Otacílio Antunes Reis Filho (Jun/02-Jul/02), Roque de Barros Laraia (Apr/00-May/00), and Ayrton Carneiro de Almeida (Apr/1985-Apr/1985).

pro-indigenous NGOs, i.e., the National Indian Support Association (ANAI) in Porto Alegre and The Indian Missionary Council (CIMI). These are the cases of the so-called sertanistas, indigenists, and sociocultural anthropologists, for instance. e.g., FUNAI employee and anthropologist Artur Nobre Mendes (Aug/2–Jan/3 and Jun/16–Sept/16).

To assess the expertise the presidents of FUNAI, my outcome of interest, biographic information on all the presidents of FUNAI was reviewed by the author. A compilation of FUNAI's history by Fundação Getulio Vargas' center of research and documentation of Brazilian Contemporary history CDPOC was used as a source (i.e., CPDOC, n.d). Also, the biographies in the publications Povos Indígenas no Brasil by the Centro Ecumênico de Documentação e Informação – CEDI (1980, 1981, 1982, 1983, 1984, 1986, 1991) and then by the Instituto Socioambiental – ISA (n.d., 1996, 2000, 2005, 2010) and online (i.e., ISA 2021) were used to complement the data.

To identify the causal conditions, I draw on measures from various disciplines.[8] Additionally, for my case study, I conducted a literature review on the dynamics between social movements, the military, the Brazilian government and appointments to FUNAI during the period of analysis (i.e., 1967 – 2021).

Furthermore, to obtain additional evidence about my hypothesized conditions, I rely on news media searches, the author's case knowledge and archival research at CPDOC in Rio de Janeiro and FUNAI's digital archives (i.e., *Museu do Indio*).

The forces driving appointments to FUNAI (1964-1985)

1.1 Administrations' ideology under the military regime

When FUNAI was implemented during the military regime (1964 to 1985), the ruling party, ARENA (National Renovating Alliance), and then Partido Democrático Social (PDS) were conservative parties, so then only right-wing

8 Sources for assessing the military influence over presidents: Amorim Neto (2015); Bruneau and Tollefson (2014); Stepan (1988); for the ideology of Brazilian parties: Power and Zucco (2009, 2012); Power and Rodrigues-Silveira, (2018); for the intensity of the social movement in Brazil: (R. Abers and von Bülow 2011; R. N. Abers and von Bülow 2018; Jackson and Warren 2005; Luciano 2006; Rodrigues 2002; Valente 2017; Vieira and Quack 2016; Yashar 1998, 1999).

presidents ruled Brazil. Thus, during the regime, it was not possible to untangle the president's ideology from the military influence over the president since the leaders were both.

The first president appointed to FUNAI was the civilian José de Queirós Campos, who ruled from December 1967 until June 1970. Queirós Campos, a conservative nationalist, was a councilman by the National Democratic Union (UDN) in the interior of the Minas Gerais state prior to the 1964 regime takeover (Valente, 2017). Despite being a journalist without previous experience in indigenous affairs, Queirós Campos was responsible for dismantling the SPI and reassembling the organization as a foundation (CPDOC/FGV, n.d.)

While a civilian had been appointed to the highest leadership of the agency, the rest of the agency was not. According to Valente (2017), the Minister of the Interior General Albuquerque Lima appointed military officers to various high-level placements in local posts (e.g., the so-called *chefias das inspetorias*). Moreover, the military occupied eight out of the eleven existing positions, the exact opposite of what experienced indigenists were advocating at the time (Valente, 2017).

Before leaving the office, Queirós Campos (Dec/1967-Jun/1970) addressed the issue and denounced publicly that three years after its creation, FUNAI still lacked trained professionals like linguists and anthropologists (Valente, 2017).

As for the presence of indigenous representatives in key positions at the SPI but also later remained at FUNAI, it is no surprise that they were also excluded from these positions (Almeida, 2017). For instance, the Brazilian state tutorship approach to indigenous groups was established by law, i.e., indigenous peoples were under legal disabilities until the 1988 constitution marked by substantial advances in legal rights.

Under the administration of the Brazilian president Emílio Médici (Oct/69-Mar/74), a hardliner, Oscar Jeronymo Bandeira de Mello, became the first general appointed to command FUNAI. Bandeira de Mello's rule marked the face of the following administrations under the military regime.

Bandeira de Mello was a former National Intelligence Service (SNI) officer and also a former head of FUNAI's security division. He was in charge of aligning FUNAI's work with the development ideals in the National Integration Plan (PIN) created in 1970 mainly to guide the state's operations in the Amazon region (CPDOC, n.d.)

Moreover, his administration targeted a quick integration of indigenous peoples into society so that they would not hinder the occupation and colonization of the Amazon. Also, under his command in FUNAI, the department of community development was created in an attempt to make the enterprise self-sustaining: the costs of governmental services to indigenous peoples should be paid by what could be generated through the exploitation of their patrimony (CEDI, 1986).

Only a few exceptions, like General Ismarth Araújo de Oliveira, FUNAI's third president (Mar/74-Mar/79) appointed by Geisel (1974-1979), sought some level of cooperation with sociocultural anthropologists and social scientists in several projects in FUNAI (CEDI, 1981; CPDOC/FGV, n.d.; Trinidad, 2016). However, the Executive was still worried about delegating control over land to FUNAI. The agency employees and sociocultural anthropologists were then responsible both for the identification of the lands and the final decision about demarcation (Trinidad, 2016). So, soon after the military realized that FUNAI career employees had significant control over the land demarcation process, an executive degree was put in order to curtail their autonomy (Araújo et al., 2006)

It's noteworthy then that Brazilian heads of state repeatedly have expelled or limited the influence of certain professionals in the indigenous politics field throughout the military government. Sociocultural anthropologists and *indigenistas,* allegedly the experts in the area, were shunned, and many only returned to the agency after the end of the military regime in 1985.

For instance, João Carlos Nobre da Veiga, a retired Colonel (president from Nov/1979-Oct/1981), after coming to the office appointed by Figueiredo's government (1979-1985), pledged to implement more discipline into FUNAI and dismissed 39 indigenist and sociocultural anthropologists due to a letter they sent to the Minister of the Interior criticizing FUNAI's policies (CEDI, 1986).

Also, during General Nobre da Veiga's administration, tension rose not only with sociocultural anthropologists but also with indigenous groups. As a result of the frustration at FUNAI's policies considered overly controlling by some, indigenous groups joined forces in several indigenous assemblies, but all were repressed by the military regime.

While there was a certain balance between civilian and military officers among the nine presidents to FUNAI appointed by the Executive during the military regime,[9] very few had previous experience in indigenous affairs. The exceptions were Paulo M. Leal (Oct/81-Jul/83), who worked as a former advisor to FUNAI during the Nobre da Veiga administration, and the lawyer Jurandy M. da Fonseca (May/84-Sept/84), who had been FUNAI's chief of staff in the Bandeira Mello and Ismarth Araújo de Oliveira administrations. Even so, they cannot be considered careerists.

So, during the military regime, it seems that the clash of goals between views about FUNAI from *indigenistas* made the military appoint their own trustees to office. While the background of these appointees – engineers, lawyers, economists and policemen and retired officers – seems aligned with the military's developmental paradigm and their view of the agency, they were less related to the core activity of FUNAI. So, it seems that the ideology of the Executive, i.e., being a right-wing military regime, contributed to the appointment of what I consider here non-experts to FUNAI.

1.2 Social movements pre-democratic transition

Besides the military, the so-called pro-indigenous movement has also remained another important pressure group that was invested in indigenous politics in Brazil, i.e., the military involvement in the agency, and the quality of its leadership

Along with the Minister of the Interior, the first president of FUNAI already faced opposition from civil society and the media. The many Parliamentary Inquiry Commissions from 1963 to 1967 set to investigate the wrongdoings of SPI agents culminated in the 1967 Jader Figueiredo report written by the namesake public attorney at the behest of the Minister of the Interior General Albuquerque Lima (Souza Lima 2015).

The report, which documented systematic abuses and violence perpetrated by agents of the SPI against indigenous groups, recommended the suspension of 17 and the dismissal of 33 SPI employees. Notwithstanding, these efforts backfired due to the decision by Minister General Albuquerque Lima to hold a

9 José de Queiroz Campos (Dec/67-Jun/70); Oscar J. Bandeira de Mello (Jun/70-Mar/74); Ismarth A. de Oliveira (Mar/74-Mar/79); Adhemar Ribeiro da Silva (Mar/79-Nov/79); José Carlos Nobre da Veiga (Nov/79-Oct/81); Paulo M. Leal (Oct/81-Jul/83); Otávio Ferreira Lima (Jul/83-May/84); Jurandy M. da Fonseca (May/84-Sept/84); Nélson Marabuto (Sept/84-Apr/85).

press conference in March 1968 to present the main findings of the report. On the occasion, "several national and international reporters were present, and some others flew into Brazil in its aftermath to investigate the findings," and so the results reverberated internationally (Vieira and Quack 2016).

The first organized reactions from civil society to FUNAI's policies date from the early '70s. It includes the July of 1971 manifest, signed by 80 professionals from the field of social sciences. The document protested the guidelines adopted by the military in Brazilian indigenous affairs and the proposal of the Indian Statute (CPDOC/FGV n.d.).

Skidmore (1990, p. 182) argues that clashes between the hardliner government of Médici (1969-1974) and Catholic activists – who defended indigenous peoples and small farmers, menaced by the large land speculators and landowners – went to a point where many from the latter group were tortured and arrested.

Several authors (Bigio 2007; Oliveira 2012; Vieira and Quack 2016) emphasize an episode that marked the intensification of the incipient indigenous rights movement: the announcement by the then Minister of the Interior Maurício Rangel Reis in February 1978 that Brazilian Head of State, President Ernesto Geisel would sign a decree to instate the feared emancipation of indigenous people. The emancipation of indigenous people meant the end of the indigenous' welfare apparatus, including the right to land tenure. Consequently, a plethora of NGOs was formed in the context of opposing this measure (e.g., *Comissões Pró-Índio* – CPIs, the *Grupo de Apoio ao Índio* – GAI) and from then on, remained present in the official indigenous affairs' debates (CPDOC/FGV n.d.).

Under the menace of the emancipation of indigenous peoples, activism on the indigenous cause got organized, including The Union of Indigenous Nations (UNI) in 1980. The UNI aimed to bring indigenous groups together to join forces and articulate their demands politically and socially. Nevertheless, the organization was criticized by many inside FUNAI, which did not recognize the movement, considering it a threat to national unity (CEDI 1981).

However, by the end of the 1980s, the regime would collapse. The social mobilization that pushed for democratization in the country also incorporated other societal demands, including indigenous rights. The country followed a transnational trend of social security advancements in Latin America (Yashar 1998, 1999).

While social mobilization failed to influence appointment patterns in a significant manner during military rule, regime transition in Brazil has. The widening of the political arena and the many new organizations formed by the effervescent civil society seem to have brought uncertainty and the contention of interest groups in bureaucratic politics. During the Brazilian regime transition, FUNAI faced a great succession crisis, where in a year, five presidents[10] occupied the position. One of them only lasted one day in the position due to the pressure of pro-indigenous actors and organizations.[11] Next section, I analyze the conditions which led to different appointment patterns for the head of FUNAI during the new democratic regime.

1.2.1 The forces driving appointments to FUNAI (1985-2021)

1.2.1.1 The military influence and the ideology of the Brazilian president

The first democratic president, the rightist José Sarney (Mar/85-Mar/90), left the conservative PDS to join PMDB right before running for the presidency in the first democratic election after the end of the military regime. His administration was greatly influenced by the armed forces' political positions due to its proximity to the past regime. Sarney, being the first civilian chief of state after 21 years, has had to cooperate with the military during the democratic transition due to the risk of being overthrown. Also, he had six ministries run by military officers, high investment in defense, and overall high dependence on the armed forces (as demonstrated by the measures of (Amorim Neto, 2015; Bruneau and Tollefson, 2014; Stepan, 1988).

Soon after the succession crisis, the economist Romero Jucá (May/86-Sept/88) was appointed by Sarney. Jucá had made a career out of holding political appointments in different public agencies – none related to indigenous politics. He was trusted with the task of incorporating the National Security Council's directives to FUNAI as part of the Calha Norte Project. The project's goal was to increase military occupation and promote the development of the Amazonian region, to

10 Those are: the police officer Nélson Marabuto Domingues (Sep/84–Apr/85); former Director of the National Agrarian Reform Institute of Brazil (Incra); Ayrton Carneiro de Almeida (18/4/1985); Sergeant and former FUNAI bureaucrat Gérson da Silva Alves (Apr/85–Sep/85); the *sertanistas* Álvaro Vilas Boas (Sep/85–Nov/85) and Apoena Meireles (Nov/85– May/86).

11 De Almeida (18/4/1985).

protect it from international greed and the misuse of Brazilian strategic natural resources. As one of the consequences of the project, the National Security Council (CSN) began to influence the demarcation processes of indigenous land directly.

The three subsequent presidents followed Jucá's and CSN's footsteps: the lawyer and former president of a branch of the National Security Council (CSN), Iris Pedro de Oliveira (Sept/88-Mar/89); Colonel Aírton Alcântara (Mar/90-Aug/90); and the retired sergeant of the Air Force, former advisor to Iris Pedro de Oliveira and ally of Romero Jucá, Cantídio Guerreiro Guimarães (Aug/90-July/91).

Notably, Colonel Airton Alcântara was the first military president of FUNAI in the democratic regime – the last one was Colonel Paulo Moreira Leal, who stepped down in 1983. Alcântara was appointed to office by the new rightist Brazilian President Fernando Collor de Mello (Mar/1990-Dec/1992).

Colonel Alcântara's policies also reflected the agency's inner conflict between indigenists and the military. He had prepared a list of 880 FUNAI employees that became "available" for allocation in other public agencies –many of these sociocultural anthropologists and indigenists (CEDI, 1991).

Also, in the same period, the Earth Summit (or Eco 92 in Portuguese), a UN conference on environmental and developmental issues held in Rio de Janeiro in 1992, put the Brazilian government in the spotlight for their practices with traditional peoples. Thus, Fernando Collor de Melo appointed the *sertanista* Sydney Ferreira Possuelo (Jun/91-May/93) to chair FUNAI to improve Brazil's image on sustainable practices. The fact that also Collor did not have close ties to leaders in the armed forces seems to have reduced the stakes of replacing a military officer by the social movement's conception of a qualified professional.

Centrist President Itamar Franco (Dec/92-Jan/95), Collors' successor after his 1992 impeachment, retained Possuelo as the head of FUNAI. Nevertheless, Possuelo was later dismissed by Justice Minister Maurício Correia for opposing the clientelistic distribution of posts by the Minister of the Civil Cabinet, Henrique Hargreaves, and also due to pressure from the military and mining companies (CPDOC/FGV, n.d.).

Itamar Franco faced an important economic crisis, a lack of popular support and political turmoil after the impeachment of Collor. As a result, he turned to the military for support, a similar strategy employed by presidents prior to 1946 (Amorim Neto, 2015).

While usually this strategy is shown by the great percentage of appointments of military officers to ministries that were expected to be run by civilians, this was not the case for FUNAI (Amorim Neto, 2015). Despite Franco's ties with the Brazilian security forces, after Possuelo, all presidents appointed to FUNAI were civilian FUNAI careerists.[12] It is noteworthy that after Franco, presidents' bond with the armed forces weakened. The military would only return to FUNAI – and other traditional civilian public agencies – in the late 2010s.

This pattern was followed by the then moderate Fernando Henrique Cardoso's administration (Jan/1995-Dec/1998; Jan/1999-Dec/2002) from the Brazilian Social Democratic Party (PSDB).[13] Exceptions were the appointments of the lawyer Sulivan Silvestre (Aug/97-Fev/99) and of the career politician José Márcio Panoff de Lacerda (Fev/99-Nov/99). In the first case, scholars argue that he represents a peculiar appointment by Minister of Justice Iris Rezende member of Fernando Henrique Cardoso's first term administration (Jan/1995- Dec/1998), who managed to show his "gunpowder" power by appointing a "loyalist and a complete stranger" to indigenist policies, despite the discontent of FUNAI employees and NGOs (CPDOC, n.d; ISA, 2000)

However, only during the leftist Lula da Silva's administration (Jan/3-Jan/11) have two anthropologists successfully stayed in office for a prolonged period: Mercio Pereira Gomes (Sep/3-Mar/7) and Márcio Meira (Apr/7-Apr/12). In total, the Brazilian worker party (PT) has ruled Brazil for 13 years, first with Lula da Silva and then with the later impeached Dilma Rousseff (Jan/11-Aug/16). During PT's administration, appointees to FUNAI's leadership either had training or some previous experience in indigenous affairs.[14]

Similar to Franco, Dilma's successor, Temer, experienced very little popular support having stepped into office after an impeachment process as well; he also turned to the armed forces for support. One of the actions that signaled an approximation to the military was the recreation of the agency responsible for direct assistance and advice to the president on military and security matters:

---

12 Claudio dos Santos Romero (May/93-Sept/93) and Dinarte Nobre Madeiro (Sept/93-Sept/95).

13 However, it is important to stress that across the years the position of parties has shifted, as argued by Power and Rodrigues-Silveira (2018), and Power and Zucco (2009, 2012).

14 Individuals with background in peripheral areas, like former President Flávio Chiarelli (Oct/2014-Jun/2015), a lawyer whose on-the-job experience was obtained as the National Chief Attorney of FUNAI.

The Office of Institutional Security of the Presidency of the Republic (GSI) (*Estadão*, 2016). Additionally, he appointed the first military president to FUNAI in 17 years (i.e., General Franklimberg Freitas – May/2017-Apr/2018; Jan/2019-Jun/2019).

After that, military influence at FUNAI continued to rise with former military, Brazilian President Bolsonaro (2018 – present), and sociocultural anthropologists and indigenists with appropriate training have been removed from technical positions in the organization (Oliveira, 2019).

Moreover, President Bolsonaro, a former military officer himself, has more than twice the number of appointees from the army in high-level bureaucratic positions than Dilma and Temer. Only in the sustainability area, by 2020, there were 99 political appointees from the military (ABRAJI, 2020; Menezes, Mello, and Couto, 2021). Under Bolsonaro's Administration, FUNAI has changed command of 20 regional coordinators; most political appointees are from the military (Leitão, 2020).

Marcelo Augusto Xavier, chief of police, was an ombudsman at FUNAI for a few months, and in 2016, his work at the Parliamentary Inquiry Commission (CPI) of FUNAI and Incra (2016) was highly controversial. Invited by Brazil's congressional farm lobby, which represents the country's powerful agribusiness sector in both houses, he was an advisor to the CPI. According to Shalders (2019), in addition to trying to criminalize indigenous peoples, civil servants and non-governmental organizations, the commission's final report would allegedly gather a series of information on what would be, in the view of its authors, irregularities in some demarcation processes.

In conclusion, after the democratization process, the inclusion of new parties and leaders with different backgrounds, including ties with the military and ideology, seems to have added more confounding factors that can drive appointments. However, it is seen that the military influence over the presidency still has led presidents to appoint non-experts to FUNAI. Also, rightist presidents that had strong ties with the military (e.g., Temer and Bolsonaro) have seemed to have promoted the most changes in the direction of the agency's leadership to align not only with the military lobby but also with the agribusiness lobby. Next section, I address the role of social movement in the politics of FUNAI.

1.2.2 Social movements post-democratic transition

With a new regime, it came a new constitution. Between 1987 and 1988, there was a constant presence of indigenous groups and manifestations in the National Congress to demand the acknowledgment of their rights in the new Constitution. In fact, the Constitution of 1988 is known for providing ground-breaking legislation towards social rights – including indigenous' - in areas like land, education, and health in Brazil.

Also, at the time, several institutions (i.e., the main author of the chapter on "Indians," the Union of Indigenous Nations – UNI, supported by the Brazilian Association of Anthropology – ABA, the National Coordination of Geologists – Conage, the Brazilian Society for the Advancement of Science – SBPC, and the Missionary Indigenous Council – CIMI) lobbied the Subcommittee on Black people, Indigenous Populations, Disabled people and Minorities, so that the chapter on indigenous rights would pass the voting (CEDI, 1991).

After the democratization period, the effervesce of social movements fluctuated. During the Brazilian Labor Party PT 13-year administration also, social movement agents were brought into the cabinet. PT's administration was marked by the appointment of public leaders associated with social movements and unions. Such a trend was also observed at FUNAI (D'Araújo, 2007, 2009; D'Araújo and Petek, 2018). Yet, throughout the PT government, occasional public protests against FUNAI policies still occurred. For instance, the Brazilian labor party also received considerable criticism over the slowness of land demarcation processes, perhaps due to the same incredibly large governmental base, which prioritized agribusiness development in exchange for political support.

However, FUNAI's policy regime drastically shifted in 2017 after center-right president Temer – who maintained a more aligned view with the military than its predecessor, Dilma – came to office.[15] For instance, the land tenure processes have come to an abrupt halt for the first time since the 1985 democratization in Brazil (Amado, 2020). As a result, the agency has faced increased criticism by indigenous peoples, advocates, and *indigenistas*.[16] The rise in tension between

15 Over the years the PSDB (Brazilian Social Democratic Party) and Brazilian Democratic Movement (MDB) went further to the right of the ideology spectrum (Power and Rodrigues-Silveira, 2018).

16 About the performance and wrongdoing of FUNAI's policies or the state's approach to indigenous affairs in Brazil, refer to de Carvalho, Goyes, and Vegh Weis (2021).

political and administrative views for the agency is also reflected in changes to FUNAI's cadre and who gets appointed to its leadership.

Moreover, during Temer's administration, political controversies over the role of the military in FUNAI resurged in media outlets again for the first time since the 1990s. Despite the criticism, Michel Temer – who maintains a close relationship with the military – went through with the appointment of a General to FUNAI's main post[17] To make amends for the public discontent, General Franklimberg Freitas (May/2017-Apr/2018) was highly publicized as the first president of FUNAI with an indigenous origin.

While national and international organizations have condemned Temer's and now Bolsonaro's environmental practices, it has not been sufficient to influence changes to FUNAI's cadres. Moreover, pro-indigenous organizations speculate that the violence against indigenous mobilization also adds to the difficulty of maintaining the relevance of contemporary activism. A 2018 ranking by the Global Witness organization puts Brazil in first place among 22 countries with a higher number of deaths of environmental activists (Global Witness, 2018)

In sum, post-democratization, the opening of the political arena has had some short-lived influence on political appointments to FUNAI. The opening of the political arena and competition has allowed more variation in the Executive, and ultimately at the pattern of appointment, leading more *indigenistas,* and FUNAI careerists to leadership positions. However, in the long term, civil society pressure is curtailed by the political interests of the Executive.

Limitations and Final remarks

The present chapter aimed to uncover under which conditions the Executive appoints policy experts – officials with technical experience and training – to leadership positions at social agencies across different regime types in Brazil. For so, a case study was conducted based on historical and scholarly data about Brazilian civil-military relations involved in indigenous politics from 1967 to 2018.

17 Organizations like the Articulação dos Povos Indígenas do Brasil (APIB) published an open letter to condemn the appointment of a military officer by Michel Temer's (Aug/2016-Dec/2017) allies from the conservative Social Christian Party (PSC).

My first hypothesis was that international and national social mobilization contributed to the appointment of experts to FUNAI. The history of appointments during the military regime indicates that social mobilization had little influence in shaping FUNAI's leadership. As for post-democratization Brazil, the impact of social movements on FUNAI's politics seems to be limited to the alignment of the Brazilian president with grassroots groups, that is, their ideological preferences. This is somehow expected as in Brazil, presidents have retained extensive powers even after the democratization process.

Moreover, compared to social movements, under a democratic regime, political ideology, i.e., a right-wing chief of the Executive, seems to have a bigger role in the appointment patterns of non-experts. Especially when the president has more incentives to be responsive to the military lobby, that is, having close ties with the armed forces. Being a rightist with no ties to the military only, like Collor, or a non-rightist (i.e., centrist) with ties with the military, as Franco, did not result in administrations where only non-experts were being appointed to FUNAI's cadre.

So ultimately, whenever these contextual conditions were present – a right-wing chief executive with ties to the military – simultaneously – either during the democratic or non-democratic regime, certain professional groups, which coincided with indigenous affairs policy expertise, remained out of leadership positions.

The background of the non-policy experts appointed either by rightist leaders during the military regime or right-wing administrations of Sarney, Temer, and Bolsonaro included engineers, lawyers, economists, policemen and retired officers. Moreover, as the policy decisions of those appointees show, the individuals selected were, in fact, aligned with the policy expectations of right-wing presidents with ties with the military.

It is important to stress that the ideology of the experts under scrutiny might also be a part of the explanation underlining their appointment. The mismatch between the military and indigenists, which shaped FUNAI's history, is also reflected in the absence of the latter class in FUNAI's presidency during the authoritarian regime, and it seems to be linked to the ideological differences between these two groups. Sociocultural anthropologists, as well as sociologists in Brazil, are mostly known for being left-wing, similar to what Amorim Neto and Santos (2005) argue about Brazilian political scientists.

While there's no systematic research that maps sociocultural anthropologists' political ideology across time, for instance, just by observing the Brazilian anthropological association's website (ABA), one can perceive that the themes debated by the professional cluster are predominantly associated with a leftist orientation, and thus, very differently from those that resonate with the military which is mostly rightist themes.

It was found here that the lack of ideological alignment shunned full categories of professionals. While often Brazilian politicians draw both from the loyalist criteria (internal networks, party membership, and regional politics) as well as competence when selecting candidates for political appointments, here it might be that the perception of competence itself changed due to their difference in goals.

Regarding policy implications, the low institutionalization of FUNAI has failed to shelter the organization from policy regime backsliding. The consequences have not stopped at policy rhetoric, but physical conflict in the region was observed during the recent conservative wave in Brazil (Betim, 2021).

However, the low institutionalization of FUNAI is neither a new nor an isolated phenomenon. State capacity has remained uneven across different agencies in Brazil. For instance, results from a study of Brazilian Federal agencies by Bersch, Praça, and Taylor (2017) suggest that sectors including economic policy, legal and foreign relations perform better in agency capacity (i.e., career strength, stability, and specialization) and autonomy from politics (i.e., the partisanship of staff) than health, security and social agencies, for instance. According to the study, FUNAI's overall capacity score is even lower than the average of the health, social security and public social organizations.

Furthermore, many of the inefficiencies and institutional fragilities of FUNAI were inherited from the SPI, the first indigenous affairs agency. Furthermore, FUNAI was structured during the military regime after a public scandal that unraveled wrongdoings from SPI employees. So, it might be that its institutional vulnerability might be greatly shaped by its structural trajectory. However, the democratic regime seems to have reshaped – even if only temporarily – the expectations towards the institutions and the role of societal agents.

Moreover, FUNAI's current policy track, including executive delegation to the bureaucracy, indicates that there is a conflict of interest between the organization and the Executive. The Executive's directions to FUNAI have clashed not only with the Brazilian Constitution but with the organization's present mission.

In sum, findings from the case study suggest that both regime and political ideology matter. So, similar to what Dargent (2014) has found, having a context where multiple agents in power can proceed as checks and balances of others seems to increase the costs of opting for solely partisan or loyalist criteria. Moreover, only after the democratization the first policy experts (e.g., *indigenists,* sociocultural anthropologists, FUNAI careerists) were appointed to the highest-level position at FUNAI.

Moreover, the case study reveals the considerable political influence of the military on fields that are not directly tied to the national defense – traditionally, the organization's main function under a democratic regime. For instance, Brazil is an exception in the Americas, together with Venezuela and, to a lesser extent Mexico, where the military occupies positions in the government (Figueiredo, 2021). Most democratic countries like Canada and the United States limit the involvement of the military in the government to safeguard civil control over the military. Thus, the high presence of the military in the Bolsonaro administration is a concern, according to civil-military scholars (See Tosta, 2020).

However, the external validity of the findings remains a limitation of this study. In order to generalize the results found here, future research is needed to compare the pattern of appointments with other social agencies. Also, due to the goal of the present case study to unravel the dynamics between specific agents involved in the agency's political arena (social movements, the military and Brazilian presidents), other explanations that might influence the appointment pattern have remained unassessed (i.e., the makeup of the congress, the ideology of the president's cabinet, Brazil's congressional farm lobby). Also, upcoming research with FUNAI's cadre to identify if there are reasons to believe that certain categories would self-select to remain out of FUNAI's administration (e.g., If *indigenistas* did not want to head FUNAI during a conservative government).

Moreover, the findings also reveal the absence of leaders from an origin descent throughout FUNAI's over its 54 years. While this is not surprising – given the state's approach to indigenous groups over the years as covered in the literature – the exact factors behind the exclusion of indigenous leadership away from the organization and other important political positions remain an empirical puzzle for forthcoming analyses.

The recent decay of the country's social policy regime, and the lack of responsiveness to social movements, phenomena that are observed in other public agencies and policies in the social field, coincide with the return to the military in civilian posts and also with overall democratic backsliding in Brazil. Future studies are needed to untangle the effects of the military as a lobby group and of regime change in Brazil.

References

ABERS, Rebecca N.; VON BÜLOW, Marisa. Movimentos sociais na teoria e na prática: como estudar o ativismo através da fronteira entre Estado e sociedade? *Sociologias*, 13(28), 2011, p. 52-84.

________; ________. Social Movements and Conventional and Contentious Politics. In AMES, Barry (ed.). *Routledge Handbook of Brazilian Politics*. London: Routledge, 2018, p. 105-117.

ALBERT, Bruce. Terras indígenas, política ambiental e geopolítica militar no desenvolvimento da Amazônia: a propósito do caso Yanomami. *Amazônia: a fronteira agrícola*, 20, 1991, p. 37-58.

ALMEIDA, Maria Regina Celestino de. A atuação dos indígenas na história: revisões historiográficas. *Revista Brasileira de História*, 37(75), 2017.

AMADO, Guilherme. Bolsonaro não demarcou nenhuma terra indígena em dois anos. *Época*, 2020.

AMORIM NETO, Octavio. *Presidencialismo e governabilidade nas Américas*. Rio de Janeiro: FGV, 2006a.

________. The Presidential Calculus: Executive Policy Making and Cabinet Formation in the Americas. *Comparative Political Studies*, 39(4), 2006b, p. 415-40.

________. Democracia e relações civis-militares. In AVELAR, Lúcia; CINTRA, Antônio Octavio (eds.). *Sistema Político Brasileiro: uma introdução*. Rio de Janeiro: Fundação Konrad Adenauer/Editora Unesp (FEU), 2015, p. 315-30.

ARAÚJO, Ana Valéria et al. *Povos indígenas e a Lei dos "Brancos":* o direito à diferença. LACED/Museu Nacional, 2006.

BARBERIA, Lorena; PRAÇA, Sérgio. Who Gets Political Appointments? Party Loyalty and Bureaucratic Expertise in Brazil. *Encontro ABCP*, 2014, p. 1-14.

BERSCH, Katherine; PRAÇA, Sérgio; TAYLOR, Matthew M. State Capacity, Bureaucratic Politicization, and Corruption in the Brazilian State. *Governance*, 30(1), 2017, p. 105-24.

BETIM, Felipe. Invasões, incêndios e ameaças de morte: indígenas vivem onda de ataques após COP26 | Atualidade | EL PAÍS Brasil. *El País Brasil*, 2021.

BIGIO, Elias dos Santos. A ação indigenista brasileira sob a influência militar e da Nova República (1967-1990). *Revista de Estudos e Pesquisas da Fundação Nacional do Índio*, 4(2), 2007, p. 13-93.

BRASIL. FUNAI*'s Statute – Decree N° 9.010*, 2017.

BRUNEAU, Thomas Charles; TOLLEFSON, Scott D. Civil-Military Relations in Brazil: A Reassessment. *Journal of Politics in Latin America*, 2014, p. 107-38.

DE Carvalho, Salo; GOYES, David R; WEIS, Valeria Vegh. Politics and Indigenous Victimization: The Case of Brazil. *The British Journal of Criminology*, 61(1), 2021, p. 251-271.

CASTRO, Celso (ed.). Apresentação. In *Amazônia e Defesa Nacional*. Rio de Janeiro: FGV, 2006, p. 7-12.

CEDI. *Aconteceu:* povos indígenas no Brasil 1980. Rio de Janeiro: CEDI/ISA, 1981.

________. *Povos indígenas no Brasil 1986*. Rio de Janeiro, 1986.

CONGRESSO EM FOCO. Indígenas entram com ação na Justiça e pedem afastamento do presidente da FUNAI. 2021.

CPDOC/FGV. Fundação Nacional do Índio. Retrieved from http://www.fgv.br/cpdoc/acervo/dicionarios/verbete-tematico/fundacao-nacional-do-indio-FUNAI, 20/1/2020.

D'ARAÚJO, Maria Celina. *Governo Lula:* contornos sociais e políticos da elite do poder coordenação. CPDOC/FGV, 2007.

________. *A elite dirigente do governo Lula*. CPDOC/FGV, 2009.

D'ARAÚJO, Maria Celina; PETEK, Júlia. Recrutamento e perfil dos dirigentes públicos brasileiros nas áreas econômicas e sociais entre 1995 e 2012. *Revista de Administração Pública*, 52(5), 2018, p. 840-62.

DARGENT, Eduardo. *Technocracy and Democracy in Latin America:* The Experts Running the Government. Cambridge University Press, 2014.

Exame. "É muita terra para pouco índio, diz Bolsonaro." 2019.

FIGUEIREDO, Janaína. Brasil é exceção nas Américas na concessão de cargos para militares no Governo. *O Globo*. 2021.

FUNAI. *Demarcação*. 2021.

GARFIELD, Seth. Where the Earth Touches the Sky: The Xavante Indians' Struggle for Land in Brazil, 1951-1979. *Hispanic American Historical Review*, 80(3) 200, p. 537-64.

GEDDES, Barbara. *Politician's Dilemma:* Building State Capacity in Latin America. University of California Press, 1994.

GEORGE, Alexander; BENNETT, Andrew. Chapter 1: Case Studies and Theory Development. In *Case Studies and Theory Development in the Social Sciences*, 2005, p. 3-36.

GLOBAL WITNESS. *At What Cost? Our Report on Attacks on Land & Environment Defenders in 2017 | Global Witness*, 2018.

IBGE. *Sinopse – Censo 2010*. 2010.

ISA. Localização e extensão das TIs. 2021a.

———. Órgão Indigenista Oficial. *Povos indígenas no Brasil*. 2021b.

JACKSON, Jean E.; WARREN, Kay B. Indigenous Movements in Latin America, 1992–2004: Controversies, Ironies, New Directions. *Annual Review of Anthropology*, 2005, 34(1): p. 549-73.

LEITÃO, Matheus. FUNAI já trocou comando de 20 coordenadorias regionais; maioria dos nomeados é militar. *G1*, 2020.

LEWIS, David E. Testing Pendleton' s Premise: Do Political Appointees Make Worse Bureaucrats? *Journal of Politics*, 69(4), 2007, p. 1.073-88.

LOPEZ, Felix Garcia; BUGARIN, Maurício; BUGARIN, Karina. Rotatividade nos cargos de confiança da administração federal brasileira (1999-2013). *Revista do Serviço Público*, 65(4), 2014, p. 439-61.

LOPEZ, Felix Garcia; PRAÇA, Sérgio. Critérios e lógicas de nomeação para o alto escalão da burocracia federal brasileira. In *Cargos de confiança no presidencialismo de coalizão brasileiro*, IPEA, 2015.

LUCIANO, Gersem dos Santos. *Coleção Educação para Todos*: O índio brasileiro: o que você precisa saber sobre os povos indígenas no Brasil de hoje. LACED/Museu Nacional, 2006.

MOE, Terry M. 1989. *The Politics of Bureaucratic Structure BT* – Can the Government Govern? Can the Government Govern? 1989, p. 267-329.

OLIVEIRA, João Pacheco de. Mensurando alteridades, estabelecendo direitos: práticas e saberes governamentais na criação de fronteiras étnicas. *Dados*, 55(4), 2012, p. 1.055-88.

________. Sem a tutela, uma nova moldura de nação. In LIMA, Antonio Carlos de Souza (ed,). *Tutela: formação de Estado e tradições de gestão no Brasil*. E-papers, 2014, p. 89-112.

________; LIMA, Antonio Carlos de Souza. Os muitos fôlegos do indigenismo. *Anuário Antropológico* (81), 1981, 277-90.

POTTER, Hyury. Quem são os índios isolados do Pará que senador diz não existirem – BBC News Brasil. 2020.

POWER, Timothy J.; RODRIGUES-SILVEIRA, Rodrigo. The Political Right and Party Politics. In AMES, Barry (ed.). *Routledge Handbook of Brazilian Politics*. London: Routledge, 2018, p. 251-68.

________; ZUCCO, Cesar. Estimating Ideology of Brazilian Legislative Parties, 1990-2005: A Research Communication. *Latin American Research Review*, 44(1), 2009, p. 218-46.

________. Elite Preferences in a Consolidating Democracy: The Brazilian Legislative Surveys, 1990-2009. *Latin American Politics and Society*, 54(4), 2012, p. 1-27.

POZZOBON, Jorge. O lumpen-indigenismo do Estado brasileiro. *Journal de la société des américanistes*, (1), 1999, p. 281-306.

PRAÇA, Sérgio; LOPEZ, Felix Garcia. Political Appointments, Political Parties, and Bureaucracy. In AMES, Barry. (ed.). *Routledge Handbook of Brazilian Politics*. London: Routledge, 2018, p. 358-372.

RODRIGUES, M. G. M. Indigenous Rights in Democratic Brazil. *Human Rights Quarterly*, 24(2), 2002, p. 487-512.

SHALDERS, André. Falhou no psicotécnico, investigou desafeto e atacou procurador: a trajetória do novo presidente da FUNAI. *BBC News Brasil*, 2019.

SHANKLAND, Alex; ATHIAS, Renato. Decentralisation and Difference: Indigenous Peoples and Health System Reform in the Brazilian Amazon. *IDS Bulletin*, 38(1), 2007, p. 77-88.

SOARES, Leonardo Barros. A ausência eloquente: Ciência Política Brasileira, povos indígenas e o debate acadêmico canadense contemporâneo. *Revista Brasileira de Ciência Política*, (33), 2020, p. 1-39.

SOUZA LIMA, Antonio Carlos de. Sobre tutela e participação: povos indígenas e formas de governo no Brasil, séculos XX/XXI. *Mana*, 21(2), 2015, p. 425-57.

Stepan, Alfred C. *Rethinking Military Politics: Brazil and the Southern Cone.* Princeton, New Jersey: Princeton University Press, 1988.

The World Bank. *Indigenous Latin America in the Twenty-First Century: The First Decade.* 2015.

TOSTA, Wilson. "Presença de militares no governo torna política menos transparente", diz analista – Política – Estadão. *O Estado de São Paulo*, 2020.

TRINIDAD, Carlos Benítez. La Fundação Nacional Do Índio al Servicio de Los Intereses Geoestratégicos e Ideológicos de La Dictadura Brasileña. *Americanía*, (3), 2016, p. 243-77.

VALENTE, Rubens. *Os fuzis e as flechas:* história de sangue e resistência indígena na ditadura. Companhia das Letras, 2017.

VIEIRA, Ana Carolina Alfinito; QUACK, Sigrid. Trajectories of Transnational Mobilization for Indigenous Rights in Brazil. *RAE-Revista de Administração de Empresas*, 56(4), 2016, p. 380-94.

YASHAR, Deborah J. Contesting Citizenship: Indigenous Movements and Democracy in Latin America. *Comparative Politics*, 31(1), 1998, p. 23.

________. Democracy, Indigenous Movements, and the Postliberal Challenge in Latin America. *World Politics*, 52(1), 1999, p. 76-104.

Threats, civil-military relations, and inequality: explaining economic development content in the declaratory defense policies of democracies (1998-2012)

Igor Acácio

Introduction

Defense and economic development are mutually reinforcing and key functions of the modern State. Yet, its association with the content of declaratory policies of democracies still remains understudied. The chapter has four guiding hypotheses. First, countries with low levels of external threats will link their declaratory defense policies with economic development issues. Second, the larger the levels of civilian control over the military the more states will link their declaratory defense policies with economic development issues. Third, the more unequal countries are, the larger the link between development and defense. Fourth, civilian control and inequality interact to jointly explain the part of the link between development and defense.

These hypotheses are tested using a dataset of declaratory defense policies gathered with web-scrapping techniques and coded with supervised machine-learning dictionary methods. To illustrate the argument, the chapter also presents qualitative evidence from Brazil, India and South Africa, highly unequal democracies, similar levels of civilian control over the military, varying levels of external threats, and variations in links between defense and development in their declaratory defense policies.

The chapter finds support for all hypotheses: countries with low levels of external threats present more development content in their declaratory defense policy, and countries where civilians oversee the defense sector portray, on average, more development content in their declaratory defense policy. Unequal countries portray intense links between defense policy and the association between inequality and developmental content in defense policy is larger if the defense sector is run by civilians.

The chapter also contributes to illustrate the application of concepts of the literature on civil-military relations – which is dominated by small-n studies – applied to the quantitative analysis of declaratory defense policies. The underlying assumption in this chapter is that analyzing declaratory defense policies is of analytical value. This is not something uncontroversial. Prominent civil-military relations scholars contend that declaratory defense policies are not meaningful in inferring the priorities of different countries unless they are followed by structures to formulate plans and material resources are committed (Bruneau, 2018; Bruneau and Matei, 2008). In other words, at the very least, countries need to care enough to put money and resources where they claim to be their priorities in declaratory documents. In countries with feeble defense policies, there is a substantial difference between what is publicized in documents and what happens in defense policies (Amorim Neto, 2019; Amorim Neto and Acácio, 2020). Yet I contend that it is still useful to dig deep into these documents and the determinants of their content because there is a substantial amount of data and meaningful variation that must be explained by social scientists. We have only begun to do so. In Brazilian political science, to the best of my knowledge, the only quantitative study that draws on declaratory defense policies is a book by Gustavo Baracho. He studied the impact of civil-military relations and other variables on declaratory defense policies, focusing on the factors shaping their diffusion internationally (Baracho, 2018). Therefore, this chapter follows up in his footsteps.

The chapter proceeds as follows. The following section discusses the links between defense policy and economic development and outlines my theoretical framework, followed by four testable hypotheses. The third section presents the measures, data and the research design in the quantitative tests. The fourth section presents the results of the quantitative analysis and is followed by a case-based analysis of Brazil, India and South Africa. The final section concludes the chapter.

Explaining declaratory the developmental content in declaratory defense policies: a theoretical framework

Issues included in defense policies vary between countries and over time, as "the domain of national security issues is variable" (Katzenstein, 1996:10). This chapter assesses the impact of external threats, inequality, and civilian control over the military on democracies' declaratory defense policy. Below, I describe my framework considering the literature.

The role of external threats

First, it is important to understand defense policies as having a close relationship with state-building. The nexus between defense and development has a solid grounding in the social science literature. War makes states. This logic relies on the relationship between the extraction dynamics by which States build up defense capabilities to justify and reinforce the extraction of resources from the citizenry, and it happened mainly during the formation of nation-states in Europe (Tilly, 1985).

Since the defense function exists to protect states from external aggression, it is conceivable that external threats are the main driver of defense policy content. Pioneering works on military doctrine argued that military doctrine tends not to change rapidly unless there is war (Posen, 1984). This "realist" view considers military doctrine as a product of an anarchic international system based on self-help. The structural realist approach pictures the State as the primary actor in the international system (Gilpin, 1984). Force – or the threat of its use – is what matters and its principal authors agree with the argument that the amplification of what analysts understand as "security" should be avoided (Art and Waltz, 1999; Walt, 1991). In an anarchic international system in which power prevails, insecurity is a permanent feature. States then seek to maximize power, as it allows them to increase autonomy and amplify influence in the international system (Mearsheimer, 2001; Waltz, 1979). This set of theories emphasizes the study of material aspects of power such as military and economic capabilities. Therefore, States adopt defensive, offensive, or deterrent postures according to their material capabilities (Posen, 1984).

Comprehending military doctrines of countries with low levels of external threats does not seem to have been a main concern for scholarship in mainstream international relations, for which the focus is deliberately on great power politics, where the threat of foreign aggression is always a given. If western powers assumed to derive their defense policies from external threats, the most critical secutity challenges countries in the developing world face are inward-focused

(Wendt and Barnett, 1993:322). Scholars of Latin America have a long-standing debate on the role of wars in state building (Centeno, 2002, 2003; Ferraro and Centeno, 2018; Kurtz, 2012; Schenoni, 2021; Soifer, 2015; Thies, 2004).

Centeno (2003) has claimed that external wars in Latin America, because of their limited nature, produced states with limited state capacity. Wars that happened in Europe during the formation of the European nation-states are arguably different from the violent processes that shaped how the third-world states were created. The distinctive domestic preconditions that exist in indicates these countries make a compelling call to evaluate the relationship between war and state-making (Sorensen, 2001). Thies (2004) and more recently Schenoni (2021) have shown compelling evidence that wars produced lasting effects on Latin American State capacity. Finally, the literature on third-world security indicates that these countries face a security predicament: defense policy favors the building of state capacity, development and political at the expense of agendas focused on the threat of interstate conflicts that might not even exist. Security and insecurity are defined regarding how vulnerable states are, both domestically and externally, based on how these factors can hamper governing regimes and the exertion of political authority (Ayoob, 1995). From a practical standpoint, linking security to development has become commonplace in the political practice of States relatively deprived of material capabilities and low threat environment. In sum, levels of threat are arguably an important driver of defense policy.

Civil-military relations in a democracy

If researchers are interested in the impact of domestic variables, they should model the determinants of defense policy by accounting for civil-military relations. The central dilemma of civil-military relations can be summarized in the following proposition: the security of the modern State is guaranteed by the creation and training of the military to protect it, but these capabilities also make the military inherently mighty to overpower the government that they are supposed to serve (Feaver, 2003; Huntington, 1957, 1995). Therefore, civilian control of the military means that at the very least the military does not plot to overthrow the government it serves; they recognize that the government officials are their principals.

In democracies, being a soldier should be a state profession like any other (Moskos, Williams, and Segal, 2000). Once converted from a menace to the regime to an instrument of policy, soldiers can be called to fight, keep the peace, build and rescue (Pion-Berlin and Martinez, 2017:19-20). The process of consolidation is done by the establishment of institutions that assert civilian control over the military, transforming the military into public employees who are experts in the use of violence but act under the direction of a democratically elected civilian government (Pion-Berlin and Martinez, 2017:22-23).

Defense policy in a democracy is, above all, conducted by the democratically elected central government. In a democracy, because the electoral cycle is meaningful, civilian politicians may use defense policy as a signaling mechanism, showing to the public that they genuinely care about the issues the public cares about. Economic development and redistribution are certainly one of them, as the prolific literature on the economic vote has found time and again (Duch and Stevenson, 2008; Lewis-Beck and Stegmaier, 2019).

The also prolific literature on the guns X butter tradeoff provides insights on how governments decide on the allocation of resources and priorities in regard to the defense policy (Gifford, 2006; Mintz, 1989; Mintz and Huang, 1991; Mintz and Ward, 1989; Ripsman, Zielinski, and Schilde, 2018; Whitten and Williams, 2011; Williams, 2019). Essentially, governments can invest or disinvest in defense at the expense of social expenditures. If external threats are not salient, it is reasonable to expect that the government priorities will shift towards disinvesting in defense, and investing in social expenditures. These tradeoffs are particularly salient in more unequal and less economically developed democracies, where governments can be under enormous popular pressures to deliver welfare programs and the like.

However, in order to prioritize "butter" at the expense of "guns" or even to use "guns" to generate "butter" (i.e., using defense policy as an auxiliary welfare program), civilian leaders must have enough control over the military. In other words, the military must be under civilian control so politicians can enact certain policies without the adamant fear of coups or deviations from governmental plans.

Civil-military relations have severe implications for a country's strategic assessment of its national security (Owens, 2017). Militaries, even under control, are influential governmental actors. They are experts in the use of force and such expertise the military offer may very well translate into policy influence. Soldiers will always have more information than civilians when it comes to technical aspects of combat and a more up-to-date assessment of military capabilities and because of that are to be allowed to give their input on civilian decisions (Feaver, 2003). It is therefore not uncommon that officers often have privileged access to the head of state and cabinet ministers.

When officers give their policy input, their views are based on their organizational culture, which can have a substantial impact on officers' willingness to support strategies developed by the governments they serve (Kier, 1995; Legro, 1994). The classic scholarship on civil-military relations makes it clear that the military profession is one where individuals are subject to a *total institution* (Huntington, 1957; Janowitz, 1960; Nordlinger, 1977). Soldiers are cast aside and become professionals in the use of violence and a considerable change in mentality must take place. They go through a substantial process of indoctrination. Their mentality and their privileged information may lead the military to consider themselves better fit to judge their material needs to defend the country, countering civilian instructions and securing first and foremost their corporate interests (Nordlinger, 1977). In addition, scholarship has argued for the idea that military disloyalty comes not from becoming intrinsically powerful while having a potential war to fight but from a possible disagreement between the military officers and government officials regarding the extent and severity of potential foreign threats (McMahon and Slantchev, 2015).

Finally, the military might just be reluctant to let civilian politicians steer the defense policy away from the defense against foreign threats because they might consider professionally diminishing, as their role is to counter foreign threats (Finer, 1976:23). Professional militaries might consider themselves autonomous from the society they are supposed to protect. Scholarship on civil-military relations provides some insights into the problem we are dealing with. Time and again, when military officers did not consider specific missions attributed by the civilian government appropriate, they exhibited a wide array of shirking, from staying quartered to picking and choosing how to execute them (Jaskoski, 2013; Pion-Berlin and Acácio, 2022; Pion-Berlin, Esparza, and Grisham, 2012; Pion-Berlin and Trinkunas, 2010).

Thinking about civil-military relations as a variable allows us to conceive how these preferences can be voiced and eventually prevail based on how little control the political leadership has over their experts on violence. At the very least, an approach like this acknowledges the military's special *status* when voicing concerns over national security. If given more leeway in drafting defense documents and conducting the defense policies, arguably the military would prefer not to include developmental elements in the defense policy.

To sum up, the possibility that the military has an intrinsic decision-making bias in regard to the use of force and a privileged position to voice its concerns and opinions to the commander-in-chief makes it so that militaries, if not under the control of the government, could steer defense policy towards externally oriented, less developmentalist declaratory defense policies.

Hypotheses

Table 1 below summarizes the theoretical expectations regarding the independent variables of interest. The most important factor in my framework is the systemic imperative, the level of external threats. Quadrants 1 and 3 present scenarios when threats are low. When threats are external threats are low and civilians run the defense sector, I expect to find the highest amount of developmental content in the defense policy.

In countries experiencing limited levels of threats, democratic leaders, constrained by the need to deliver for their electorate will insert developmental content in the defense policy. Per quadrant 3, when threats are low, if the armed forces possess control of the defense sector, they will lobby to keep elements of their professional function – national defense – that could counter the systemic factors that disincentivize more developmental content in the defense policy.

Table 1
Summary of Theoretical Expectations

<table>
<tr><td></td><td></td><td colspan="2">External Threats</td></tr>
<tr><td></td><td></td><td>Low</td><td>High</td></tr>
<tr><td rowspan="2">Civilian Control over the Military</td><td>High</td><td>(1)
Highest Development Content, particularly if highly unequal or poor</td><td>(2)
Second Lowest Development Content</td></tr>
<tr><td>Low</td><td>(3)
Second Highest Development Content, particularly if highly unequal or poor</td><td>(4)
Lowest Development Content</td></tr>
</table>

Source: elaborated by author.

Quadrants 2 and 4 present scenarios when threats are high. In quadrant 4, external threats are high and the military controls the defense sector. Therefore, the declaratory defense policy should exhibit a low amount of developmental content. If civilians have a grip over the defense sector, given the strong incentives of the democratic regime to deliver public goods that are not national defense, we would see the second lowest level of development content in the defense policy. We can therefore list two baseline testable implications of this chapter.

H1: The lower the level of external threats the higher the developmental content in the declaratory defense policies.

H2: Control over the military is positively associated with high developmental content in the declaratory defense policies.

In addition, we care about the role of an important economic variable – inequality – which can constrain governments to act regarding policy. I test its direct impact on the dependent variable and an interactive hypothesis seeking to get at the economic mechanisms shaping the impact of civilian control. If civilian control over the military is informed by features of the economy that put pressure on democratically elected leaders to signal that they care about priorities affecting the electorate, then economic variables should matter. Therefore, we can state the hypotheses:

H3: The higher the level of inequality, the higher the developmental content in the declaratory defense policies.

H4: Civilian control over the military magnifies the impact of the level of inequality on the association between development and defense in the defense policy.

Measures, Data and Modeling Strategy

The dependent variable in this chapter seeks to capture the degree of developmentalism in the declaratory defense policies. The source to measure the dependent variable is a database of declaratory defense policies collected by ETH Zürich, and it covers the period between 1998 and 2012 (ETH Zürich Center for Security Studies, 2021). The White Papers from the ETH Zürich database that was available in either English or Spanish were obtained via web scrapping techniques.

All documents were unified based on the variables "year" and "country" for every country that had more than one declaratory defense policy is published in the same year. For example, Hungary in 2012 published two documents relative to its armed forces, and the documents were merged to obtain a country-year observation. Given this treatment of the data, we ended up with 162 usable documents. Fourteen were discarded because they were not machine-readable. The global superpower, the United States, was also excluded and so were non-democracies (polity V indicator <6), leaving us with a sample size of 120. Non-democracies are excluded because democracy is a key scope condition of how mechanisms outlined by the civil-military relations literature take place, as they are grounded in democratic theory. As for the exclusion of the United States from the sample, the defense policy of the United States is *sui generis* due to its *status* as a global superpower as well as its high levels of military expenditures and its global military presence.

Using the Quantitative Analysis of Textual Data package (*quanteda*) (Benoit et al., 2018), available in the statistical software R (R Core Team, 2020), each document was transformed into a *corpus*. Later, the set of *corpus* was *tokenized* along with the removal of *stopwords*, symbols, and numbers. Then, with the data ready for analysis, a dictionary with a "development vocabulary" was created using stems and case insensitivity for each word. The terms included are as follows:

Table 2
Development vocabulary inserted in *Quanteda*

```
```{r}
token_development <- token_geral %>%
tokens_select(pattern = c("develop*",
"desaroll*",
"econo*",
"econó*",
"civic*",
"cívic*",
"infrastr*",
"infraes*",
"grow*",
"crec*"),
case_insensitive = TRUE)
print(token_development)
```

Source: elaborated by author.

The dictionary, written in *glob* patterns, was applied to all documents in the corpus set, obtaining a word count of words related to economic development in the declaratory defense policies. The resulting database linking the observed countries with the Correlates of War code for each country was generated with given variables, so it could easily be merged with data from other datasets to in-
```

clude the covariates in the model.[1] Table 3 below portrays the summary statistics of all variables used in the statistical analysis.

Table 3
Descriptive Statistics

Variable	Obs	Mean	Std. Dev.	Min	Max	Source
Dependent Variable (Level of Development in the Declaratory Defense Policy)	120	.635	.329	.088	1.64	ETZ Zurich Dataset, Web scrapped
External Threat	120	.262	.259	.025	.912	Kim and Lang (2021)
Civilian Control	120	.875	.332	0	1	Database of Political Institutions (2021) + Original Data
GDP Percapita	120	17047457	12818504	516306.72	64777428	Kim and Lang (2021)
Inequality	120	.4773411	.0846436	.2474818	.7369977	Solt (2020)
Democracy	117	9.111	1.173	6	10	Polity V Project
Military Expenditures as a Share of GDP	119	1.728	1.018	.574	10.471	Kim and Lang (2021)
Composite Index of National Capabilities (CINC)	120	.006	.009	0	.074	Correlates of War Project
Conscription	120	.517	.502	0	1	Kim and Lang (2021) + Original Data

Source: elaborated by author.

The chapter has three independent variables of interest: the level of external threats, civil-military relations and economic inequality. How are they measured? Measuring the degree of external threats is not trivial. A recent dataset for it has been created by Kim and Kang (2021). They create an index encompassing three factors influencing external threats: the degree of hostility, the relative distribution of military capabilities and the distance between the pair of countries. This weighted index varies from 0 to 1, where 0 means the lowest level of threats and 1 means the most threatened. The measure has substantial construct validity with a materialist view of national security and threats and is appropriate for conducting statistical tests: it has been tested, is freely available and its coding scheme is transparent (Kim and Kang, 2021).

We must measure civilian control over the military accurately and consistently. This is a complex variable to operationalize and measure with comparable indicators valid for large samples, partially explaining why small-n studies dom-

1 The measure of developmentalism follows this formula. $Developmentalism_{ij} = \frac{WordCount\ Development_{ij}}{WordCount\ Total_{ij}}$, where i is the country and j is the year.

inate the literature. To measure the concept of civilian control over the military, one must balance concept validity with feasibility in data collection to yield the largest sample size possible.

The measure used in this study is relatively straightforward: a binary indicator of whether the person responsible for the defense ministry in each country is a civilian. The Database of Political Institutions (DPI) collects such data for the period between 1975 and 2020, and it has been used by recent studies (Amorim Neto and Accorsi, 2020; Beliakova, 2021). In addition, relying on names provided by the WhoGov dataset (Nyrup and Bramwell, 2020), I manually recoded all the data for the countries in the sample so that the measure includded retired military officers. The source for the recodes included official gazettes, local press sources and government websites. This insight proved to be fruitful, as the correlation between these the original and the new measure is 0.55. Therefore, an additional empirical contribution of this chapter is to produce hand-coded data on retired military officers available for future scholarship. Figure 1 displays a scatterplot of the dependent variable and two independent variables of interest, showing a suggestive association per the line of the linear.

Figure 1
Scatterplot of the dependent variable, level of external threat and civilian control

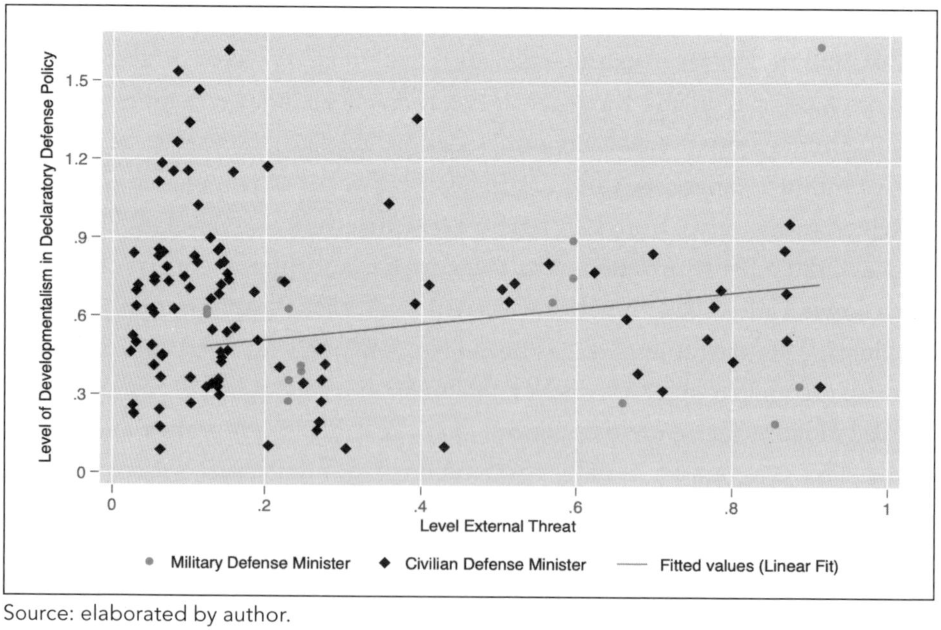

Source: elaborated by author.

The measure for inequality, the third independent variable of interest was obtained from Frederick Solt's SWIID dataset on inequality measures (Solt, 2020). It is defined as the "Estimate of Gini index of inequality in equivalized (square root scale) household market (pre-tax, pre-transfer) income, using Luxembourg Income Study data as the standard" (Solt, 2021:1).

In terms of theory, credible statistical analysis must control for potential confounders (i.e., variables that could theoretically affect both the independent variables of interest and the dependent variables being analyzed). We must first control for wealth, measured by GDP per capita. This is a known proxy for wealth and a readily available proxy for state capacity (Dincecco and Katz, 2016; Hendrix, 2010). The source for this data is Kim and Lang (2021), which sources it from the World Bank.

Second, we must control for the relative power states possess in the international system. The composite index of national capabilities (CINC), developed by the project *Correlates of War* (Singer, Bremer, and Stuckey, 1972), includes the production of iron and steel, urban population, military expenditures, number of troops and energy production of a country with relation to the total of resources available in the international system, representing the structural limits to which State action is subject to (Amorim Neto, 2013). It is an index that shows the share of material capabilities a country has relative to others. Data available for this variable range from 1816 to 2016 allowing us full coverage over our sample.

Third, the levels of democracy can also influence both the levels of civilian control over the military and the content of the defense policy. Its source is the Polity project (Marshall, Jaggers, and Gurr, 2011). We must also include a control because it is standard in the literature regarding public expenditures and allocations. I include a measure of the military expenditures as a share of the country's gross domestic product. The source for this data is the SIPRI dataset (Stockholm International Peace Research Institute, 2021). Finally, since defense documents are often inward facing seeking to justify defense spending and even the existence of the armed forces' recruiting programs, we must also control for conscription. The source for the data is Kim and Lang (2021), with additional research to complete the dataset for all countries in the sample.

The choice of statistical models to analyze data depends on the data structure, which can induce biases in the coefficients and error terms, rendering inaccurate inferences. The chapter draws a cross-national dataset for all democracies with declaratory defense policies included in the ETH dataset for the period 1998-2012 (table A1 in the appendix shows the cases and years). Therefore, choosing an econometric technique entails an assessment of whether there is a need to account for the heterogeneity in the sample of countries.[2] Finally, the findings of the statistical analysis shown below are correlational, not causal.

Results: the determinants of the level of developmentalism of declaratory defense policy

Figure 2 presents the results of the statistical tests with the determinants of the level of developmentalism in declaratory defense policies for all democracies that had a declaratory defense policy from 1998 to 2012. Since it is of interest to compare the relative sizes of the coefficients, the continuous independent variables were all standardized. This means the effect sizes are shown in terms of standard deviations of those variables. Coefficients correspond to the impact of an increase in one standard deviation in the continuous independent variables on the values of the dependent variable (i.e., the degree of development content in the declaratory defense policy). The coefficient for civilian control, since it is a categorical variable, represents the value of having civilian control over the military compared to the baseline (military control over the defense policy).

---

2 A Breusch and Pagan Lagrangian multiplier test for random effects indicates that simple ordered-least squares regression is not indicated (Prob>chibar2=0.0028). The results of the Hausman model specification test (Hausman 1978) supports the hypothesis that there a need to use the model country-fixed effects (Prob>chibar2=0.0028), but time fixed effects are not necessary (Result from command *testparm i.year* in Stata: Prob > F =0.2889). A standard Breusch-Pagan test for heteroskedasticity (Breusch and Pagan 1979) (Result from command *testparm i.year* in Stata: Prob > F =0.2889) indicated the need for the models to include country fixed effects and cluster the robust standard errors at the country level, which should also dispel concerns regarding the possibility of some serial correlation in the panel (Wooldridge test for autocorrelation in panel data: Prob > F = 0.0018).

Figure 2
Determinants of Developmentalism, 90% CI

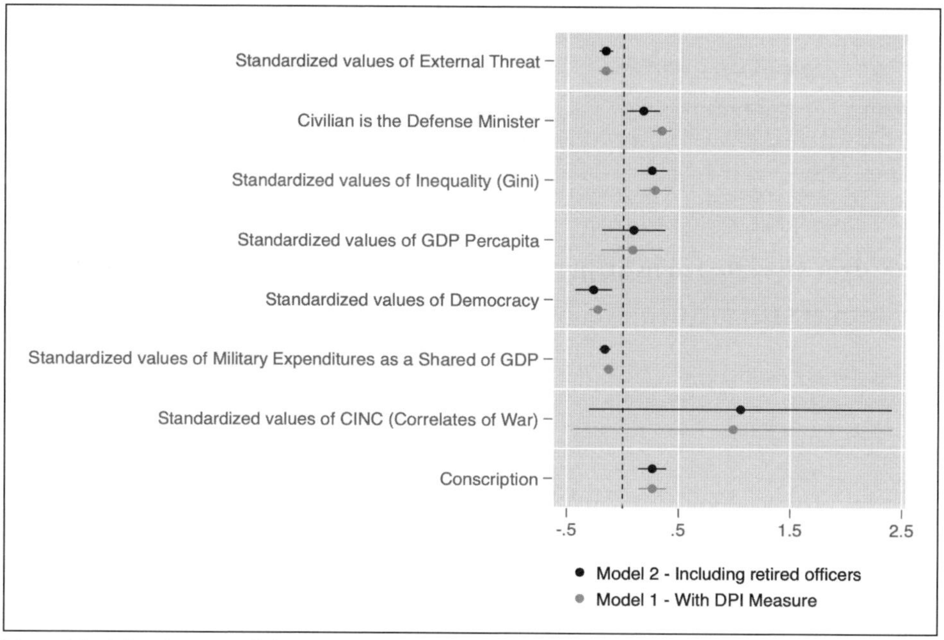

Note: Model 1. 90% Confidence Intervals, N=116, R^2= 0.35 N of countries=46, Avg N obs per country: 2.6. Model 2: 90% Confidence Intervals Country fixed effects, Std. Err. adjusted for 46 clusters, N=116, R^2= 0.34, N of countries=46, Avg N obs per country: 2.5. Criteria for democracy polity score equal or above 6.
Source: elaborated by author.

In support of my first hypothesis, external threats are negatively correlated with degree of developmental content in declaratory defense policies. In support of my second hypothesis, having a civilian as the head of the defense minister is *ceteris paribus* associated with more developmental content in the defense policy. Figure 3 below displays the results calculating the marginal effects of the independent variables of interest with the values for all variables held at their means.

Figure 3
Marginal Effects Plots with average values of variables, based on model 2

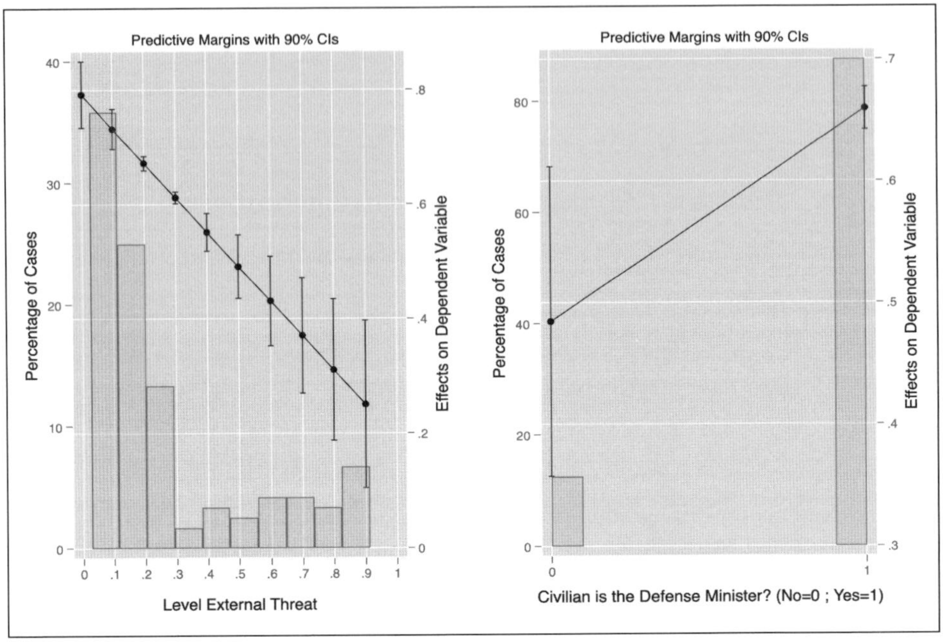

Source: elaborated by author.

In support of my third hypothesis, the level of inequality is positively associated with the developmental content in the declaratory defense policy of these 46 democracies. Note that the tests were run without the recoded values for civilian control, yielding similar results for key variables. Coefficients for External Threat are statistically significant and virtually the same in size and direction; coefficients for civilian control are also statistically significant, positive and double in magnitude. Substantively this means that either with a restrictive or a generous coding rule regarding who is considered a military officer in charge of the defense ministry the coefficient for this variable is still positive and statistically significant: on average when civilians are in charge, the declaratory defense policy will portray more content on economic development.

Now we must discuss the potential mechanism informing civilian control: the role of inequality, which may magnify the role of civilian control in shaping the content of declaratory defense policy. Figure 4 below portrays a third model that includes a multiplicative interaction, to test whether there is moderation between civilian control and the level of inequality. The coefficient of the interaction term is statistically significant at the 90% level with the predicted signal. The coefficients of the other variables remain consistent with models 1 and 2.

Figure 4
Model 3 – Testing the interactive hypothesis

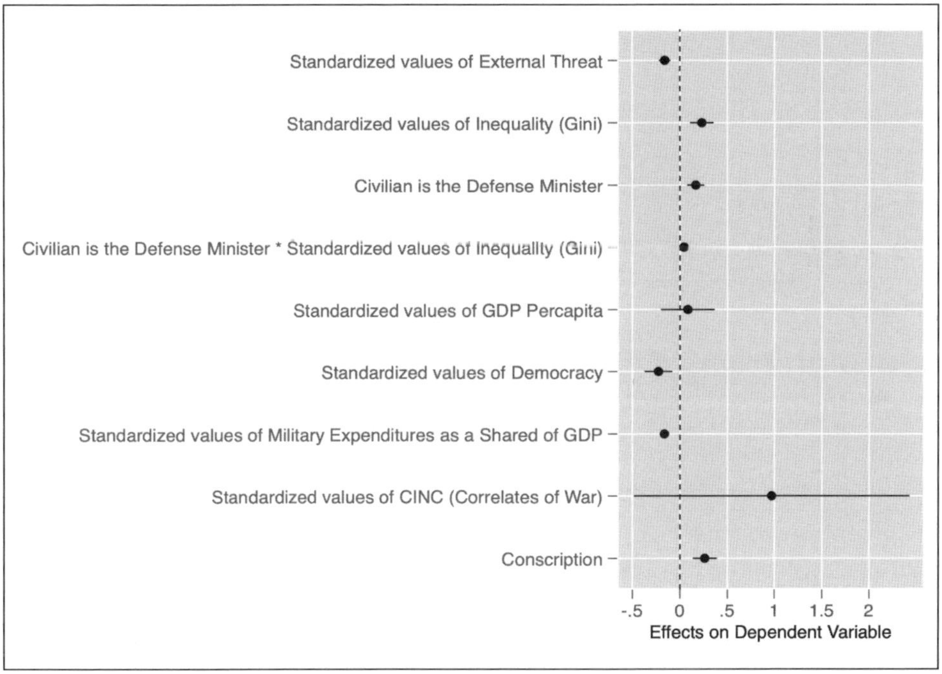

Note: Model 3. 90% Confidence Intervals, N=116, R^2= 0.34, N of countries=46, Avg N obs per country: 2.5. Country fixed effects, Std. Err. adjusted for 46 clusters. Criteria for democracy polity score equal or above 6.
Source: elaborated by author.

In terms of the constitutive terms of the interaction term – civilian control and inequality – the values of their coefficients cannot be interpreted as the average marginal effects (Brambor, Clark, and Golder, 2006; Hainmueller, Mummolo, and Xu, 2019). Instead, what they mean is the average marginal effect when the value for the variable in the interactive term is zero. In other words, the coefficient for civilian control on model 3 assumes the value for inequality is zero.

Conversely, the coefficient for inequality on figure 4 represents the marginal effect of civilian control over the military.

Figure 5
Marginal effects plot, based on model 3

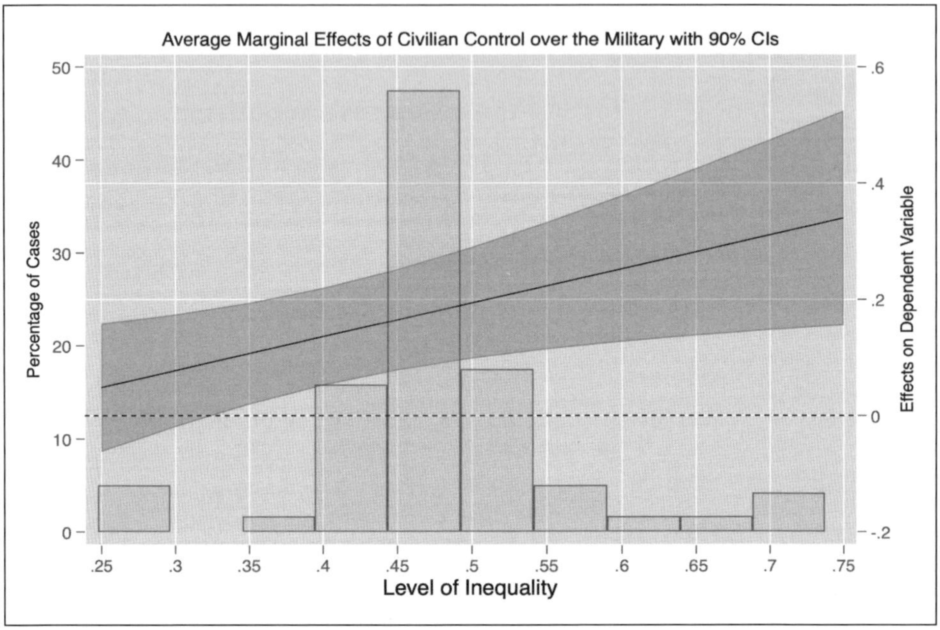

Source: elaborated by author.

Crossing the zero thresholds on figure 5 means that as inequality grows the positive impact of civilian control on the level of development in countries' declaratory defense policy also grows. Civilian control magnifies the impact of inequality, which provides evidence in support of hypothesis 4.

Illustrating the role of threats: qualitative evidence from Brazil, India and South Africa

This section analyzes the content of the declaratory defense policies of three highly unequal countries, where civilians were at least formally in charge of the defense sector but with varying levels of external threats and developmental content in the declaratory defense policy. It serves as an illustration of the argument regarding the role of external threats in explaining the outcome while isolating by design other important variables. In other words, it presents as a most similar systems design (Seawright, 2018; Seawright and Gerring, 2008). It also shows the type of content such documents portray regarding threats and economic development, giving this chapter a descriptive component beyond the numbers and statistical analysis it has relied on so far.

The White Paper of Defense of Brazil (2012) represents the continuation and deepening of a process initiated in 2005 with the II National Defense Policy and strengthened in 2008 with a National Defense Strategy. The country took steps to be more explicit about its priorities in the defense sector. It makes substantial progress if compared to the first national defense policy crafted by the Fernando Henrique Cardoso administration, in 1996, which contained a set of vague and anodyne formulations (Alsina Jr., 2006). Empirical evidence collected by Amorim Neto (2019) shows that the elaboration of the White Paper 2012 received sizeable civilian input. Brazil's White Paper of National Defense is a 275-page document divided into six chapters, annexes, and at the end, a list of the scholars, politicians and diplomats involved in the debates upon which the document was developed. This chapter focuses on the sections "The Brazilian State and National Defense" and "The Strategic Environment of the XXI Century" because they contain the most general formulations and considerations regarding potential threats Brazil faces.

In the South African case, the South African Defense Review 2013 was drafted long after the institutional framework of the defense policy defense was established, in comparison to Brazil: the post-Apartheid defense policy was made in 1996 and revised in 1998 and 2012-2015. The version analyzed in this chapter is from April 2013. The focus of analysis is the introduction of chapters 1, 2, 3 and 9 entitled, respectively: "The South African State 'a developmental perspective,'" "The Strategic Environment," "Drivers of Insecurity" and "Developmental and Order Tasks."

India does not possess a declaratory defense policy in the same shape as Brazil and South Africa. Instead, the annual reports released by the Ministry of Defense were analyzed. These documents with content superior to two hundred pages have been released annually since 2000. This analysis looked at sections of those documents where the sources of threat and priorities of the Indian defense policy are pointed out. They appear in the chapter entitled "Strategic Environment" or "National Security Environment." For this chapter, 14 versions of the initial chapter of those reports were studied.

The External Threat Environment

Table 4 below summarizes the findings regarding threats in the three cases. South America presents a unipolar distribution of capabilities (Malamud and Alcañiz, 2017) and a small number of interstate conflicts (Pion-Berlin, 2016). From the standpoint of regional security, the perception of threats in the Brazilian State, evidenced by analysis of declaratory policy, is that there are no foreign threats. On the other hand, the document is clear that the mission of the armed forces is to protect Brazil's economic development.

Brazil asserts the importance of stability in the South America explicitly. In this region, Brazil perceives itself as a regional leader on a continent with a low degree of interstate conflicts (Government of Brazil 2012:34). The strategy coined by Brazilian foreign policy at the time was to cooperate with South American States (and the extended region, the west coast of Africa) and to deter the non-South American states from acting in the region. With the systemic constraint of low external threats, the incentives are for the defense policy in Brazil to have high developmental content.

The systemic incentives to have a declaratory defense policy with more development content are even more intense for South Africa. Southern Africa, from the viewpoint of material capabilities, presents a unipolar distribution in favor of South Africa. From the viewpoint South Africa's regional security agenda, regional and domestic problems are intimately related (Government of South Africa, 2015, Intro 7).

Table 4
Perceptions of threats in the cases' declaratory defense policy

	Brazil	India	South Africa
What is threatened?	Economic development, to raise living standards for the population	The Indian State, which exists to protect the population	The population
Sources of threats	State-related, but not declared. The potential threat is Brazil not having enough resources to develop the economy due to the intervention of foreign powers in South America.	State-related – unstable neighborhood surrounded by two nuclear powers; Non-state related – terrorism and guerillas.	Non-state, mainly crime, health epidemics, forced migration, violations of human rights and poverty.
Actions recommended by the State	Strategy to fight possible classic foreign threats by mitigating vulnerabilities. Cooperation with South America and deterrence to other foreign powers.	The defense force is very operational and tasked with fighting wars and terrorism. Internal security tasks are increasingly important.	Widest array of tasks that range from classic defense to activities related to human security.
International Insertion ambitions	Regional Power with global aspirations. The region is stable Brazil needs to contribute to keeping it like that.	Global Power, as a region is seen as a burden and unstable, as India sees itself as culturally and politically isolated.	Regional Power. Stability is necessary, and that justifies the need to take the lead in Southern African issues

Source: elaborated by author.

South Africa's defense document states that non-military issues are the primary drivers of insecurity in that country. Security there is not just the absence of war but is to pursue the eradication of poverty, sustainable development, and Strengthening of democratic governance. In the context of transnational threats, collaborative and multilateral action is the only option to solve these security issues, not unilateral military action (SADR 2013, Chap2:18).

Under the guise of human security, domestic and foreign aspects are barely separated, evidenced by the discourse that South Africa is a developmental state. South Africa adopts a developmental perspective for defense as well as favors multilateralism for the conduction of regional foreign policy since many of the issues are shared by other southern African states.

Finally, India's security environment, per its declaratory policy, is the most threatening. Pakistan is a fundamental preoccupation and so is a concern with instability in South Asia more generally (Government of India. Ministry of Defence, 2012:5). The document also increasingly encompasses internal security threats, as India sought to frame part of its defense policy in terms of the post 9-11 security agenda, as in the following excerpt, from the 2011 report:

> Even though the probability of conventional full-scale inter-state wars is reckoned by many analysts to have reduced, the security environment has become complex, with incidence of low-intensity conflicts and asymmetric threats taking various forms, including domestic and trans-national terrorism, narco-terrorism, cyber warfare and piracy [Government of India. Ministry of Defence, 2011:3].

The "Defense-Development" nexus in declaratory defense policies

Is the variation in the threat environment perceptions portrayed in the previous section reflected in the variation on developmental content in the declaratory defense policies? They are summarized in table 5.

Table 5
Perceptions on the security-development nexus

	India	Brazil	South Africa
Defense-development nexus?	Low	Medium	High
Bottom line of the Defense-development nexus	Defense is the priority because it is a precondition for development.	Defense protects development – Brazilian priority – as it protects natural resources, helps cooperate with neighbors and deters foreign threats.	Development creates Defense

Source: elaborated by author.

In Brazil, the defense apparatus must protect the country from threats posed by non-South American states to the region. Also, the political legitimization of defense policies by a developmental discourse is justified because the country needs to safeguard its natural resources for economic development. The discursive nexus between defense and development presents itself in the following logic: the political-economical rise of Brazil makes the need for natural resources to be safeguarded by Brazilian defense and foreign policies (Government of Brazil, 2012:22). The documents show the Brazilian society the importance of an effective defense system with a force designed based on capabilities, given the fact that Brazil officially has no potential foes.

South Africa is the least threatened country and the one with the strongest link between defense and development in the declaratory defense policy. There are two tasks for the defense force in South Africa, according to its declaratory policy: deter foreign threats by other countries – which are non-existent – and developmental tasks. The term *"Developmental State"* is constantly used in the document analyzed, and according to it, the South African threat perception includes themes such as epidemics, criminality, and poverty. Development is the central topic of defense policy. Directed by the government, the defense forces must contribute to the development primarily by generating conditions necessary to it and through more specific actions (Government of South Africa, 2015:10). Beyond the arguments that development is a necessary condition for security, there is a set of actions listed by the document to be taken by the defense force targeted at helping a country's development.

Finally, the link between defense and development in India's declaratory defense policy is very low, mainly observed in the issue of energy security (Government of India. Ministry of Defence, 2001:16) and alternative measures to deal with the Naxalite insurgents (Government of India. Ministry of Defence, 2008:5). Therefore, the threat perception in Indian defense policy matches the elements of a traditional military power embedded in a high threat environment.

Conclusion

This chapter sought to study the declaratory defense policies of democracies and the nexus between defense and economic development in them. The heuristic proposition that countries with low levels of foreign threats would have their declaratory defense policy logically associated with economic development was tested more broadly in the context of quantitative data and qualitative evidence from three developing democracies.

It is useful to study declaratory defense policies because we can identify meaningful variations to be explained by social scientists. This chapter empirically tested hypotheses with quantitative and qualitative evidence. To do so, I built a database on declaratory defense policies and applied a supervised machine learning method to measure the degree of developmentalism in the declaratory defense policies. Using statistical analysis, I found support for all my hypotheses in the declaratory defense policies of more than 46 countries. Democracies with low levels of external threats portray more economic development content in their declaratory defense policies. When civilians oversee the defense sector, declaratory defense policies are more developmentalist. The impact of civilian control is larger in democracies with high levels of inequality.

The chapter also illustrated the argument with case-based evidence analyzing the declaratory defense policies of Brazil, South Africa and India. These are democracies with high level of economic inequality, at least nominal civilian control over the military and substantial variation in the defense policy content and the level of external threats. The results of this most-similar systems comparative design confirms insights shown in the quantitative analysis.

The next steps following up on this research agenda should broaden the dataset of declaratory defense policies with sources beyond the ETH Zurich database and do more fine-grained content analysis to identify the degree, for instance, of focus on internal security and other missions in the declaratory defense policies. That should combine more sophisticated text-as-data models using computational social science methods but also draw on empirically rich qualitative evidence that is available from the case-based on civil-military relations and defense policy.

References

ALSINA Jr., João Paulo Soares. *Política externa e política de defesa no Brasil:* Síntese Imperfeita. Brasília: Câmara dos Deputados, 2006.

AMORIM NETO, Octavio. *De Dutra a Lula:* La Conducción y Los Determinantes de La Política Exterior Brasileña. Buenos Aires: Editorial Universitaria de Buenos Aires, 2013.

________. The Impact of Civilians on Defense Policy in New Democracies: The Case of Brazil. *Latin American Politics and Society*, 61(3), 2019, p. 1-28.

________; ACÁCIO, Igor. Política de defesa e política nacional, 2008-2020. *IREE Defesa & Segurança*, (2), 2020, p. 1-15. Retrieved from https://iree.org.br/defesa/octavio-amorim-neto-e-igor-acacio/.

________; ACCORSI, Pedro. Presidents and Generals: Systems of Government and the Selection of Defense Ministers. *Armed Forces and Society*. 2020.

ART, Robert J.; WALTZ, Kenneth N. *The Use of Force:* Military Power and International Politics. New York: Rowman e Littlefield Publishers, 1999.

AYOOB, Mohammed. *The Third World Security Predicament:* State Making, Regional Conflict, and the International System. London: Lynne Rienner Publishers, 1995.

BARACHO, Gustavo. *Livros brancos de defesa:* realidade ou ficção. Curitiba: Appris, 2018.

BELIAKOVA, Polina. Erosion of Civilian Control in Democracies: A Comprehensive Framework for Comparative Analysis. *Comparative Political Studies*, 54(8), 2021, p. 1.393-1.423.

BENOIT, Kenneth et al. Quanteda: An R Package for the Quantitative Analysis of Textual Data. *Journal of Open Source Software*, 3(30), 2018.

BRAMBOR, Thomas; CLARK, William Roberts; GOLDER, Matt. 2006. Understanding Interaction Models: Improving Empirical Analyses. *Political Analysis*, 14(1), 2006, p. 63-82.

BREUSH, T. S.; PAGAN, A. R. A Simple Test for Heteroscedasticity and Random Coefficient Variation. *Econometrica*, 47(5), 1979.

BROOKS, Risa A. *Shaping Strategy:* The Civil-Military Politics of Strategic Assessment. Princeton, NJ: Princeton University Press, 2008.

BRUNEAU, Thomas C. A Conceptual Framework for the Analysis of Civil-Military Relations and Intelligence. *Defense & Security Analysis*, 34(4), 2018.

________; MATEI, Florina Cristiana. 2008. Towards a New Conceptualization of Democratization and Civil-Military Relations. *Democratization*, 15(5), 2008, p. 909-929.

CENTENO, Miguel Angel. *Blood and Debt:* War and the Nation-State in Latin America. University Park: The Pennsylvania State University Press, 2002.

________. Limited War and Limited States. In DAVIS, Diane E.; PEREIRA, Anthony W. (eds.). *Irregular Armed Forces and Their Role in Politics and State Formation*. Cambridge: Cambridge University Press, 2003, p. 82-95.

DINCECCO, Mark; KATZ, Gabriel. State Capacity and Long-Run Economic Performance. *Economic Journal*, 126(590), 2016, p. 189-218.

DUCH, Raymond M.; STEVENSON, Randolph T. *The Economic Vote*. Cambridge: Cambridge University Press, 2008.

ETH Zürich Center for Security Studies. National Security and Defense Strategies Database. 2021. Retrieve from https://css.ethz.ch/en/services/digital-library/series.html/154839. October 20, 2021.

FEAVER, Peter D. *Armed Servants:* Agency, Oversight, and Civil-Military Relations. Cambridge: Harvard University Press, 2003.

FERRARO, Agustin E.; CENTENO, Miguel Angel (Eds.). State and Nation Making in Latin America and Spain. *State and Nation Making in Latin America and Spain. The Rise and Fall Of the Developmental State*. 2018. Cambridge: Cambridge University Press, 2018.

GIFFORD, Brian. Why No Trade-off between "Guns and Butter"? Armed Forces and Social Spending in the Advanced Industrial Democracies, 1960-1993. *American Journal of Sociology*, 112(2), 2006.

GILPIN, Robert G. The Richness of the Tradition of Political Realism. *International Organization*, 38(2), 1984.

GOVERNMENT OF BRAZIL. *White Paper on National Defense*. Brasília, DF. 2012. Retrieved from https://www.gov.br/defesa/pt-br/arquivos/2012/mes07/lbdn.pdf. April 6, 2021.

GOVERNMENT OF INDIA. Ministry of Defence. *Annual Report (2001)*. New Delhi: Ministry of Defence of India, 2001.

________. *Annual Report (2007-2008)*. New Delhi: Ministry of Defence of India, 2008. Retrieved from https://www.mod.gov.in/documents/annual-report?page=1. October 30, 2021.

________. *Annual Report (2010-2011)*. New Delhi: Ministry of Defense of India, 2011. Retrieved from https://www.mod.gov.in/documents/annual-report. October 30, 2021.

________. *Annual Report (2011-2012)*. New Delhi: Ministry of Defense of India, 2012. Retrieved from https://www.mod.gov.in/documents/annual-report. October 30, 2021.

GOVERNMENT OF SOUTH AFRICA. *South African Defence Review 2015*. Pretoria: Ministry of Defense and Veterans Affairs of the Republic of South Africa, 2015.

HAINMUELLER, Jens; MUMMOLO, Jonathan Mummolo; XU, Yiqing. How Much Should We Trust Estimates from Multiplicative Interaction Models? Simple Tools to Improve Empirical Practice. *Political Analysis*, 27(2), 2019, p. 163-192.

HAUSMAN, J. A. Specification Tests in Econometrics. *Econometrica*, 46(6), 1978.

HENDRIX, Cullen S. 2010. Measuring State Capacity: Theoretical and Empirical Implications for the Study of Civil Conflict. *Journal of Peace Research*, 47(3), 2010, p. 273-285.

HUNTINGTON, Samuel P. *The Soldier and The State*. Cambridge, MA: Harvard University Press, 1957.

________. Reforming Civil-Military Relations. *Journal of Democracy*, 6(4), 1995, p. 9-17. Retrieved from http://muse.jhu.edu/content/crossref/journals/journal_of_democracy/v006/6.4huntington.html.

JANOWITZ, Morris. *The Professional Soldier:* A Social and Political Portrait. New York: The Free Press, 1960.

JASKOSKI, Maiah. *Military Politics & Democracy in the Andes*. Baltimore: John Hopkins University Press, 2013.

KATZWNSTEIN, Peter J. *The Culture of National Security:* Norms and Identity in World Politics. New York: Columbia University Press, 1996.

KIER, Elizabeth. Culture and Military Doctrine: France between the Wars. *International Security*, 19(4), 1995, p. 65-93.

KIM, Nam Kyu. Are Military Regimes Really Belligerent? *Journal of Conflict Resolution*: 62(6),2017, p. 1151-1178.

________; KANG, Alice J. External Threat Environments and Individual Bias against Female Leaders. *Political Science Research and Methods*, 2021.

KURTZ, Marcus J. *Latin American State-Building in Comparative Perspective*. Cambridge: Cambridge University Press, 2012.

LEGRO, Jeffrey W. Military Culture and Inadvertent Escalation in World War II. *International Security*, 18(4), 1994, p. 108-142.

LEWIS-BECK, Michael S.; STEGMAIER, Mary. Economic Voting. In CONGLETON, Roger D, GROFMAN, Bernard; VOIGT, Stepan (eds.). *The Oxford Handbook of Public Choice, Volume 1*. Oxford University Press, 2019.

MALAMUD, Andrés; ALCANIZ, Isabella. Managing Security in a Zone of Peace: Brazil's Soft Approach to Regional Governance. *Revista Brasileira de Política Internacional*, 60(1), 2017.

MARSHALL, Monty G.; JAGGERS, Keith; GURR, Ted Robert. Polity IV Project Dataset Users' Manual, v. 2010. *Polity IV Project*, 2011, p. 1-86.

MCMAHON, R. Blake; SLANTCHEV, Branislav L. 2015. The Guardianship Dilemma: Regime Security through and from the Armed Forces. *American Political Science Review*, 109(2), 2015, p. 297-313.

MEARSHEIMER, John J. The Journal of Military History *The Tragedy of Great Power Politics*. New York and London: W. W. Norton and Company, 2001.

MINTZ, Alex. Guns *versus* Butter: A Disaggregated Analysis. *American Political Science Review*, 83(4), 1989.

________; HUANG, Chi. Guns *versus* Butter: The Indirect Link. *American Journal of Political Science*, 35(3), 1991.

________; WARD, Michael D. The Political Economy of Military Spending in Israel. *American Political Science Review*, 83(2), 1989.

MOSKOS, Charles C.; WILLIAMS, John Allen; SEGAL, David R. *The Postmodern Military:* Armed Forces after the Cold War. London: Oxford University Press, 2000.

NORDLINGER, Eric. *Soldiers in Politics:* Military Coups and Governments. New York: Prentice Hall, 1977.

NYRUP, Jacob; BRAMWELL, Stuart. Who Governs? A New Global Dataset on Members of Cabinets. *American Political Science Review*, 114(4), 2020, p. 1.366-1.374.

OWENS, Mackubin Thomas. Civil-Military Relations. *Oxford Research Encyclopedia of International Studies*, 2017, p. 1-30.

PION-BERLIN, David. *Military Missions in Democratic Latin America*. New York: Palgrave Macmillan US. 2016. Retrieved from http://link.springer.com/10.1057/978-1-137-59270-5.

________; ACÁCIO, Igor. Explaining Military Responses to Protests in Latin American Democracies. *Comparative Politics* (Forthcoming). 2022. Retrieved from https://doi.org/10.5129/001041522X16195268352999. June 26, 2021.

________; ESPARZA, Diego; GRISHAM, Kevin. Staying Quartered: Civilian Uprisings and Military Disobedience in the Twenty-First Century. *Comparative Political Studies*, 47(2), 2012, p. 230-259.

________; TRINKUNAS, Harold. Civilian Praetorianism and Military Shirking during Constitutional Crises in Latin America. *Comparative Politics*, 42(4), 2010, p. 395-411.

POSEN, Barry. *The Sources of Military Doctrine*. Ithaca: Cornell Univesity Press, 1984.

R CORE TEAM. R: A Language and Environment for Statistical Computing. 2020.

RIPSMAN, Norrin M.; ZIELINSKI, Rosella Cappella; SCHILDE, Kaija E. In REVERON, Derek S.; GVOSDEV, Nikolas K.; CLOUD, John A. (eds.). *The Political Economy of Security*. 2018. Retrieved from http://oxfordhandbooks.com/view/10.1093/oxfordhb/9780190680015.001.0001/oxfordhb-9780190680015-e-38. October 30, 2021.

SCHENONI, Luis L. Bringing War Back in: Victory and State Formation in Latin America. *American Journal of Political Science*, 65(2), 2021.

SEAWRIGHT, Jason. Why Cross-Case Qualitative Causal Inference Is Weak, And Why We Should Still Compare. *Qualitative and Multi-Method Research*, 16(1), 2018, p. 8-15.

________; GERRING, John. Case Selection Techniques in Case Study Research. *Political Research Quarterly*, 61(2), 2008, p. 294-308. Retrieved from http://journals.sagepub.com/doi/10.1177/1065912907313077.

SINGER, J. David; BREMER, Stuart; STUCKEY, John. Capability Distribution, Uncertainty, and Major Power War, 1820-1965. In RUSSETT, Bruce (ed.). *Peace, War, and Numbers*. Beverly Hills: Sage, 1972, p. 19-48.

SOIFER, Hillel David. *State Building in Latin America*. Cambridge: Cambridge University Press, 2015.

SOLT, Frederick. Measuring Income Inequality Across Countries and Over Time: The Standardized World Income Inequality Database. *Social Science Quarterly*, 101(3), 2020.

________. *Using the SWIID in Stata*. Iowa City, 2021.

SORENSEN, Georg. War and State-Making: Why Doesn't It Work in the Third World. *Security Dialogue*, 32(3), 2001, p. 341-54.

STOCKHOLM INTERNATIONAL PEACE RESEARCH INSTITUTE. SIPRI Military Expenditure Database. 2021. Retrieved from https://www.sipri.org/databases/milex. March 29, 2021.

THIES, Cameron G. State Building, Interstate and Intrastate Rivalry: A Study of Post-Colonial Developing Country Extractive Efforts, 1975-2000. *International Studies Quarterly*, 48(1), 2004.

TILLY, Charles. War Making and State Making as Organized Crime. In EVANS, Peter; RUESCHEMEYER, Dietrich; SKOCPOL, Theda (eds.). *Bringing the State Back In*. Cambridge: Cambridge University Press, 1985, p. 169-186.

WALT, Stephen M. The Renaissance of Security Studies. *International Studies*, 35(2), 1991, p. 211-239.

WALTZ, Kenneth. *Theory of International Politics*. New York: McGraw-Hill, 1979.

WHITTEN, Guy D.; WILLIAMS, Laron K. Buttery Guns and Welfare Hawks: The Politics of Defense Spending in Advanced Industrial Democracies on JSTOR. *American Journal of Political Science*, 55(1), 2011, p. 117-134. Retrieved from https://www.jstor.org/stable/25766258?seq=1#metadata_info_tab_contents. October 30, 2021.

WILLIAMS, Laron K. Guns Yield Butter? An Exploration of Defense Spending Preferences. *Journal of Conflict Resolution*, 63(5), 2019.

Appendix

Table A1
Countries and years included in the dataset for statistical analysis

Country	Declaratory Defense Policy Documents
Albania	2004, 2005, 2012
Argentina	2010
Australia	2000, 2007, 2009, 2010, 2012
Austria	2001
Belgium	2000
Bolivia	2003
Bosnia-Herz	2005
Brazil	1996, 1998, 2005, 2008
Bulgaria	2002, 2010
Canada	2005,2008, 2012
Chile	2002
Colombia	2007
Croatia	2005, 2006
Czech Rep.	2002, 2004, 2008, 2011, 2012
Denmark	2005, 2010
Ecuador	2006
Estonia	2004, 2009, 2010
Ethiopia	2009
Finland	2001, 2004, 2006, 2009, 2012
France	2008
Georgia	2007, 2012
Honduras	2005
Hungary	2004, 2012
India	2004
Ireland	2000, 2003, 2007, 2008, 2011
Italy	2004, 2005
Jamaica	2006
Japan	2011

Latvia	2003, 2012
Lithuania	2002, 2009, 2011, 2012
Macedonia	2005, 2012
Malaysia	2012
Netherlands	2000, 2008, 2010
New Zealand	2000, 2001, 2002, 2003, 2004, 2006, 2008, 2010
Norway	2004, 2006, 2008, 2012
Paraguay	2005
Peru	2005
Philippines	2011, 2012
Poland	2003, 2007, 2009
Romania	2005, 2006, 2007
S. Africa	1996, 1998, 1999, 2010, 2011, 2012
Slovakia	2001, 2003, 2005
Slovenia	2004
Spain	2000, 2003, 2004, 2008, 2012
Sweden	2004
Turkey	2000, 2007
United Kingdom	2008, 2010
Ukraine	2005, 2006, 2007, 2009, 2010, 2011
Vietnam	2009

Note: some of the countries in the table above were excluded because they did not meet the criteria for democracy (Polity score above or equal to 6).

Transparency and Civil-Military Relations: assessing civilian access to military records in Brazil and Mexico (1981-2012)

Karina Furtado Rodrigues[1,2]

Introduction

How did civil-military relations shape access to military information in Latin America in its democratic consolidation (1981-2012)? The general lack of interest in defense affairs from Latin-American civilians has already been identified by the literature, and some of the listed reasons are: Latin American countries do not experience a foreseeable possibility of war, its defense industry does not create a sufficiently expressive number of employments to call the attention of politicians and, consequently, the subject does not attract votes (Bruneau, 2005; Pion-Berlin, 2005).

Despite this unawareness of defense, transparency is seen as a democracy and policy-enhancing tool; and it is a consensus that unrestricted powers to operate in secrecy can create spaces that favor corruption, inefficiency (Michener, 2010) and the impossibility to make judgments regarding the success of military strategies. The dilemma is that transparency should be the rule, but secrecy is also necessary and can also be democratically legitimate. The nature of the work of military institutions is somewhat related to being able to surprise the enemy or build deterrence capabilities, things that are impossible to make without secrecy (Colaresi, 2014).

---

1 The views expressed in this chapter are those of the author and do not necessarily reflect the official policy or position of the Brazilian Army High Command and General Staff College, the Brazilian Army, the Ministry of Defense nor the Brazilian government. This research does not make any use of classified information.

2 This research is a result of my Ph.D dissertation at EBAPE/FGV, funded by two research grants from the Brazilian Ministry of Education: the Pró-Estratégia grant and the PDSE fellowship (*Programa de Doutorado-Sanduíche no Exterior*). I would like to thank all who made comments in the drafts of this study: Prof. Octavio Amorim Neto (EBAPE/FGV), Prof. David Pion-Berlin (UC Riverside), Prof. Luiz Goldoni (Eceme), Igor Acácio (UC Riverside) and Pedro Accorsi (University of Minessota).

I argue that, depending on how the relationship between civilians and the military is structured, more or less access to military records will be rendered to civilians. Two opposing patterns of civil-military relations can be used to better understand these differences in military records' transparency: the separation model of military behavior (Pion-Berlin et al., 2012; Huntington, 1957), in which civilian control functions in terms of objective control (the more professional autonomy the military have, the more control of the military there will be) and subjective control (the settlement of legal and institutional boundaries at their discretion); and the integration model (Janowitz, 1960; Pion-Berlin et al., 2012; Moskos, 1977), which advocates for a less marked dichotomy between civilians and the military.

The integration model, however, can only be used to understand Latin America if we analyze integration in a broader way, in terms of how closely civilians and the military work together in the conduct of public policy. I argue that in the region we experience a *reverse Janowitzian integration model*, which means that while the integration model advocates for a civilianization of defense in Latin America we find a militarization of many civilian affairs. Then I propose that this model of civil-military relations will result in such an equation: the more reverse integration, the less transparency in military records will be.

I analyze two Latin American cases in their democratization periods: Brazil and Mexico. Both countries have strong freedom of information laws, with Mexico's law among the strongest laws in the world, much stronger than the Brazilian one (Gutiérrez, 2010; Rodrigues, K. F., 2020a), and both represent the separation model of civil-military relations with isolated military institutions; however, they present different levels of integration between civilians and the military, that may have directly influenced transparency on defense issues. E.g., a 2011 study on defense budget transparency classified Mexico as within "medium to low transparency," together with countries such as Afghanistan and Venezuela, while Brazil figured among "Moderate to high transparency" (Transparency International, 2011). More recently, the 2020 Government Defence Integrity Index, from which I collected the data for Brazil, showed the same discrepancy between these two countries: Mexico was classified as having a very high risk of corruption, while Brazil had a moderate risk classification (Transparency International, 2020).

Due to the ongoing character of the recent government militarization and the apparent erosion of many democratic institutions in both countries, I chose to analyze a completed historical process to generate more solid observations. Thereafter, my analysis goes from the start of important democratic reforms in both countries (1981 for Mexico, 1985 for Brazil) until 2012, which is the period before the very beginning of the political crisis in Brazil and the end of the two consecutive terms of *Partido Acción Nacional* (PAN) in Mexico.

The study undertakes two independent explaining-outcome process tracings (Beach; Pedersen, 2013) using the gradual institutional changes theory as a theorized causal mechanism (Mahoney; Thelen, 2010). I assess civilian access to military records in Brazil and Mexico using historical and legal analysis, together with primary data from 24 semi-structured interviews conducted between 2013 and 2016 in both countries.

I conclude that, from 1981/85 to 2012, Brazil's model of civil-military relations produced more transparency in defense than Mexico's model, despite Mexico's stronger Freedom of Information (FOI) legislation. In Mexico, the higher integration between civilians and the military made political confrontation deeply homogeneous. Brazil, in turn, presented more political competition, and many policies within a wide political spectrum gained traction in the political agenda. Nevertheless, both countries still have isolated military institutions, which means that despite any legislation, there is still great discretion in the internal application of these rules.

This chapter is organized as follows: the following section presents the theoretical framework, exploring what transparency in defense means, how information availability is linked with civil-military relations and how we can use the literature on gradual institutional change to answer the research question; the third section contains methodological procedures; the fourth section presents Brazil's and Mexico's cases; the fifth section presents a straw-in-the-wind assessment of military transparency in the recent past; and, finally, the sixth section presents comparisons and concluding remarks.

Theoretical frame

This section aims to better define which theoretical fields the civilian access to military records touch and how these fields interconnect, exploring what is considered transparency in terms of military classifiable records; debating civil-military relations and their relation to information disclosure; and, at last, presenting mechanisms of institutional change that I will use to understand both cases.

Transparency of military records

If democracies cannot survive without transparency, neither can they live without secrecy. Nevertheless, it is known that giving unlimited discretion to a bureaucracy in restricting access to information can be a formula for ineffectiveness, corruption and institutional self-interest. "Officials' ability to make optimal judgments is undercut by their obligation to disregard many relevant concerns and by their largely unchecked freedom to base conclusions on political and personal self-interest" (Schulhofer, 2010:10).

Globally, standards on access to restricted documents have already been a topic of international debate, formalized in documents such as, among others, the Global Principles on National Security and the Right to Information (the Tshwane Principles) (Osji, 2013). The impact of these standards and ranking on *de facto* transparency on defense is still unknown, but they generally include provisions such as limits to classification, a public listing of motives to classify, the publication of a list of classified documents, automatic disclosure of declassified records, among others (Rodrigues, K. F., 2017).

Theoretically, it is already clear that transparency is not a dichotomous variable: there can be as many forms of transparency as one can imagine. Hood and Heald (2006), e.g. explore the many directions transparency can take: it can be horizontal, vertical, inward, outward, or any combination of the first two with the other two. Transparency can also be different depending on the level of information *visibility* or on the capacity to make inferences from information (*inferability*, using Bersch and Michener's (2013) terminology).

In this sense, K. F. Rodrigues (2020b) contends that if democracy needs to make room for access restrictions to information, neither classified information nor institutions that generate many secrets should be seen necessarily, as opaque or not transparent. This is because classifiable information has a different nature; the restriction of access is part of the policy itself, and at first, its visibility and inferability are legitimately reduced to a code or a list of codes referring to classified or declassified documents. Most importantly, however, is that if a citizen or other third party cannot have full visibility of, or inferability from a public record, the *classification* **process** should be transparent to the general public and should also be *accountable to a third party* – which can be called horizontal accountability. If a country does not have a transparent classification process and a functioning horizontal accountability towards classification, then one can consider these institutions opaque – which is different from saying that all institutions that generate secrets are non-transparent.

Civil-military relations and civilian access to records

Depending on how the relationship between civilians and the military is structured, more or less access to military records will be rendered to civilians. Considering a separation model of military behavior (Pion-Berlin et al., 2012), which follows Huntington's (1957) perspective on civil-military relations, the more professional autonomy the military has, the more objective control of the military there will be. There is a sense that professionalization and specialization should be respected, and too much civilian interference would probably be considered inappropriate civilian interference on military expertise. From this perspective, subjective control also needs to be in place, which is the settlement of legal and institutional boundaries at their discretion.

There is a consensus that Latin American countries follow a separation model of military behavior (Pion-Berlin et al., 2012), with military institutions operating as total institutions. However, when civilian elites grant objective civilian control while granting only loose subjective control it generates military-bureaucratic insulation,[3] full of incentives for them to resist subjective control.

The other classical civil-military relations approach is the one of Janowitz (1960) – which Pion-Berlin, Ugues and Sparza (2012) call the integration model of military behavior – which, differently from Huntington's view, advocates for a less marked dichotomy between the two groups. This means, as explored later by Moskos (1977), that the military should not be an isolated institution

3 Bureaucratic insulation (in Portuguese, *insulamento burocrático*) means the creation of specialized institutions that would be specialized and institutionally designed to act as state (and not political) institutions, shielded from political turnover as their autonomy is guaranteed.

– instead, it should reflect the whole society's values, avoiding institutional isolation and making the military profession no more than another occupation. However, we can use Janowitz's take on *integration* to better understand the Latin American context only if we analyze integration more generally, in terms of how close civilians and the military work together in the conduct of public policy. This is because in Latin America, I argue, there is a *reverse Janowitzian integration*: if Janowitz (and Moskos) advocated for a civilianization of defense, in Latin America we experience a militarization of many civilian affairs, which, for transparency, results that the more reverse integration, the less transparency in Defense issues will be.

Civilian engagement with defense issues, as suggested by the integration model, is growing, but it is historically weak. In most Latin American countries civilians simply do not have enough incentives – defense is not easily transformed in votes – to know about defense and national security, especially when there is an absence of inter-state conflicts (Pion-Berlin, 2005). According to Bruneau (2005), however, in a consolidated democracy there should not exist parts of the state "not controlled" by civilians. Politicians are expected to know little about many issues but should know sufficiently about defense to be able to maintain democratic civilian control. The author also stands for the fact that not everything is about control: military effectiveness and efficiency should be the subject of civilian accountability.

These studies do not take into account that the lack of civilianization of defense affairs might not be a product of civilian lack of interest in defense affairs. If the military has veto powers about transparency regulations, but civilian groups advocating for more transparency are present, the real issue turns out to be agenda power. In this context, civilians who are interested in defense issues might not be considered legitimate actors to have access to some information and to influence defense decision-making.

In addition, the armed forces are one of the most trusted institutions in Latin America, and they are often deployed in internal missions, whether of public security, insurgency or natural disaster management nature. Besides the lack of other functioning institutions to do the job, it is common for elected representatives to try to borrow prestige from the armed forces, to raise numbers on popularity and election pools. Scholars have been worried about the impacts of this type of integration on civil-military relations (Nóbrega Júnior, 2010; Hachemer, 2017).

Thereafter, I propose that, *in a context of isolated military bureaucracies under wide objective control and loose subjective control, the more integration between civilians and the military, the less transparency on defense there will be.*

Among Latin American countries, Brazil and Mexico represent two countries known for following a separate model of civil-military relations; with military institutions organized as total institutions; with a lack of civilian control over doctrine and training; with constant military deployments on public security operations; but with different levels of integration (towards militarization) between civilians and the military for the period of study – and this difference was the crucial element for the case study selection.

In Brazil, scholars agree that civilian control might have been perfect, but it was improving. Recent research has shown that civilian participation in defense policy formulation is growing and can change its orientation (Amorim Neto, 2019). The country has a Ministry of Defense and, despite the maintenance of the Amnesty Act – an act that gave pardons to civilians and military officials involved in human rights abuses during the military regime – the state was still able to undertake many other reparation policies, and also to open intelligence archives (D'Araújo, 2010; Zaverucha, 2005a). Mexico, in turn, has extensive use of the military in internal deployments and has been persistently criticized for giving a *carte blanche* to military officials, regardless of human rights crimes (Astorga, 2007, 2015; Freeman; Serra, 2005; Hachemer, 2017).

Access to military records and institutional change theory

This study aims to understand how civil-military relations influence transparency on defense by analyzing how military and civilian actors engaged and reacted to transparency regulation proposals and enactments. Thereafter, the analysis makes use of the institutional change theory and, especially, the gradual institutional change theory.

Neo-institutionalists argue that institutions tend to last – as a set of values, culture and formal and informal norms that guide human actions to some predictability (Scott, 2008), that often get "locked-in," "like 'frozen' residues, or 'crystallizations' of previous political conflict" (Streeck; Thelen, 2005:6). However, change happens, and the literature on path dependence presented important theoretical developments in explaining them, emphasizing mechanisms such as *exogenous shocks, increasing returns* and *positive feedback*, and highlighting that there can be self-reinforcing mechanisms that promote changes within institutions (Page, 2006).

These works, however, left uncovered gradual changes, which are those made from within and not necessarily from an exogenous incremental self-reinforcing variable. Streeck and Thelen (2005:8) contend that "equating incremental with adaptative and reproductive minor change, and major change with, mostly exogenous, disruption of continuity, makes excessively high demands on 'real' change to be recognized as such." The fact is that, through the years, little changes can evolve into big structural changes. In this regard, the authors suggest scholars make a distinction between an analysis of the *processes of change* (which can be either abrupt or incremental) and the results of change (which can be either continuity or discontinuity).

Mahoney and Thelen (2010) state that these gradual changes are only accessible through the eyes of history. Institutional changes would be a result of changes in the balance and distribution of power, also influencing the relationship between one institution and a set of other institutions, and actors in disadvantaged groups within an institution can use their *status* to promote change through other institutions. In addition, institutions are not simply self-enforcing: rules can carry a spectrum of different understandings, which means they can be enforced to different degrees depending on the actors within the institution. Therefore, change is expected in the soft spots or gaps between rules and their interpretation, and that is precisely where institutions take place (Mahoney; Thelen, 2010; Streeck; Thelen, 2005). Mahoney and Thelen (2010) contend that there are four modes of gradual institutional change, which are:

(1) **Displacement:** displacement happens when there is the removal of existing rules with the introduction of new ones. In this context, actors that were "losers" in previous changes introduce new rules and, in the absence of resistance, can promote change.

(2) **Layering:** this happens when there is the introduction of new rules without removing previous ones. The new rules are on top of or alongside the old ones, changing the impact the original rules had. "Losers" cannot introduce a whole new institution.

(3) **Drift:** occurs when existing rules assume new meanings and impact due to changes in the environment. Actors neglect changes that already occurred.
(4) **Conversion:** occurs when there is an intentional and strategic redeployment of existing rules. Henceforth, actors explore ambiguity to minimize the impact of existing rules.

To establish which type of change is happening, Mahoney and Thelen (2010) make use of two variables: (1) political context, which is related to the veto possibilities of the change-actors; and (2) characteristics of the targeted institution, which is the degree of discretion they have in interpreting and implementing a rule. Depending on the configuration of these two variables, a certain type of dominant change-agent and mode of change is likely to occur. Having said that, the next section aims to present the methodological procedures used to identify a gradual change in defense transparency.

Methodological Procedures

This study undertakes two explaining-outcome process tracing analyzes (Beach; Pedersen, 2013). The process tracing method proposed by Beach and Pedersen (2013) is mainly mechanism-centered, single-case oriented and follows a Bayesian rationale. Saying that process tracing is *single-case oriented* means that all conclusions taken from one case have issues travelling around, e.g., the same evidence can mean different things for each of the cases. Therefore, they contend that process tracing can be used to identify the presence of certain mechanisms in a case, but it needs other comparative methods, in addition to the first method, to ensure that the findings can really be general enough so they can be considered, at most, medium-range theories (Beach; Pedersen, 2013).

This debate in the research design implies that the study presents two separate process tracings, one for each case. Contexts are different, and so are the types of evidence that can actually explain why and how parts of the causation mechanisms influenced Y – which, in this case, is transparency in defense. They then suggest that other comparison methodologies should be used after the process tracing application. Thereafter, in the concluding remarks there will be a comparison assessment that will confront both cases to the proposition made in the theoretical section.

Saying that process tracing is *mechanism-centered* means that it is interested in discovering the black box of events that led X to cause Y. There is a realm of already hypothesized mechanisms in the literature. Thereafter, this study assumes an institutionalist view of organizational change, seeing gradual institutional change theory as a theorized mechanism. The analysis of such mechanisms aims to uncover the nuances of power disputes of the military transparency agenda, in such a fashion that it is still open to finding new context-oriented mechanisms.

Finally, to say that process tracing follows a *Bayesian rationale* at heart means that, when testing a theory, we have prior expectations regarding the explanatory power of its statements, and while process tracing, new sets of an evidence update our belief in the propositions or hypothesis established before. These expectations, for some authors, should be formalized with numbers. However, some scholars question the researcher's ability to properly infer an amount of probability or belief, advocating just for *some* formalization – such as *high* or *low* expectations, due to the disbelief in the capacity for an accurate assessment of these numbers in qualitative research – which will be the perspective considered in this study (Beach; Pedersen, 2013; Fairfield; Charman, 2017; Mahoney, 2016). We set an expectation that Mexico, due to its deeper integration between the military and civilian elites, will have less formal transparency on defense than Brazil, even though having much stronger freedom of information law (RTI Rating, 2021).

Data recollection comprised a bibliographic search, legislation analysis and 24 semi-structured interviews conducted between 2013 and 2016 in both countries, including military officials, public servants, diplomats, archivists, specialists in civil-military relations and archives. Not all interviews are listed; only interviews that generated unofficial information, interpretations of legislation and political decisions are mentioned in the text; end notes contain the interviewee credentials in those cases where interviewees allowed identification.

Results

This section aims to identify and understand the changes in civilian access to military records both in Brazil and Mexico. At the beginning of each subsection a summary of changes, together with the type of change and the process/result of the change, is displayed. Later, I present a brief description of the change regarding civil-military relations.

Brazil

Since the foundation of the Brazilian republic, the military has had the tradition of being a prominent and proactive actor in politics (Santos, 1986). The rhetoric of military disengagement in politics emerged only with the democratization of the post-military regime (1964-1985). The main changes in civilian access to military records in Brazil between 1985 and 2012 are listed in Table 1.

The *first change* (displacement) of the democratic period occurred with the 1988 Constitution, which concluded the transition from the military regime to democratic rule. The first civilian president of the newborn democracy was president José Sarney, which was indirectly elected under an informal military tutelage. The Constitutional Assembly that wrote the constitution created many checks and balances in the federal government with no exemptions to military institutions. However, objective civilian control was not on the agenda. There was little interest from the main civilian leaders to engage in defense affairs, and the Constitution sections related to the topic were written mostly by the military themselves (Oliveira, 1994).

The overall result is that the Constitution accommodated both right and left-wing demands (Zaverucha, 2005b). In terms of transparency, it established the right-to-information in article 5, line XIV nevertheless, it did not establish a process to accede to information.

Table 1
Gradual changes in civilian access to military records in Brazil from 1985 to 2012

	Description	**Change**
1	1988 Constitution	Displacement
2	8.159 (1991) Archives Law	Layering
3	Political disappearances' Law 9.140 (1995)	Layering
4 / 5	Decree 2.134 (1997) and Decree 2.910 (1998)	Displacement and Layering
6 / 7	Creation of the Amnesty Commission in 2001 and the Decree 4.553 (2002).	Layering
8 / 9	11.111 (2005) Law and Decree 5.584 (2005).	Displacement and Layering
10 / 11	Human Rights National Plan (2009) and ICHR condemnation (2010).	Layering
12/ 13	12.527 (2011) Law the Decrees 7.724 (2012) and 7.983 (2012), the creation of a Truth Commission.	Displacement

Source: the author.

The *second change* (*layering,* since it did not revoke previous legislation) occurred with the enactment of the Archives Law (Act 8.159/1991), elaborated by archivists, jurists and activists. This was the first piece of legislation that established an (unclear) process to accede to public records, subordinating military archives to the Executive branch, creating Permanent Commissions for the Evaluation of Documents,[4] establishing a 30-year maximum limit plus one renovation for the classification of documents, and creating the Archives National Council.[5] However, these institutions had (and still have) no sanction powers, affecting superficially civilian access to military records and archives (Hott, 2005).

The country just had its first directly elected president after the military regime, Fernando Collor de Melo, who tried to exercise authority by extinguishing the National Intelligence Service (SNI) – a symbol of the military regime – transforming the agency into an intelligence department within the presidency's Secretary of Strategic Issues. The military still had veto possibilities in some policy arenas, such as the endurance of the Political Amnesty legislation and

[4] In Portuguese, *Comissões permanentes de avaliação de documentos.*

[5] In Portuguese, *Conselho Nacional de Arquivos* (CONARQ).

the postponement of the creation of a Brazilian Ministry of Defense (D'Araújo, 2012; Oliveira, 1994).

The positioning of the Brazilian government regarding crimes committed during the military regime was being questioned by the "political disappearances" Law 9.140 (1995), our *third change (layering),* which recognized disappearances during the military regime as deaths, establishing financial compensations to citizens (both military and civilian) who suffered damages during this period.

The *fourth change (displacement)* occurred in 1997 with Decree 2.134 – the "access decree," which revoked previous legislation that ruled secrecy, guaranteeing public access to archives and establishing secrecy tiers, a set of restrictions to secrecy and also administrative punishments for noncompliance; but established the necessity of giving motives to access documents (Hott, 2005).

One year later, the *fifth change (layering)* occurred as a response to the third change, with the enactment of decree 2.910 (1998). The military was concerned with decree 2.134 (1997) because it revoked rules and procedures for maintaining and managing classified information of the previous Decree 79.099 (1977), which the Regulation for Safeguard of Secretive Issues.[6] Thereafter, two servants of the Brazilian National Archive and two military officials elaborated this new decree, which stipulated the publication of a list of declassified documents open to consultation every six months; the establishment that declassified documents should be automatically public; among others (Hott, 2005).

The fifth change was a turning point for access to military and diplomacy records because, for the first time, there was a clear link between civilian legislation regarding access to public records and some risk of exposure of these institutions, whether from the Paraguay War or of the military regime. The following debates on the transparency of public records were all marked by strong resistance from the military and diplomats (Rodrigues, 2020b).

Between the fifth and the sixth changes, during the two presidential terms of Fernando Henrique Cardoso, there were important events for the country's civil-military relations. Brazil published its first National Policy on Defense in 1996 and was able to create a civilian Ministry of Defense in 1999. There were also challenges to civilian control. In 2000, president Cardoso fired Army General Gleuber Vieira due to public insubordinate declarations. From this point on,

6 In Portuguese, *Regulamento para a Salvaguarda de Assuntos Sigilosos.*

a series of retaliation started to come from the military, who even scheduled a meeting of 155 generals in Brasília (Brazil's capital) without calling the civilian Defense Minister (Zaverucha, 2005a).

In this context, the *sixth change* (*layering*) was the creation of the Amnesty Commission within the Ministry of Justice in 2001. In addition to that, a deputy presented a draft bill that put transparency as means of questioning the Amnesty Law (draft bill 2.649/2002). Then the *seventh change* (displacement) came inadvertently: in the very last moments of Cardoso's term, he signed decree 4.553 (2002), which allowed unlimited classification renewals for documents, eliminated the publication of lists of declassified documents, competing with several provisions of the Archives Law (Hott, 2005). The president contended that he signed the decree "by mistake." The ones signing the decree together with the president were the president's Chief of Staff and the Minister of Institutional Security, who was an Army General (Rodrigues, K. F., 2013).

President Luiz Inácio "Lula" da Silva, whose term began in 2003, had the chance to abrogate the secrecy decree. Nevertheless, the president did not want to create tensions with the military right at the beginning of his term, and the decree persisted for three years (Hott, 2005). In 2004, however, there was the leaking of photos of a hanged man locked in a prison of the military regime, which revived the shadows of the probability of an annulation of the unrestrictive political amnesty given in the democratization process.

Thus, the leak was followed by the attempt to calm emotions down with a new access-to-information law, Law 11.111 (2005), our *eighth change (displacement* and *layering* at the same time, since it established a maximum secrecy tier of 30 years – instead of 50 years, established automatic disclosure of declassified documents, but, at the same time maintaining the possibility of unlimited classification renovations) (Hott, 2005; Rodrigues, K. F., 2013). G. M. Rodrigues (2011) asserts that most of the laws and decrees in this period were "reactive" ways to contain general dissatisfaction that was careless of public debate and long-term planning. As a result of this reactive behavior, Lula enacted decree 5.584 (2005), our *ninth change* (*layering*), which stipulated the recollection of many documents produced by specific institutions which were responsible for the repression during the military regime.

The *tenth (layering) and the eleventh (drift) changes* were the launching of the Human Rights National Plan (2009) and the condemnation of Brazil by the Inter-American Court of Human Rights (2010), respectively. The first one envisioned the creation of a Truth Commission in Brazil, which led to many criticisms from the Armed Forces. The condemnation, in turn, damaged Brazil's image internationally and helped the coalition in favor of the enactment of the FOI law (Rodrigues, K. F., 2020a).

The enactment of the Brazilian Freedom of Information (FOI) Law 12.527 (2011) and decrees 7.724 (2012) and 7.983 (2012) compose, together, the *twelfth change (displacement)*. This legislative process faced strong resistance from the Senate's Commission of Foreign Affairs and National Defense (CRE), which acted on behalf of the military and the diplomatic corps. According to one interviewee,[7] the military resisted the legislation because they had an unimaginable amount of information and difficulties in sharing it timely as the law required. Another argument was the *revanchismo* against the military regime[8]. In the end, the minister of defense was somehow able to convince the forces that the law would do no harm to the military.[9]

President Dilma, a former political prisoner of the military regime, was one of the main supporters of the law and set a strategy to pressure the Senate: first, she enacted the Decree on a National Plan for Open Government, with the support of eighteen ministries (Prete, 2011); second, she called for international pressure by signing and co founding the Open Government Partnership (OGP), together with the United States (Rodrigues, K. F., 2020b).

In October 2011, the Senate voted against the eternal secrecy prerogative and Dilma enacted the Brazilian Freedom of Information law in November 2011. The two 2012 decrees were following many international standards on FOI, establishing clear guidelines for classification and its management, and establishing an interministerial commission to be the last instance of appeals in the case of declassification requests made by citizens. The classification should not exceed 50 years (for top-secret documents with one classification renovation), *ex-ante* classification was not allowed, and fewer ranks and positions could classify information in the higher secrecy tiers.

7 Interviewee from the Ministry of Justice, who participated in the discussions of the draft bill. Rio de Janeiro, May 2013.

8 Interview with a military official allocated in the Brazilian Army Command and General Staff College. Rio de Janeiro, May 2013.

9 Interview with Nelson Jobim, Minister of Defense at the time the FOI Law was enacted. Rio de Janeiro, May 2013.

The creation of a Truth Commission is our *thirteenth change (layering),* which occurred on the on same day of the FOI Law enactment, challenging the stable veto power the military has in reconciliation issues. However, during its existence, the Commission lacked powers to criminally prosecute anyone who committed crimes related to torture and murder; it did not have the power to demand the presence of repression agents in its audiences and had no special access to military archives. Access to military documents was difficult even when the requested information was not classified,[10] and many were denied information requests by the National Truth Commission due to the non-existence of the information or an alleged documental elimination.

Mexico

Mexico was considered for a long time the Latin American haven of civil-military relations. While most countries were struggling with military and civilian coups, the Institutional Revolutionary Party (under its many versions) governed peacefully (Ackroyd, 1991).

However, Ronfeldt (1975) contends that researchers should analyze military subordination in Mexico carefully: it exists, but also do the residual political roles of the military. The Mexican army was indeed less political than its Latin American neighbors at the federal level. Nevertheless, in lesser political conflicts the Mexican army was historically more involved. The deployment of the armed forces in a specific region has always been a political currency for the central government to preserve power.

The war on drugs (Astorga, 2005) paved the importance of the military for Mexican politics, and the constant military support to the Mexican political hegemony protected them from public scrutiny. Little is known about the Mexican military, and even "routine activities" tend to be classified "as highly sensitive and subject to security restrictions" (Claire, 1992:17). The main changes in civilian access to military records in Mexico between 1981 and 2012 are listed in Table 2.

10 Interview with Nadine Borges, former member of the regional Truth Commission of the Rio de Janeiro state. Rio de Janeiro, February 2015.

Table 2
Gradual changes in civilian access to military records in Mexico from 1981 to 2012

	Description	Change
1	Media draft law which included right-to-information provisions (1981)	Drift
2	Drug-trafficking started to be considered a national security threat (1985)	Layering
3	The creation in 1990 of the Federal Electoral Institute and the National Commission for Human Rights, among other institutions.	Conversion
4	Media draft law which included right-to-information provisions, in 1997	Drift
5	Strengthening of Human Rights institutions, and settlement of a minority government, in 1999.	Displacement and Layering
6	The enactment of the Mexican Freedom of Information Law (2002)	Displacement
7	National Security Law (2005)	Layering and Displacement
8	National Archives Law (2012)	Layering

Source: the author.

The *first change (drift)* occurred in 1981, with the first attempt to regulate access to public records. There was an intense debate for the next four years until 1981 when president Portillo presented a draft bill that was more about controlling the media than ensuring freedom of information. Part of the media – around 30% of the press – was coopted and was in favor of the bill. However, the other 70% of the press made a massive campaign against it, which took the voting off the agenda (Michener, 2010).

The 1980s and the 1990s saw an increase in drug trafficking in Mexico: Colombian Cartels were dissolved, and Mexico became the main route to deliver drugs to the US American market. The government kept using the military to solve public security crises; however, in 1985, with the murder of a DEA agent on Mexican soil, the United States became even more strict in its policy of militarizing counternarcotic actions in Mexico (Claire, 1992; Freeman; Serra, 2005). Miguel de la Madrid's presidential term (1982-1988) also increased the possibilities of internal deployment of the armed forces, besides establishing drug trafficking as a national security threat (Andersen, 1996; Freeman; Serra, 2005), which can be considered our *second change (layering)*.

Camín (2002) contends that the population was not satisfied with the country's electoral frauds, which fueled strong pressure toward the implementation of anticorruption reforms and electoral neutrality in the country. After the last and most scandalous electoral fraud – the election of Salinas de Gortari (Fuser, 1995), the *third change* (layering) emerges as a result of some acquiescence from the president to some of its population reclaims. Thereafter, Gortari created a few democratic institutions at the end of the 1990s, such as the Electoral Federal Institute[11] and the National Commission for Human Rights. This change is important to transparency regulations because it would not be possible to break political hegemony without fair elections. Civilian elites and the military continued to be aligned with Gortari. The support resulted in a military modernization agenda carried out in 1989, by National Defense Secretary General Antonio Riviello Bazan, who reinforced a doctrine of internal deployments of the armed forces (Andersen, 1996; Velásquez, 2009).

Mexico's next president Ernesto Zedillo inherited the Tequila crisis,[12] so, to restrain damages, he showed commitment to building institutional trust and credibility by diminishing presidential powers, setting the political agenda with anticorruption reforms, and even appointing an opposition member to be the Federal Attorney General. In 1997, the *fourth change (drift)* consisted of the government's attempt to enact a media law that set right-to-information provisions under Zedillo's term. This new draft suffered from the same disease as the as last draft: it had many provisions setting press regulation, which communication companies and newspapers were against. Between a mediatic turmoil, much of Zedillo's will to support the law vanished, even with key legislative supporters' appeals to the Organization of American States in favor of the proposal (Michener, 2010).

The military's roles were broadened and strengthened under Zedillo's presidency: he put the military on the front lines of the drug war through the Chihuahua Pilot Project,[13] created the National Public Security Council and allocated military officials to Mexico's Attorney General.[14] Later these reforms made things even

11 In Spanish, *Instituto Federal Electoral* (IFE).

12 The Tequila effect was a currency crisis which generated an increased capital flight.

13 The Chihuahua Pilot Project replaced many officials from the Federal Justice Police by army officials. Nevertheless, a few months later there were accusations that the military officials in this project had links to the Juárez Cartel (Freeman; Serra, 2005).

14 In Spanish, *Procuraduría General de la República* (PGR).

more complicated for Vicente Fox's administration to establish civilian control of the armed forces (Artz, 2003; Freeman; Serra, 2005, Hachemer, 2017).

In 1999, the National Human Rights Commission gained full constitutional autonomy; and in the same year, an Organic Law was able to institutionalize a minority government, putting a pause in the decades of one-party rule. The debate on the right to information was still alive, and during 1999 and 2000, several meetings with scholars, the press and NGOs were mobilized around the topic of freedom of information (Michener, 2010).

The election of Vicente Fox (PAN, *Partido Acción Nacional*) on July 2, 2000, was one of the most important recent democratic milestones of Mexican history and it changed the context of power balance in the country with the confirmation of PRI's loss of influence and the end of 71 years of the party in power. The president won with the proposal to lead a country in a more parliamentary way, as state institutions were already more balanced and independent (Camín, 2002). It is only after the end of PRI's one-party rule that Polity IV considers Mexico a democratic state.

The influence of the US was still strong and, especially at the beginning of Fox's administration, boycotted the president's intent to take steps back regarding the use of the armed forces in counterdrug efforts. This influence in this special moment was quite disappointing since much was expected from this political change (Amorim Neto; Malamud, 2015; Astorga, 2007). Hachemer (2017) points out that the pressure from the US was not the only determinant for this absence of change. Historically,

> [...] the military supported the regime to the extent of self-abandonment, but this also came at a price for civilian leaders: rising military influence in the decision-making process and the importance of the armed forces in the intensifying "War on Drugs" in the 2000s left civilian decision-makers unable to "break" military prerogatives. Quite contrary to the theoretical argument that civilian actors would always seek to enforce oversight and civilian decision-making after a democratic transition, comprehensive reform of the Mexican armed forces is stalled for as long as civilian authority depends on military fealty. [Hachemer, 2017:92]

Vicente Fox also promised, in his first presidential speech in December 2000, to create a Truth Commission to investigate abuses from security forces.

Nevertheless, he only created a weaker substitute for a Truth Commission, which he called Special Prosecutor for Social and Political Movements of the Past (FEMOSPP).[15] FEMOSPP was created to investigate and prosecute public officials responsible for human rights violations in the presidential terms of Gustavo Díaz Ordaz, Luís Echeverría and José Lopez Portillo. However, no one was convicted after four years of the existence of the special prosecutor (DOYLE, 2006; VIVANCO, 2001).

The *sixth change (displacement)* occurred when the Mexican Congress approved the Freedom of Information Law in 2002. By the time of its enactment, it was the strongest FOI law in the media, and organized civilian groups world. Some sectors of the bureaucracy, the media and organized civilian groups had a decisive role in enacting such a strong law. Civil society lobbying and massive media coverage, especially due to a group of experts called *Grupo Oaxaca*, were able to make the draft presented by the government stronger (Michener, 2010).

The law did affect the military: it created a Federal Institute of Access to Information[16] capable of searching for documents in military units to challenge classification and restriction decisions. Nevertheless, there was no single sign of resistance or attempt of interference in the enactment process of the law.[17] There was a perception that the law did not affect the military since the Mexican FOI Law allows the classification of laws and decrees; the 12-year time limit to restrict a document worked only in theory since an agency could request IFAI for an unlimited extension (article 15), and the FOI Law did not establish clear classification tiers. In addition to that, the nomination of the five commissioners responsible for deciding appeals, including the ones related to national defense, is made by the Executive and confirmed by the Legislative. In majority governments, the nominations of IFAI's commissioners might suffer from political biases.[18]

15 In Spanish, *Fiscalía Especial para Movimientos Sociales y Políticos del Pasado* (FEMOSPP).

16 In Spanish, *Instituto Federal de Acceso a La Información* (IFAI), which turned into a national institute in 2015.

17 Interviews with (i) a former Commissioner at IFAI during Vicente Fox' administration – Mexico City, May 2016; and (ii) a member of CISEN, the Mexican intelligence agency – Mexico City, May 2016.

18 Interviewee who worked as a commissioner at IFAI during Vicente Fox' administration. Mexico City, May 2016.

Fortunately, the FOI law also showed some positive impact on civilian access to information about the military. Doyle (2004) contends that some scholars were able to access data that were never public before with the Mexican FOI law, such as the names of military zone commanders, among others.

The *seventh change (layering and displacement)* occurred three years later, in 2005 under Fox's term, with the National Security Law (LSN).[19] Gutiérrez (2010) contends that the LSN pretended to be about transparency, but in fact, created many legitimate instances to increase governmental secrecy. There was an increase in the number of the reasons to restrict access to information; it expands classification motives; allows *ex-ante* classification of all the information generated by their intelligence agency, their National Security Council, and budgetary information of all activities related to national security. Thereafter, the military used the international context and the increasing internal violence to modify the rules. Unlimited secrecy also pleased US and its counternarcotic efforts in the country (Astorga, 2007; Freeman; Piñero; Barajas, 2008).

During PAN's term (from 2000 to 2012), the party did not question military autonomy. On the contrary: from 2007 on, under Felipe Calderón's term (also from PAN), the country expanded internal military deployments and increased cooperation the with US, through *Iniciativa Mérida*.

In 2012, Calderón enacted the Federal Archives Law,[20] the first federal law regulating the archives of the public administration in the country, establishing a definition of historical archives and giving the National Archive (AGN) the responsibility to define which records should be discarded (Murguía, 2011). Researchers started to have access to lists of military records held by AGN but still had no direct access to military archives themselves. Even when a researcher is allowed to access them, they generally get lost in an infinite number of unimportant documents.[21]

19 In Spanish, *Ley de Seguridad Nacional.*

20 In Spanish, *Ley Federal de Archivos.*

21 Interview with American scholar specialized in Mexican archives. Mexico City, May, 2016.

Military transparency after 2012

This section aims to explore straw-in-the-wind evidence[22] from the recent past in order to make initial descriptive inferences. If my theoretical proposition is right also for this period, we can expect that any processes of militarization of civilian policies and institutions will produce less transparency in the defense realm. Is it the case?

Figure 1 shows data from the beginning of the period comprised by this study until 2020.

Figure 1
Liberal Democracy Indicator for Brazil and Mexico – 1981-2020

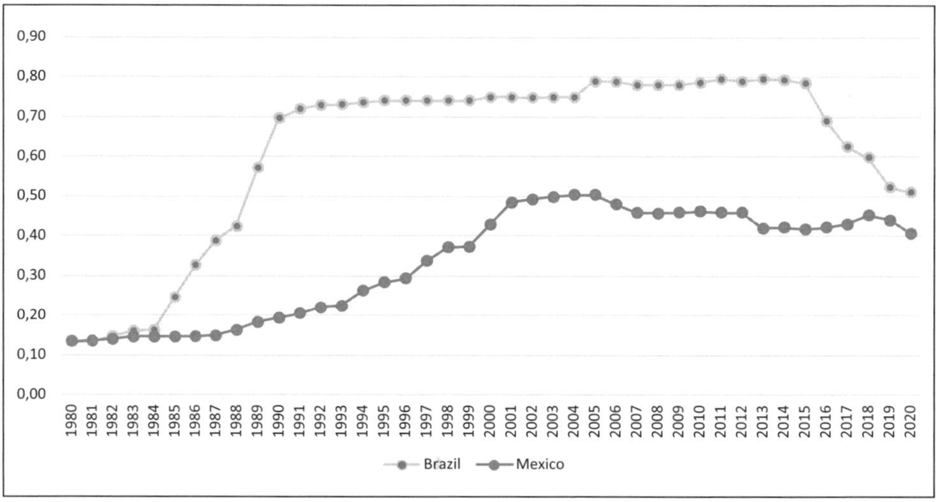

Source: Varieties of Democracy Institute (2021).

Both countries present a decrease in their Liberal Democracy Indicator since 2012. Brazil scores now similar to what it scored in 1989 as a result of a democratic representation crisis that began in 2012 with the Mensalão trials, followed by massive street protests in 2013, the impeachment of president Dilma Rousseff in 2016, culminating with the election of an extreme-right wing presidential

22 In process tracing, straw-in-the-wind evidence are those that passed the straw-in-the-wind test, which is the most superficial of the four existing ones. It shows the plausibility of a hypothesis, without eliminating other hypotheses; it is a collection of general information that supports the hypotheses (Rodrigues, K. F, 2017).

candidate, Jair Bolsonaro (Mourão, 2019). The election of Bolsonaro and his vice-president, who is a former army general, might be considered a turning point in the process of gradual rapprochement between civilians and the military in the sense of militarization of civilian policies. Changes after the election confirm this trend since in 2020, there was more than six thousand military personnel allocated to civilian positions within the Brazilian federal government, many of them unlinked with the positions' need for professional specialization (Número de militares em cargos..., 2020).

In terms of federal legislation, there was only one attempt to make classification more flexible, through decree 9.690 (2019), but in the face of pressure from civil society and the overall political context, it was rapidly revoked. However, new forms of restrictions to information emerged, such as the undue use of FOIA's personal data protection clause, in such a fashion that there is no distinction between private actions (which would harm one's intimacy) and actions derived from exerting a public position (Sigilo de 100 anos... 2021). This subterfuge has been used to restrict all types of information, such as the list of the president's visitors, and the president's vaccination records, among many other examples unrelated to national security. There are other cases where the government started to require a "confidentiality agreement" from servants of civilian ministries and agencies under Brazil's National Security Law (Opacidade..., 2021).

Thereafter, with high veto powers to change transparency legislation, there has been changing in the application of existing rules (as for personal data protection) in all sectors of government – through *conversion*. There is also a change in the meaning of existing rules, with a "securitization" of what has always been considered civilian and unrestricted information, such as health information – through *drift*.

However, it is still soon to make optimistic or pessimistic predictions on the results of this process: with such a strong political and mediatic focus on military institutions during the last four years – due to the president's attempted to reliance on the military prestige –, for the first time in a long time, civilians bothered to look at, or even be curious about, defense institutions, which could change civilian defense attention deficits in the long run. One must also be careful with the public perception distortions related to transparency, e.g., the more transparency you have, the more undue behavior is uncovered, and the greater will be the general perception of corruption. We cannot assume causality from this relation – often, ***being able*** to uncover and investigate government corruption or inefficiency is precisely the sign of well-functioning oversight institutions and, consequently, less corruption.

Mexico, in turn, scored lower in the Liberal Democracy Indicator in the period from 2013 to 2020 than from 2001 to 2012. Mexico's democratization, from 2000 on, did not change any of the military prerogatives, despite a wider political heterogeneity. "This was because not a single political actor included in defense in their agenda, nor defense's institutional organization" (Manaut, 2021:3, our translation).[23]

The year 2012 ended with a new president from PRI, Enrique Peña Nieto, who expanded *Iniciativa Merida*'s war on drugs also to states that had lower crime rates. In 2018, Andrés Manuel López Obrador (known by the acronym AMLO), from the left-wing Morena party (*Movimiento Regeneración Nacional*), was elected. The relationship between AMLO and the military is unclear since, while one of the few politicians in Mexico that openly criticized the military, he also mentioned a possible unrestricted amnesty regarding crimes against human rights. In effect, AMLO continued to deploy the military internally, also promoting many structural reforms which helped to deepen militarization, counting on popular support (Manaut, 2021). Mexico also presents a high level of militarization of governments, especially public security, with more than 130 civilian positions occupied by military personnel and the transfer of expressive amounts of funds and public assets for military organizations and endeavors (Militares por toda..., 2021).

In terms of transparency, there were important or changes in Mexico, such as the promulgation of a national (and not only federal) FOI law in 2015, turning IFAI (Federal Institute on Access to Information) into INAI (National Institute on Access of information, also with constitutional autonomy. However, there were no changes in classification procedures or the overriding character of the National Security Law. INAI's decisions on the disclosure of some information are not always complied with, their use of public money is complexly classified and recent research still shows the difficulty in acceding to military intelligence information (López, 2017).

---

23 Original excerpt in Spanish: "Ello se debió a que ninguna fuerza política incluyó en su agenda legislativa la defensa y su organización institucional."

Comparison and discussion

This chapter aimed to discuss how civil-military relations affect transparency provisions that rule civilian access to military records in Latin America. I proposed that *in a context of isolated military bureaucracies under wide objective control and loose subjective control, the more integration between civilians and the military, the less transparency in defense would be.* These expectations shaped case selection, with Mexico representing a more integrated (and coopted) model of military behavior and with Brazil representing a separate model. For its historical analysis, this chapter makes use of the gradual institutional change theory, undertaking two independent explaining-outcome process tracings.

The comparison between both cases confirms the proposition and initial expectations. Even though the Brazilian FOI law is weaker than the Mexican one in general *de jure* terms when it comes to classification systems and transparency in defense, the evaluation is the opposite: Mexico was way behind in promoting transparency of their military institutions.

In Brazil's democratization, political heterogeneity made possible gradual changes in the subjective control of the armed forces, together with the non-exclusion of the armed forces from general checks and balances. The separated model of military behavior ensured that, even with loose subjective control and strong veto powers over reconciliation policies, the military could not prevent or suppress changes in some of their prerogatives and in the political organization of groups with different views, including the ones related to transparency. A myriad of legislation on access to information emerged in the agenda over the years, mostly through layering and displacement.

Mexico, in turn, was one of the first Latin American countries to enact a FOI law, but is still the one that maintains its main strategic defense document almost fully classified. Mexico presented fewer meaningful changes in terms of access to military records over the years, which can be explained by the historical cooptation between governments and the armed forces, which shows an increasing and constant deepening. The major advancement in this topic was the 2002 FOI law that, unfortunately, was overruled by the 2005 National Security Law, which established, e.g., *ex-ante* secrecy for many types of documents and meetings. In such an environment, civil-society advocacy was not enough to promote gradual changes.

Straw-in-the-wind evidence from 2012 until 2020 shows a militarization process in Brazil, which might be affecting transparency under conversion and drift types of change. However, since the present political context has been forcing civil society to improve its knowledge of defense, it is too soon to conclude that these setbacks in transparency will remain and increase. In Mexico, the hopes of more openness that emerged from Obrador's election were frustrated, with the continuity of the alliance between the government and the armed forces, with no significant improvements in defense transparency.

Two context-oriented mechanisms that cannot travel between cases emerged from process tracing. The first, present in the Brazilian case, was the tension between some civilian groups and the military regarding reconciliation policies, an issue present in almost all discussions about regulations of the freedom of information. The second, present only in the Mexican case, is the influence of the United States in shaping Mexico's defense and security doctrine toward public security. The powerful neighbor can be held partially responsible for the increasing reliance of civilian elites in the armed forces through its resource induction policies directed to counternarcotic efforts and public security.

We can conclude that the militarization of governments, at least in the two cases studied, can generate less transparency in defense and also in other areas of government. In the face of these findings, it is good to remember that the *modus operandi* of military institutions and doctrine is **war**, which is, appropriately, the most secrecy-driven state endeavor, even when secrecy is correctly limited to the exception. What civilian representatives seem to forget is that this rationale is not fully adaptable to the horizontality required by liberal democracies; thus, it should exist only within the limits of its suitable policy sector.

References

ACKROYD, William S. Military Professionalism, Education, and Political Behavior in Mexico. *Armed Forces & Society*, v. 18, n. 1, 1991, p. 81-96.

AMORIM NETO, Octavio. The impact of civilians on defense policy in new democracies: The case of Brazil. Latin American Politics and Society, v. 61, n. 3, 2019, p. 1-28.

________; MALAMUD, Andrés. What Determines Foreign Policy in Latin America? Systemic *versus* Domestic Factors in Argentina, Brazil, and Mexico, 1946-2008. *Latin American Politics and Society*, v. 57, n. 4, 2015, p. 1-27.

ANDERSEN, Martin Edwin. Las relaciones entre civiles y militares y la seguridad interna en México: la reforma sin hacer. In ROETT, R. (org.). *El Desafío de la Reforma Institucional en México*. Washington: Siglo Veintiuno Editores, 1996, p. 238.

ARTZ, Sigrid. *La Militarización de la Procuraduría General de la República*: Riesgos para la Democracia Mexicana. Project on Reforming the Administration of Justice in Mexico. La Jolla: Center for U.S. Mexican Studies, 2003.

ASTORGA, Luis. *¿Qué Querían que Hiciera?* Inseguridad y delincuencia organizada en le gobierno de Felipe Calderón. Mexico City: Grijalbo, 2015.

________. *Mitología del "narcotraficante" en México*. Ciudad de Mexico: Universidad Autónoma de México, 1995.

________. *Seguridad, Traficantes y Militares*: el poder y la sombra. Mexico City: Tusquets Editores México, 2007.

BEACH, Derek; PEDERSEN, Rasmus Brun. *Process-tracing Methods*: Foundations and Guidelines. The University of Michigan Press, 2013.

BRUNEAU, Thomas C. Civil-Military Relations in Latin America: The Hedgehog and the Fox Revisited. *Revista Fuerzas Armadas y Sociedad*, v. 19, n. 1, 2005, p. 111-131.

CAMACHO, Zósimo. El documento oficial más secreto de la Sedena. Contralínea, Ciudad de México, 7 Fev 2016, p. 1-8. Retrieved from http://www.contralinea.com.mx/archivo-revista/index.php/2016/02/07/el-documento-oficial-mas-secreto-de-la-sedena/.

CAMÍN, Héctor Aguilar. *México*: a cinza e a semente. São Paulo: BEI, 2002.

CLAIRE, Robin. *The Mexican military and political transition*. Monterrey: Naval Postgraduate School, 1992.

COLARESI, Michael P. *Democracy Declassified*: The secrecy Dilemma in National Security. Nova Iorque: Oxford University Press, 2014.

D'ARAÚJO, Maria Celina. *Militares, democracia e desenvolvimento*: Brasil e América do Sul. Rio de Janeiro: Editora FGV, 2010.

________. O estável poder de veto Forças Armadas sobre o tema da anistia política no Brasil. *Varia História*, v. 28, n. 48, 2012, p. 573-597.

DOYLE, Kate. *Impunity's Triumph:* The Failure of Mexico's Special Prosecutor. Washington: National Security Archive, 2006.

________. *The Blind Man and the Elephant:* reporting on the Mexican Military. Washington: National Security Archive Eletronic Briefing Book n 120, 2004.

FAIRFIELD, Tasha; CHARMAN, Andrew E. *Explicit bayesian analysis for process tracing:* Guidelines, opportunities, and caveats. Political Analysis, v. 25, n. 3, 2017, p. 363-380.

FREEMAN, Laurie; SERRA, Jorge Luis. Mexico: The Militarization Trap. In YOUNGERS, C. A.; ROSEN, E. (org.). *Drugs and Democracy in Latin America:* the impact of U.S. Policy. Boulder: Lynne Rienner Publishers, 2005.

FUSER, Igor. *México em transe.* São Paulo: Scritta, 1995.

GUTIÉRREZ, Eduardo Guerrero. Transparencia y seguridad nacional. *Cuadernos de transparencia*, n. 18, 2010.

HACHEMER, Peter. Mexico: A Civil-Military "Pact" Unravelling? In CROISSANT, A.; KUEHN, D. (org.). Reforming Civil-Military Relations in New Democracies. Gewerbestrasse: Springer, 2017, p. 83-101.

LÓPEZ, Lucía Carmina Jasso. Seguridad nacional, inteligencia militar y acceso a la información en México. *URVIO – Revista Latinoamericana de Estudios de Seguridad*, n. 21, 2017, p. 140.

HOOD, Christopher; HEALD, David (org.). *Transparency*: the key to better governance? Oxford: Oxford University Press, 2006.

HOTT, Daniela Francescutti Martins. *O acesso aos documentos sigilosos:* um estudo das comissões permanentes de avaliação e de acesso nos arquivos brasileiros. 145 f. Universidade de Brasília, 2005.

HUNTINGTON, Samuel P. *The Soldier and the State.* Cambridge: Harvard University Press, 1957.

JANOWITZ, Morris. *The Professional Soldier:* A Social and Political Portrait. Free Press, 1960.

MAFEI, Rafael; BARRETO, Marina S. Opacidade Fardada. *Revista Piauí*, November 14, 2021. Retrieved from https://piaui.folha.uol.com.br/opacidade-fardada/. November 18, 2021.

MAHONEY, James. Mechanisms, Bayesianism, and Process Tracing. New *Political Economy*, v. 21, n. 5, 2016, p. 493-499.

________; THELEN, Kathleen. *Explaining Institutional Change:* Ambiguity, Agency, and Power. New York: Cambridge University Press, 2010.

MANAUT, Raul Benítez. Militarización con respaldo popular: La transición militar en México, 2000-2020. In GRABENDORFF, Wolf (org.). *Militares y gobernabilidad:* Como están cambiando las relaciones cívico-militares en América Latina. Bogotá: Friedrich Ebert Stiftung, 2021.

Marinha pede "só" 93 anos para entregar documentos que perderam sigilo. *Fiquem Sabendo* , March 31, 2019. Retrieved from https://fiquemsabendo.com.br/transparencia/newsletter-edicao-5/. November 3, 2021.

MICHENER, Robert Gregory. *The Surrender of Secrecy:* Explaining the Emergence of Strong Access to Information Laws in Latin America (PhD thesis). 512 f. University of Texas at Austin, 2010.

________; BERSCH, Katherine. Identifying transparency. *Information Polity,* v. 18, n. 3, 2013, p. 233-242.

Militares por todo lado. Silber Meza. *Revista Piauí,* November 15, 2021. Retrieve from https://piaui.folha.uol.com.br/militares-por-todo-lado/. January 14, 2022.

MOSKOS, C. C. From Institution to Occupation: Trends in Military Organization. *Armed Forces & Society,* v. 4, n. 1, 1977, p. 41-50.

MOURÃO, Rachel R. From Mass to Elite Protests: News Coverage and the Evolution of Antigovernment Demonstrations in Brazil. *Mass Communication and Society,* v. 22, n. 1, 2019, p. 49-71.

MURGUÍA, Ramón Aguillera. Se aprueba la Primera Ley Federal de Archivos del México Independiente. *Rendición de Cuentas,* Mexico City, December 12, 2011, p. 6-9. Retrieved from http://rendiciondecuentas.org.mx/se-aprueba-la-primera-ley-federal-de-archivos-del-mexico-independiente/.

NÓBREGA JÚNIOR, José Maria Pereira da. A militarização da segurança pública: um entrave para a democracia brasileira. *Revista de Sociologia e Política,* v. 18, n. 35, 2010, p. 119-130.

Número de militares em cargos civis cresce e passa de 6 mil no governo Bolsonaro. Renata Agostini. CNN Brasil, July 17, 2020. Retrieved from https://www.cnnbrasil.com.br/politica/numero-de-militares-em-cargos-civis-cresce-e-passa-de-6-mil-no-governo-bolsonaro/. November 3, 2021.

OLIVEIRA, Eliézer Rizzo de. *De Geisel a Collor:* Forças Armadas, transição e democracia. Campinas: Papirus, 1994.

Opacidade Fardada. Rafael Mafei e Marina Slhessarenko Barreto. *Revista Piauí*, November 14, 2021. Retrieved from https://piaui.folha.uol.com.br/opacidade-fardada/. January 12, 2022.

OSJI., Tshwane. *Principles:* Global Principles on National Security and the Right to Information. New York: Open Society Justice Initiative, 2013.

PAGE, Scott E. Path dependence. *Quarterly Journal of Political Science*, v. 1, n. 1, 2006, p. 87-115.

PIÑEYRO, José Luis; BARAJAS, Gabriela. La Seguridad Nacional con Fox: Avances Analíticos, Retrocesos Reales. *Foro Internacional*, v. XLVIII, n. 1-2, 2008, p. 209–237.

PION-BERLIN, David. Political management of the military in Latin America. *Military Review*, v. Jan-Feb, 2005.

PION-BERLIN, David; UGUES, Antonion Jr.; ESPARZA, Diego. Self-Advertised Military Missions in Latin America: What is Disclosed and Why? In: KARAKATSANIS, N. M.; SWARTS, J. (org.). *Political and Military Sociology.* Transaction Publishers, 2012.

RODRIGUES, Georgete Medleg. Legislação de acesso aos arquivos no Brasil. *ACERVO – Revista do Arquivo Nacional*, v. 24, n. 01, 2011, p. 257-286.

RODRIGUES, Karina Furtado. Informações de Defesa e Segurança Nacional: entre a legitimidade do segredo e o direito à informação. In REIA, J. et al. (org.). *Horizonte presente:* tecnologia e sociedade em debate. Brasília: Letramento, v. 19, 2017, p. 1-18.

________. *Relações civis-militares e as leis de acesso à informação na América Latina e no Brasil.* 2013, p. 1-107 f. (Master thesis). Fundação Getulio Vargas, 2013.

________. The politics of Brazil's access to information policies: history and coalitions. *Journal of Public Administration*, v. 54, n. 1, 2020a, p. 142-161.

________. Unveiling the concept of transparency: its limits, varieties and the creation of a typology. *Cadernos EBAPE*, v. 18, n. 2, 2020b, p. 237-253.

RONFELDT, David F. *The Mexican Army and Political Order Since 1940.* The Rand Paper Series, 1975.

RTI RATING. *Global Right to Information Rating.* Available in http://www.rti-rating.org/. April 9, 2021.

SANTOS, Wanderley Guilherme dos. *Sessenta e quatro:* anatomia da crise. São Paulo: Vértice, 1986.

SCHULHOFER, Stephen J. Secrecy and Democracy: Who Controls Information in the National Security State? NYU School of Law, Public Law Research Paper, n. 10-53, 2010.

SCOTT, W. Richard. Approaching adulthood: The maturing of institutional theory. *Theory and Society*, v. 37, n. 5, 2008, p. 427-442.

SERRANO, Monica. The Armed Branch of the State: Civil-Military Relations in Mexico. *Journal of Latin American Studies*, v. 27, n. 2, 1995, p. 423-448.

Sigilo de 100 anos: entenda os critérios para tornar um documento secreto. CNN Brasil, June 10, 2021. Retrieved from https://www.cnnbrasil.com.br/politica/sigilo-de-100-anos-entenda-os-criterios-para-tornar-um-documento-secreto/. November 12, 2021.

STREECK, Wolfgang; THELEN, Kathleen Ann. Introduction: Institutional Change in Advanced Political Economies. In STREECK, W.; THELEN, K. A. (org.). *Beyond Continuity:* Institutional Change in Advanced Political Economies. Oxford University Press, 2005.

TRANSPARENCY INTERNATIONAL. *The Transparency of National Defence Budgets.* 2011.

TRANSPARENCY INTERNATIONAL. *Government Defence Integrity Index*. 2020. Retrieved from https://ti-defence.org/gdi/. January 17, 2021.

VARIETIES OF DEMOCRACY INSTITUTE. V-Dem Online Graphing. Available in https://www.v-dem.net/en/online-graphing/. November 3, 2021.

VELÁZQUEZ, Ernesto. Puntos de Vista: los retos de la democracia en México. Volume 1. Mexico: Teveunam, 2009.

VIVANCO, José Miguel. *Mexico:* Truth Commission Call – Letter. Human Rights Watch, Mexico City, 2001. Retrieved from https://www.hrw.org/news/2001/08/21/mexico-truth-commission-call-letter. June 14, 2021.

ZAVERUCHA, Jorge. A Fragilidade do Ministério de Defesa Brasileiro. *Revista Sociologia Política*, v. 25, n. novembro, 2005a, p. 107-121.

________. *FHC, Forças Armadas e polícia:* entre o autoritarismo e a democracia, 1999-2002. Rio de Janeiro: Editora Record, 2005b.

Brazil, Colombia, and the Korean War: small powers' reasons for joining military coalitions, and what do they gain?

Pedro Accorsi

On July 17, 2017, former Brazilian president Lula da Silva shared a story on his Facebook page about the Iraq War. He mentioned that former US president George W. Bush insinuated that Brazil should join the US in that war. According to Lula, he answered that Iraq was not Brazil's problem and that his war was against hunger and poverty.[1] Although one can speculate what the true reasons for Brazil's refusal to participate in this conflict were, decisions in the opposite direction are not unprecedented. In fact, they are quite common – small powers often send troops to fight in important conflicts alongside great powers. Poland, for example, participated in the Iraq War, among other countries. Belgium, Colombia, and Ethiopia were also among the countries which sent troops to the Korean War, as did Brazil in World War II. Examples also abound in more recent conflicts, such as Afghanistan, the Gulf War, among others. Still, as Lula's example shows, smaller powers also say no quite often. In the Korean War, for example, the US was quite unsuccessful in recruiting allies from Latin America. In the Iraq War, Washington offered astronomical material benefits for Turkey to participate in what was called the "deal of the century" (Henke, 2018). But Turkey still refused the request.

How to explain this variation? Works on alliances, which see them as a result of common interests, threat perceptions, reliability and reputation, ideology, identity, norms, and values (Morrow, 2000; Snyder, 2007; Telhami and Barnett, 2002; Walt, 1990), cannot account for it. The same applies to works that focus on the demand side of coalitions (Henke, 2017) or works on small powers and alliances (Amstrup, 1976; Fox, 2018; Keohane, 2005; Liska, 1968; Rothstein, 1968). A small body of work has been approaching the question of coalition-building

1 https://www.facebook.com/Lula/posts/1377452145657115/.

during crises (Corbetta and Dixon, 2004; Henke, 2018, 2019; Pilster, 2011; Tago, 2007; Vucetic, 2011), but the subject is still underexplored.

Moreover, when smaller states do comply, are they rewarded? Although there is a sizeable literature linking political compliance with material rewards such as foreign aid (e.g., Henke, 2017, 2018; Wolford, 2016), one could make the case that such rewards are not so straightforward. Not only there are mechanisms that would suggest an effect in the opposite direction, but there is evidence that participation in coalitions does not lead to an increase in aid (Tago, 2008).

In this chapter, I analyze the decisions of Brazil and Colombia to participate (or not) in the Korean War. This design is appropriate for causal inference – it analyzes two opposite outcomes taking place at the same time in two similar countries with similar systemic incentives. I also examine whether they were rewarded or punished for their decisions in the form of foreign aid. For each of these research questions, I examine the relevant literature, elaborate hypotheses, and examine them against empirical evidence.

Small Powers and Big Wars: Making the Decision To Go or Not

Because there is so much variation in smaller powers' decisions to join military coalitions, it is essential to emphasize the autonomy that they have to make this decision, especially because great powers do not have any tool to force decisions upon them. Once a great power has made the request, there are many reasons a small power can provide for not participating in a war. A refusal does not characterize non-alignment, and states in this position can continue to be close allies with the great power and offer other types of support, such as providing raw materials and access to strategic geographic locations and voting together in international organizations, among others. Likewise, there is nothing about state identities that force them into this type of decision. One could even state the opposite: it is often the case that nobody expects that small powers that are not directly involved in major wars to send troops to them. As Keohane (2005:162) explains, "it is clear that possession of superior military or economic force cannot guarantee small-power compliance with big-power interests."

But which variables affect their decisions? Aside from the classical works asserting the autonomy of small powers, not many scholars have been engaging with how states (especially smaller powers) decide to join coalitions. Some works have connected the likelihood of joining military coalitions with language and culture (Vucetic, 2011), being part of the same formal alliance (Corbetta and Dixon, 2004), having similar domestic institutions (Mousseau, 1997), and issue characteristics (Tago, 2007). Additionally, Kim (2016) has outlined factors that increase the bargaining power of security providers in alliances. These works assess what makes military coalitions valuable to countries joining them. It is surprising, then, that very few of them speak about specific rewards, especially material ones (also called side payments, issue linkage or selective incentives).

Nonetheless, one can find, in the literature on military coalitions, approaches quite similar to the one I propose, which see them as transactions (Henke, 2017, 2018, 2019; Poast, 2012; Wolford, 2016). This view recognizes that "coalition partners come with varying price tags" (Wolford, 2016:55) and explains coalition formation using the idea that coalition builders are willing to pay to have other states join them. When the costs they are willing to incur match the demands of potential allies, the latter join the coalition.

Although I agree with the above understanding of coalitions, these arguments are incomplete. First, many coalitions are formed based on promises, or even implied promises, a fact that is often overlooked. Thus, what matters is not only whether the coalition builder is willing to pay the price of its allies but also whether these allies believe that the great power is going to honor its promises. In many cases, foreign aid is not even negotiated explicitly – countries meet the request of the great power hoping to be able to gain more aid in the future.

Second, my theory is close to a description of countries that join military coalitions as "opportunistic states" (Henke, 2019) – in other words, these countries negotiate side deals to join coalitions. The current literature, however, fails to provide a detailed and explicit theory of decision-making in these states and how they decide not only to accept these bargains but to engage in them in the first place.

In sum, I join those who describe coalitions as transactions. Nevertheless, I argue that what drives leaders' utilities and explains coalition formation are *both* perceptions about the likelihood that the coalition builder will provide specific rewards and how high the demand for such rewards is. These are usually material rewards, given that leaders almost universally benefit from increasing material resources. Then, when the expected utility derived by the leader is sufficiently positive, we should expect troops to be sent. This argument leads to a more fine-grained understanding of these decisions and, to the best of my knowledge, this is the first article on coalitions that breaks down the transaction into both demand and attainability.

I also include a domestic variable in the argument – namely, the interests and the role of the military in politics. Because leaders usually want to remain in power, they value both increasing their resources and respecting *de facto* veto players in domestic politics. For these reasons, small powers are transactional, and leaders will be more likely to send troops to major conflicts if they see rewards as attainable and if their demand for the expected benefits is high. Also, they will need the agreement of the military if the armed forces – the organization responsible for implementing this decision - are not under civilian control.

My argument is based on the fact that small powers' decisions to send troops to major conflicts take place in both an "uncertainty reduced" and "internally oriented" context, which facilitates deliberative decision-making. Goods other than security are at stake for them in this situation. First, when smaller powers participate in a major conflict, they send military forces only for support. Consequently, there are no risks for state integrity – the war is usually distant, and a defeat is improbable to result in state death or damage to their territory. Second, the costs of participating in the conflict are somewhat fixed and negotiated directly with the great power. Third, the possible benefits are also different. Like costs, they are not directly connected to the outcome of the war and will arise from an improvement in the relationship with the great power. Fourth, their participation will not be decisive for the outcome of the conflict. Finally, timing is unique. Small powers can decide to send or withdraw troops – they are not tied to the imperatives of the conflict.

Therefore, the calculation of costs, risks, and benefits in this scenario is entirely different from countries directly involved in wars – small powers in this situation are not pressured by the typical urgency of decision-making related to international conflicts. This situation then presents more pronounced domestic than international consequences for decision making, a controlled environment where costs are somewhat fixed, expected benefits are inferred, and an incentive for other goods to be negotiated other than security.

However, how exactly do the theory's mechanisms work? The first variable, the expected rewards, can be divided into two components: the perception of the leader about the likelihood of the benefit as a result of sending troops and how high her demand for this benefit is. As previously argued, military participation in a distant conflict cannot bring direct benefits to a country – that is, benefits resulting from the outcome of the conflict. Thus, the leader must view military participation as an action that achieves another specific goal of hers. If a goal can be defined as "a desirable future state of affairs one intends to attain through action" (Kruglanski, 1996:600), the difference of between wanting something and having it as a goal is in the attainability of the future benefits through one's actions. Because attainability is related to expectancy and desirability to the value of the benefit, the former is related to how much the leader thinks it is likely that the benefit will be given as a result of her decision, and the latter refers to how valuable this benefit is (or how high is the demand for that benefit). The action through which the leader achieves the desired outcome (a specific reward) is sending troops to the conflict. Therefore, it is necessary to establish that both desirability and attainability are decisive for goal setting and thus, action. The leader, then, must value the benefit she will get from the great power and must believe that this benefit is likely enough to be given as a result of the sending of troops.

The second variable that explains why a leader would choose to send troops to a distant conflict is civil-military relations – more specifically, whether a government possesses assertive control over the armed forces (see Desch, 2001; Feaver, 2003; Huntington, 1957). Civilian control usually entails: "1) a high level of military professionalism and recognition by military officers of the limits of their professional competence; 2) the effective subordination of the military to the civilian political leaders who make the basic decisions on foreign and military policy; 3) the recognition and acceptance by that leadership of an area of professional competence and autonomy for the military; and 4) as a result, the minimization of military intervention in politics and of political intervention in the military" (Huntington, 1995:9-10).

The ideal state of democratic civilian control is the capacity of civilian authorities to limit the autonomy of the armed forces and successfully establish a relationship pattern in which the military obeys civilian commands. This state is part of a continuum, in which the other extreme is a successful military coup. Many works, then, focus on an intermediate situation in which the armed forces exercise political influence and power (Colton, 1979; Feaver, 1999; Finer, 2002; Nordlinger, 1976; Perlmutter, 1977; Pion-Berlin, 1992; Rice, 2016; A. Stepan, 1988; Welch, 1976).

It is common for the military gives up being part of the government but maintain autonomous "bubbles" of political power, not touched by democratic oversight. Here, the armed forces exercise political influence by having their opinions considered in political matters and possessing institutional prerogatives. These prerogatives can be defined as areas in which the military, as an organization, assume to have the right and privilege of governing (Stepan, 1988). Thus, they possess autonomous behavior and the institutional capacity to defend their objectives. The government's capacity for making decisions is then limited since they have to share power with the armed forces. Whether military or civilian preferences prevail when there is a policy dispute can vary: "there are many times when civilian governments defer to a military demand rather than test military subordination" (Feaver, 1999:221). These dynamics are also consistent with a distinction between political dominance and shared power: "in the first configuration, political leaders retain the authority to regulate relations with their military leaders. In the second, military leaders are themselves politically powerful and can contest civilian control" (Brooks, 2007:106-7).

I argue that whenever there is a lack of civilian control, leaders must have the consent of the military before deciding to commit troops to a major conflict. Here, the military has the autonomy to say "no" to governments – they are not like other bureaucracies that only provide options for actions and opinions and implement the chosen strategy by the government. Hence, they are *de facto* veto players.

Figure 1 sums up the theory proposed in this article. Note that the argument of the first part of the theory can be represented by a simple expected utility calculation, where the utility of the leader is given by the multiplication of the value of the benefit by its likelihood. In the second part of the theory, civilian control takes the value of zero when it is absent, rendering the interests of the armed forces irrelevant. When present, however, it would be coded with the value of one and the interests of the military matter.

Figure 1
The Theory

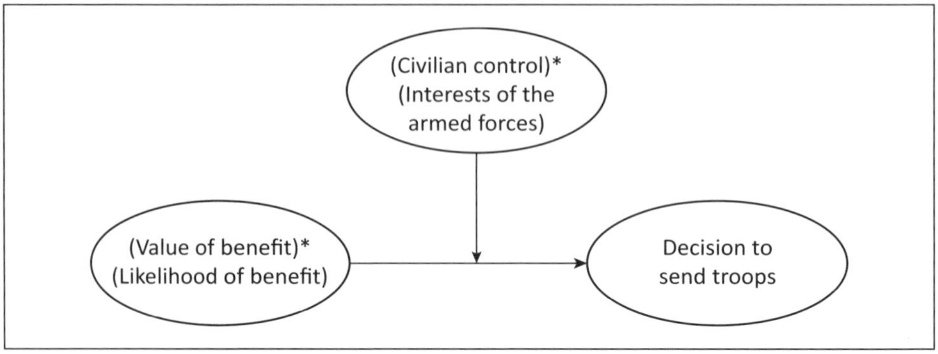

Source: elaborated by author.

The entire combination of factors is a set of sufficient conditions for small states to participate – as Mahoney defines, an "INUS package" (Mahoney, 2015, 203).[2] Given that there are other possible causal pathways for small power participation in coalitions, these are not necessary conditions – only sufficient.

In sum, small powers are transactional and will send troops to war if they receive sufficient rewards. For the sending of troops to take place, high demand for the reward and a high perceived likelihood of increased assistance from a great power as a result of this decision is the main explanatory variables. Nonetheless, whenever there is no civilian control over the military, the agreement of the armed forces is necessary for the decision to be made. When all conditions are present, participation should occur.

Method and Case Studies

In this section, I use case studies to test my theory. Case study research consists of the use of single (or few) case(s), usually to establish the veracity of a causal relationship.[3] It is stronger in internal validity – it is typically easier to establish the veracity of causal relationships with fewer cases, as one can study its details and

2 See explanation below.

3 I use the terms cross-case and case study research. Although I am aware that these terms do not necessarily equate, respectively, with quantitative and qualitative work, they overlap enough so that, for the sake of simplicity, I use them interchangeably.

several types of evidence.[4] Alternatively, cross-case research has, by definition, more cases, which makes this approach more representative of the population of cases. However, authors such as Gerring (2006) and Slater and Ziblatt (2013) challenge the notion that case studies cannot generate external validity.

Relatedly, case studies are better suited to identifying causal mechanisms. These mechanisms connect a variable with another in a credible fashion, thus showing whether a pattern of covariation is genuinely causal and what the causal interaction is (Falleti and Lynch, 2009; Mahoney, 2001). Alternatively, cross-case studies usually rely on correlations of unit-level outcomes without necessarily proving (or even explaining) causal mechanisms.

To be more specific, I use process tracing, which Mahoney (2015) defines as a set of procedures to formulate and test explanations with case studies, often making causal inference. Mahoney and Vanderpoel (2015) explain that process tracing encompasses the systematic examination of diagnostic evidence from within a case in order to evaluate a hypothesis about that case. Causes, here, can take different forms. First, a cause can be a necessary or sufficient condition. A second approach sees causes as contributing factors for the outcome, increasing its probability of happening or making it more likely. Third, causes can be treated as INUS conditions, meaning each is not individually necessary nor sufficient, but an essential part of a package that is sufficient but not necessary. INUS conditions necessarily imply equifinality since there must be at least two different combinations of factors that cause the outcome (Mahoney, 2015; Mahoney and Vanderpoel, 2015). As I mentioned in the previous section, I argue that the set of conditions for my theories consists of an INUS package.

Here, a caveat is necessary. One could argue that this section is an example of comparative historical methods, not case study research as defined by Gerring (2006). Although comparative-historical methods could be considered a middle ground between case study and cross-case research, here I consider it to be in the same category as the former. This is because it is still case study research, but with more than one case – and, as Slater and Ziblatt (2013) note, the best works in this tradition always involve rich narratives and process tracing. Therefore, it could be argued that it is even a superior design for inference than single case

4 See Dunning (2014), Gerring (2006, Ch. 7), Waldner (2014) for more detailed accounts of how different types of evidence make process tracing a powerful technique for causal inference, including using it in multi-method designs.

studies – one can increase the number of cross-case comparisons without losing the advantage of a detailed examination of cases. Comparative historical analysis, thus, allows for an additional type of leverage in comparison to singles cases. While the latter relies on temporal comparisons, the former allows for both temporal and spatial comparisons (see Gerring, 2006, Ch. 6; Rueschemeyer, 2003). As Rueschemeyer (2003) explains, this setup also allows for the testing of hypotheses about macrosocial phenomena, which usually remain constant in single cases.[5]

The selection of cases was thus made to maximize leverage for causal inference and because they constitute an empirical puzzle. Brazil and Colombia are quite similar in many respects, such as level of income, region, and systemic pressures, among others, which makes them comparable. However, they presented opposite outcomes, as Colombia sent troops to the Korean War, and Brazil decided not to. These cases, then, provide us with a between-case variation that can be leveraged.

Here, one could ask why Brazil, given that all other Latin American countries refrained from sending troops to Korea. Not only was Brazil the largest country in the region, but it had sent troops to World War II. Thus, there is a precedent that allows us to conclude that sending troops is certainly a possibility for the country.

In the case studies, I expect the leaders of Brazil and Colombia to negotiate and determine their decisions based on (material) benefits from the US and to make inferences about the likelihood of receiving these benefits. I also expect to find evidence that the military's agreement was a necessary condition for sending troops whenever there was no civilian control over the military. This can include leaders justifying decisions or trying to convince the military, stating that the military's agreement was necessary for the decision, and reversing a decision because of the armed forces. To verify these hypotheses, I use process tracing (see Mahoney, 2015).

[5] This is not to say that single cases cannot generate valuable theoretical insights. Temporal analysis is a useful method of inference in itself (see Geddes, 2003), and techniques such as counterfactual comparison can be used (see Goertz and Mahoney, 2012, Ch. 9; Mahoney, 2015:213; Mahoney and Vanderpoel, 2015:84-87; Tetlock and Belkin, 1996). Finally, research always involves practical concerns. When one is analyzing a specific historical event, there is often only one case available. Other impediments for the addition of cases might include time or financial constraints, or ethical concerns.

Brazil in the Korean War

During the decision to send troops to the Korean War, Brazil was a democracy, and Getulio Vargas was the president. The military had deposed Vargas in 1945, and General Dutra ruled Brazil until 1950 when Vargas was elected president in clean elections. Vargas had been responsible for sending troops to WWII. Thus, we can "control" for the leader. There was nothing about Vargas that determined the decision – instead, something must have changed between WWII and the Korean War.

Additionally, in 1950, the military consolidated as a political actor even more after deposing the president in 1945. Here, the armed forces were still political players, and every political group tried to co-opt them according to their interests. Military governments were seen as a legitimate solution for political problems and as a method to solve crises (Stepan, 1975).

Nonetheless, during WWII, the army was conducted by firm leadership and acted as a cohesive organization; this was not true during the Korean War. With the end of Vargas' dictatorship in 1945 and the re-democratization of the country, political debates spread to the armed forces and became even more intense after the election of the former dictator in 1950. The nucleus of political conflicts was the Military Club, a class organization that became a relevant political body of the army. The sharp political division that took place inside the club was between "nationalists" and "liberals." The former did not see firm commitments to the US through a positive lens, while the latter did. The nationalists, who were the usual supporters of Vargas, acted as the dominant group for many years and managed to win the club's elections in 1950 with General Estillac Leal when tensions were at their peak. However, nationalists rapidly lost ground, and the liberals won the 1952 elections (see Carvalho, 2005; Skidmore, 1999; Stepan, 1975).

One of the most important military figures in the negotiations to send troops to Korea was Góes Monteiro, appointed by Vargas as Chief of the Joint Staff. He was perceived to be opposed to sending troops to Korea, even though he was of a liberal inclination. Monteiro had been critical of the Brazilian troops' participation in WWII after the war, calling it "bizarre" (Alves, 2008:163-64). American officials from the State Department also showed disappointment after meeting with him. Assistant Secretary of State for Inter-American Affairs Edward G. Miller had had the impression that the idea of sending Brazilian troops to Korea was supported by the country's Minister of Foreign Affairs João Neves da Fontoura but considered it almost impossible to materialize after speaking with Monteiro. Miller wrote that the General "[...] spent most of the time [...] restating the well-known Brazilian complaints about the US. All of this could be a prelude to future requests of military equipment, which of course we will probably not be able to meet" (Alves, 2008:162). Miller also stated that Monteiro mentioned several domestic difficulties for the sending of troops, and Secretary of State Dean Acheson affirmed that Monteiro had made a list of demands (Alves, 2008:162). In the late 1940s, there had been a relative distancing between the military leadership from Brazil and the United States, given that "Brazil-US military links did not always meet the interests formulated by the Brazilian military leadership" (Svartman, 2011:80; see also Svartman, 2014:93, 97-99).

In sum, the High Command of the Army was critical to the sending of troops to Korea. The nationalists, which were the supporters of Vargas, did not support it, which was also the case for many liberals that desired a polite refusal of the US request. That was the case of Góes Monteiro, still one of the most influential officials at that time.

External pressures were strong nonetheless. During the Korean War, US president Truman wanted to form a multinational coalition. An international effort would demonstrate that a possible attack from the Soviet Union would be answered by as many United Nations (UN) members as possible and indicate that the US would not fight alone in a possible war against the Soviets. Moreover, Washington wanted to ease the pressure on the country's finances. Symbolically, support for the US would also help to legitimize its actions in the Korean War (Coleman, 2008:74).

For the reasons above, the US directly requested the Brazilian government to send troops to the conflict, with Truman even mentioning the possibility of providing future economic aid and promoting military cooperation with Brazil. However, even though Vargas' demand for foreign assistance was quite high, the perceived likelihood that the US would reward Brazil for this effort was demolished after WWII. Thus, the president decided not to send troops to Korea, even though he wanted to keep the best possible relations with the US. In May 1951, he vetoed the approach of the Ministry of Foreign Affairs for being too open to interpretations by the US. In a note for his Chief of Staff, he wrote: "Brazil cannot commit to sending troops abroad without being economical, financially and militarily prepared for its own defense. [...] And the lessons from the past are sufficient to instruct us" (Alves, 2008:170).

The expression "lessons from the past" is highly suggestive: it implies that Vargas perceived the sending of troops in WWII to have been a mistake. Further notes from Vargas confirm this impression. He affirmed that Brazil had "fought in the last war and was completely forgotten and refused in the sharing of spoils" (Alves, 2008:190). This is a smoking gun type of evidence and is consistent with the historical consensus. According to McCann (2018), Vargas "understood that American promises, real and implied, were not always fulfilled" (p. 55). The author also argues that "a sense of unfulfilled wartime promises were the backdrop for a heated debate over Korea" in Brazil (p. 254) and that "unfulfilled American promises weighed heavily on the side of staying out of it" (p. 256). The same conclusion is reached by Weis (1993:31, 46), who sees the Brazilian attitudes as a result of the postwar experience and states that Vargas "felt betrayed because he believed Truman had reneged on FDR's promise." Even Ardent pro-Americans, such as Foreign Minister João Neves da Fontoura, believed that Brazil should not repeat the mistake made in 1942 by going to war without guarantees that it would benefit from doing so (McCann, 2018:254). Oswaldo Aranha, a pro-American who had been responsible for the World War II alliance, was also opposed to committing troops (McCann, 2018:257) and saw it as "devoid of military sense" (Weis, 1993:47).

Thus, we can state that, for Vargas, the likelihood that sending troops to Korea would result in more material benefits from the US was very low. Washington neglected Latin America as a whole after WWII. After the rise of communism, the region was not a top priority nor a security concern – between 1946 and 1950, it received, on average, 0,68 percent of the US global spending on foreign aid, while Brazil received 0,13 percent.[6] These numbers can help explain why many Latin American countries were willing to send military contributions to WWII but not to Korea. Regarding Brazil, American officials had implied that the country would have a privileged position after the war, and expectations were high regarding military and economic assistance. But nothing happened, and "post-war requests for assistance were sidelined" (McCann, 2018:254; see also Svartman, 2011:77-78; Weis, 1993, Ch.1).

6 U.S. Agency for International Development (USAID) n.d.

For these reasons, Vargas made strong demands for the US. When instructing Góes Monteiro for the negotiations with Washington, the president wanted the General to emphasize the domestic difficulties of the country and the fact that aid for industrialization, infrastructure, domestic security, and military readiness was necessary. He would not settle for vague promises, however. Vargas told Monteiro that he would demand "[...] concrete action regarding the financing and transfer of capital to our industries [...] – actions that must have effects on the short-term and be undertaken *before* any military contribution [...]" (Alves, 2008:173). Monteiro went to Washington with instructions to obtain this type of agreement (McCann, 2018:257).

Regardless of whether Vargas was sincere or whether these excessive demands were only a polite refusal to the US request, this article's theory explains these facts well. If this was a polite refusal, it was because Vargas did not believe that the effort would be rewarded. If he was sincere, the fact that he wanted to ensure *ex-ante* benefits was due to the same reason.[7]

In sum, Vargas' demand for aid was high, but the experience in WWII had made the perceived likelihood that going to Korea would increase material benefits from the US to be very low. I then argue that the difference between both decisions to have been due to learning[8] – it caused the perceived likelihood of future benefits as a result of the sending of troops to Korea to be low. Not only that, but the armed forces were politically divided, and Vargas' supporters opposed the decision. Counterfactually, even if the Brazilian president wanted to go to Korea, the military's preferences would have most likely impeded him. It is worth remembering that he had been deposed by the armed forces only five years before. In fact, he was again deposed by them in 1954. Moreover, Goes Monteiro was a vital part of negotiations, dealing directly with US officials with a high degree of autonomy.

---

7 It is more likely that this was a polite refusal, given that McCann (2018:257) and states that Monteiro's "instructions specified delaying matters until the fighting ended or until World War III broke out". Weis (1993:47) makes a similar point.

8 As argued in (Alves, 2008).

Colombia in the Korean War

In Colombia, the conservatives had won the 1946 elections with Mariano Ospina Perez. As of 1930, outbreaks of violence began to occur in the country. On April 9, 1948, while Colombia was receiving the IX Pan-American Conference, Jorge Eliécer Gaitan, the most popular liberal leader at the time, was shot and killed in downtown Bogota. A massive popular fury took place, leading the country to chaos. This episode left thousands of civilians dead and became known as *El Nueve April* or *Bogotazo*, and marked the beginning of *La Violencia*, a domestic conflict that lasted until 1958.

The country was in a state of siege when Laureano Gómez, the president responsible for the decision to send Colombian troops to the Korean War, came to power on August 7, 1950. He was a controversial and popular conservative leader who served as the leader of the Conservative Party between 1939 and 1945. Gómez had some sympathy for the Axis powers and was an admirer of Franco in Spain – he shared their hatred towards communism and skepticism towards the Western model of democracy. However, he did not fully support these regimes (Bushnell, 1993:196). Previous leaders were targets of several critiques by Laureano Gómez due to their alignment with the US during WWII – the new leader had advocated for a neutral policy of non-alignment, which at the time was seen as anti-American.

The role of the armed forces in Colombian society had also changed at that point. When the *Bogotazo* took place, protesters reached the presidential palace, and the government of Ospina Perez managed to survive only because the president was able to secure the army's loyalty (Palacios, 2006:142). Gómez then heavily relied on the military to stay in office, and civilian control over the armed forces was no longer present. In fact, a coup from the army in 1953 would depose him.

Because of *La Violencia*, the demand for foreign assistance from Gómez was remarkably high, and the only possible external ally for Colombia was the US. Washington, however, saw the new Colombian president with suspicion, a scenario that he was not able to modify via diplomacy – Gómez even attempted to create a public relations campaign alongside the Ministry of Foreign Affairs to improve his relationship with the US (Coleman, 2008:88). He was denied a visit to Washington, which was customary and had taken place regularly – the US ambassador in Bogota was instructed to try to avoid this meeting at all costs

(Urán, 1986:28-29). The Colombian leader was seen as a dictator by Washington and had made several public demonstrations of affinity for fascist governments while harshly criticizing the Liberal Party for being too submissive to the US and advocating for a neutral position in WWII.

As previously mentioned, it was imperative for the US to secure troops from other countries and to have every continent represented in Korea. Thus, sending troops to the Korean War was the only possible way of securing more foreign assistance from the US for disliked president. Gómez released statements in support of the UN mission in Korea and mentioned the possibility of contributing. In his initial speeches, there was no mention of military contributions. The president made no statements on the issue before announcing the military contribution officially (Coleman, 2008:78-79).

The armed forces were consulted and supported this idea. The navy, for example, saw the conflict as an opportunity to modernize and improve its position within the Colombian Armed Forces. Admiral Antonio Taco, Chief of the Navy, believed that combat experience would help a naval program that was taking place and encourage the US to contribute to it. He had supported a naval contribution to WWII (Coleman, 2008:80). The first possibility of military support from Colombia was then explored precisely as a naval contribution. In addition to the uncertainty about the financial costs of sending ground troops, Admiral Tanco had advocated for sending a warship to Korea even before Gómez became president, and many officers had been in contact with Tanco to volunteer for service. The Conservative Party readily supported the idea, and the Admiral participated in the negotiations with the US. In September, Gómez decided to send a frigate to the conflict. Roberto Urdaneta Arbalaez, Minister of War, made the official announcement, putting the frigate Almirante Padilla under the UN command. Washington accepted the offer on September 29 (Coleman, 2008:81; Urán, 1986:29).

Equipping and sending soldiers to fight on the ground involved a significantly higher cost than sending a frigate. Nonetheless, Gómez and his Minister of Foreign Affairs, Eduardo Zuleta, discussed this possibility when the US adopted more favorable financial terms. The Chief of the Army, General Gustavo Rojas Pinilla, came out in favor of the idea, a fact that carried considerable weight with the president and played an essential role in the decision. Rojas' reasons were similar to the ones of his counterpart in the Navy – he wanted to modernize the

Army and was influenced by the almost unanimous willingness of officers to participate in the operation. Participation in the conflict presented an opportunity to train the troops, tighten military relations with the US, and increase the prestige of the army (Coleman, 2008:82-83).

After the initial contact between the Colombian officers and UN Secretary-General Lie, the Colombian Minister of War traveled to Washington to discuss the contribution in detail. In the meeting between Minister Urdaneta and General Ridgway on October 24, it was proposed that the US provide transportation, weapons, and logistical support for Colombian soldiers in Korea. The contribution had the support of General MacArthur. In November, Colombia made the final decision to offer troops to Korea (Coleman, 2008:84; Urán, 1986:32).

Gómez's decision can only be explained as an attempt to increase material benefits from the US to Colombia. Importantly, as was the case with Brazil in WWII, this was perceived to be the only way of achieving this goal. Evidence for this can be found in the Colombian aid requests after sending troops to Korea. Official documents show that Colombia started making military equipment purchase requests immediately after the decision. Minister Eduardo Zuleta sent a note to the US State Department with a request for the approval of a petition from Colombia to purchase a frigate. He specifically mentioned that the refusal of such request would be inappropriate, given that the Colombians had just assisted the US during a global crisis (Urán, 1986:31). Colombia even made a deposit for the US State Department to try to force the sale (Urán, 1986:36). The pressure was finally successful, and the purchase was completed. In April 1951, Colombia's Minister of Foreign Affairs delivered a list of military equipment needed to equip an infantry division while visiting Secretary of Defense General Marshall. Shortly after, a petition was issued requesting the purchase of several aircraft. The US government became alarmed by the Colombian petitions related to the purchasing of weapons and recommended the country reassess its immediate needs and ability to bear those costs. Colombia even requested napalm, which was denied by Washington (Urán, 1986:40-41).

Hence, there is strong evidence for the fact that the relationship between Gómez and the US government was negative, that the president wanted to improve this relationship to receive more foreign aid, and that he used Korea to achieve this goal. In a counterfactual analysis, it is virtually impossible to argue that the

Colombian president, who was not even allowed to visit Washington, would have put so much pressure on Washington for military aid.

The armed forces, in this case, were *de facto* veto players, as civilian control was not in place in Colombia. The army was decisive during the *Bogotazzo* and staged a successful coup against Laureano Gómez in 1953. It was clear that the conservative government needed the support of the military, which had the power to remove Gómez from office. As for the direct influence of the armed forces in the Colombian decision, official records show that the leaders of the armed forces were eager to obtain more training and equipment and actively lobbied in favor of sending troops to Korea (Bushnell, 1993:213). The army's chief of staff Gustavo Rojas Pinilla came out strongly in favor of the idea, an endorsement that greatly influenced the president. A US embassy report states that General Rojas "played an important role" in the decision during many private meetings with Gómez (Coleman, 2008:83).

Discussion

The variables proposed in this chapter are highly consistent with the evidence. When Brazil decided not to go to Korea, the perceived likelihood of receiving benefits for sending troops was low, which caused the president to request an extensive list of *ex-ante* benefits. The armed forces were still not under civilian control and opposed the decision – it was unlikely that the president could have sent troops even if he wanted to. When Colombia sent troops to the Korean War, alternatively, both conditions were high, and the president – who was not well regarded by the US – believed that going to Korea was the only way to gather more foreign assistance from Washington. The armed forces were not under civilian control, and their support was crucial for the decision. Table 1 shows how the theory's variables and possible alternative explanations perform in each case.

Table 1
Alternative Explanations

	Is the variable consistent with Brazil's decision about Korea?	Is the variable consistent with Colombia's decision about Korea?	Can the variable explain variation among cases?	Can it explain every case and variation?
Future benefits	Yes. Demand for aid was high, but Brazil did not expect to be rewarded with it.	Yes. Demand for aid was high, and sending troops was seen as the best way to increase it.	Yes. Countries sent troops when demand was high and they expected to be rewarded for it.	√
Armed forces	Yes. Their support was a necessary condition, and they did not agree with the idea.	Yes. Their support was a necessary condition, and they agreed with the idea.	Yes. Only when there was no civilian contol was their agreement necessary and their preferences influential.	√
External Pressures	No. The US pressured Brazil, and the president denied the request.	Not necessarily. The US wanted Latin American troops, but Gómez took the initiative.	No. Both countries dealt with the same external pressure but reached different decisions.	-
Leader ideology	Not necessarily. Vargas only wanted to keep a good relationship with the US.	Not necessarily. Gómez was a critic of the US model but profoundly anti-communist.	No. Brazil had the same leader in different decisions.	-
Norms	Not necessarily. The request came formally through the UN, but no norm required the sending of troops. There was some pressure framed in terms of collective responsibility.	Not necessarily. The request came formally through the UN, but no norm required the sending of troops. There was some pressure framed in terms of collective responsibility.	No. Although the same norms applied to Brazil and Colombia, the countries made different decisions.	-
Regime	Yes. Brazil was a democracy, and the domestic context posed challenges for Vargas.	Yes. However, public opinion supported the US in any case.	No. In Colombia, public opinion supported the US in any case.	-
Public opinion	Not clear, although the Brazilian population supported the US in the war.	Yes. The Colombian population supported the US. However, the president never announced his intentions publicly.	No. Brazil and Colombia made different decisions with similar public opinions. Moreover, presidents did not lend primacy to this variable.	-

Small powers after big wars: are they rewarded?

Intuitively, joining great powers in military coalitions should increase the number of material benefits that a country receives. Is this expectation correct? In one instance when this hypothesis was tested, results showed to be inconclusive, with no evidence of rewards for participation, although statistical tests presented several negative coefficients (Tago, 2008). If one examines a the broader literature, there is plenty of evidence for foreign aid as a result of political compliance. The US mainly provides aid based on strategic considerations, and Israel and Egypt receive historically disproportional amounts of benefits – if one "controls" for these countries, US aid is used based on poverty, democracy, and openness (Alesina and Dollar, 2000). In any case, the effect sizes are multiple times bigger for strategic reasons than for the latter (Vreeland and Dreher, 2014). Foreign aid can enhance the probability of political survival for the donor's leader by gaining concessions from the recipient leader – thus, it is given when the concessions are worth more to the donor's winning coalition than spending the same amount of money on domestic programs (Bueno de Mesquita and Smith, 2012).

Using the idea of exchanging aid for political compliance, also important is the literature that analyzes the relationship between foreign assistance and UN voting. Although this is not the same as linking participation in war coalitions with foreign assistance, this line of research is useful here since it measures compliance. The literature shows consistent and robust support for the idea that countries are rewarded for political compliance, especially when the value of the action is considered high by foreign aid donors. Members of the United Nations Security Council (UNSC), for example, receive more aid from the US (Kuziemko and Werker, 2006). Many variations of this idea followed from these findings, examining different country donors (Dreher, Nunnenkamp, and Schmal, 2013; Lim and Vreeland, 2013), international organizations (Dreher, Sturm, and Vreeland, 2009a, 2009b; Kuziemko and Werker, 2006), development banks (Bland and Kilby, 2012; Hernandez, 2013; Lim and Vreeland, 2013), among others. The US also uses aid to buy votes in the UN General Assembly (Dreher, Nunnenkamp, and Thiele, 2008). A noteworthy study on this subject is from Vreeland and Dreher (2014), who engage in an in-depth and systematic examination of the use of aid to buy support in the UNSC, providing a solid theoretical background on the politics of foreign aid, including international organizations. The idea that aid was being used for buying support in international organizations became so entrenched in the literature that Bueno de Mesquita and Smith (2010) used the election of countries to the UNSC as an instrument for foreign aid in their attempt to measure the impact of aid in development.

In short, when examining the works above, we are once more left with the impression that joining military coalitions should increase the amount of aid a country receives. These findings, combined, seem to be solid.

Why, then, would it be possible the argue otherwise? First, it is worth mentioning, again, that there are instances in which aid is not found to be given as a result of compliance (e.g., Nielsen and Simmons, 2015; Tago, 2008). Additionally, other findings in the literature could support an opposing view. The first is the fact that the US provides less foreign aid to close allies. This might sound counterintuitive, but the logic is simple: if aid is used to buy political compliance, it will not be used with countries that one already expects support. As an analogy, think of campaign financing in the US. It usually makes more sense to spend more resources in swing states or districts than in places that one already expects to win. This mechanism is corroborated by the findings of Vreeland and Dreher (2014): the authors show that the US does not use aid to buy the support of close allies or enemies in the UNSC. Because Washington already expects support from allies and does not expect to be able to buy its enemies, it aims countries somewhere "in the middle." Hence, when a country sends troops to an important conflict alongside a major power, it establishes itself as a close ally, and one of the consequences is receiving less foreign aid.

The second mechanism is related to the nature of military coalitions. Aid is usually not given *ex-ante* conflicts since side payments are often long-term. Moreover, the sending of troops from a coalition partner usually does not take too long to materialize once both sides agree to it.

Therefore, participation in a coalition usually comes *ex-ante* any financial compensation, which is an expected gain. In many cases, foreign aid is not even negotiated explicitly – countries meet the request of the coalition leader hoping to be able to gain more aid in the future. As we saw, in the Korean War, Colombia did not negotiate material rewards directly with the US before sending troops, but the country clearly expected them and started to pressure Washington on this matter right after the sending of troops. Even when rewards are negotiated, there is no guarantee that promises will be delivered. For the coalition leader, then, there is no reason to invest resources in a country that is already in the coalition. If the country has already abided regarding this important issue, resources will be better spent on those who did not. This is not to say that there are no cases in which countries are rewarded with aid for participation – still, it is plausible that the relationship between these variables is, on average, negative.

Having taken these opposite mechanisms into account, I test whether Colombia was rewarded for its participation in Korea and compare it with Brazil.

Methodology and Data

To examine the effects of sending troops to Korea on foreign aid, I use the synthetic control method (see Abadie, Diamond, and Hainmueller, 2010, 2015; Abadie and Gardeazabal, 2003). In short, this is a method to construct suitable comparison groups. The ideal scenario for establishing a causal relationship would be to compare Colombia to a very similar country – let's call it Country X – in all the factors which determine the amount of foreign aid received from the US, except for the fact that Colombia sent troops to Korea. If this was the case, one could argue that the difference in foreign aid between Colombia and Country X was the result of Colombia's sending of troops. This idea is based on Rubin causal model (Rubin, 2005), based on the framework of potential outcomes, and which informs several methods of causal inference.

Country X, however, does not exist. In the synthetic control method, then, the researcher selects a number of observable variables that are known to be able to predict the dependent variable (here, foreign aid), including the dependent variable itself before the treatment (here, sending troops to Korea). Then, the researcher selects a donor pool (here, Latin American countries), which is a group of units (here, countries) that are comparable to the treated unit (Colombia) but did not receive the treatment (sending troops to Korea). Through statistical techniques, an artificial country is built using percentages of the units in the donor pool. This synthetic country – let's call it Synthetic Colombia – will be more similar to the treated unit (Colombia) than any country in the donor pool alone. Finally, a comparison between the treated unit and the synthetic unit is made – the goal is to check if there is a change in the dependent variable (foreign aid) at the moment of the treatment. This technique is especially useful for small-sample comparative studies.[9]

Synthetic control is especially useful for studies like this. Colombia is the only treated unity, there are few (twenty-one) control units (Latin American countries), and none of them is exactly like Colombia. Hence, the synthetic control method provides us with the opportunity to build the Synthetic Colombia based on the values of a set of predictors of economic and military aid from the US, which include GDP, level of democracy, military expenditure, and ideology of the head of state. I will estimate the effect of the participation in the Korean War as the difference in the levels of aid between Colombia and its synthetic version in the years after the treatment. I will then perform a series of placebo tests to confirm if the estimated effects are unusually large relative to the distribution of the estimate that we obtain when we apply the same analysis to the other countries in the donor pool. In other words, I will apply the same tests in every Latin American country and see if the effects we find in Colombia are unusually large.

Colombia was selected as the case study because it was the only country to send troops to the Korean War, which is the treatment. The treatment year was 1951, when Colombian troops were sent to Korea. The control units, which are part of the donor pool to form synthetic Colombia, are 21 Latin American countries: Argentina, Bolivia, Brazil, Chile, Costa Rica, Cuba, Dominican Republic, Ecuador, El Salvador, Guatemala, Haiti, Honduras, Jamaica, Mexico, Nicaragua, Panama, Paraguay, Peru, Trinidad and Tobago, Venezuela, and Uruguay. The remaining Latin American countries were dropped from the analysis because they were very small. Furthermore, there is no available data for those countries for economic and demographic indicators from 1946. It is also important to mention that some studies use all countries available as the donor pool (see Abadie, Diamond, and Hainmueller, 2015). However, I have decided to include only countries in the same continent as Colombia, given that the data on foreign aid suggests a strong regional component – thus, countries in the same region

9 The assumptions of this model are similar to other statistical techniques such as regression. First, I assume (and verify to the extent possible) that other countries are not affected by the event of interest in Colombia, or by events of a similar nature. In addition, that other countries have not suffered large idiosyncratic shocks to the outcome of interest during the study period. More generally, I assume that the error terms are independent across units and in time. In other words, that possible results are not being driven by omitted variables or reverse causality.

should be more comparable to Colombia.[10] However, including countries from all regions in the analysis does not affect the results presented below.

The dependent variable is data measuring the amount of foreign aid given by the US, which is a public database from the United States Agency for International Development (USAID) covering the years from 1946 to 2016. Data on GDP was taken from Bolt, J. and J. L. van Zanden (2014). Data on the level of democracy is based on the liberal democracy index of the V-Dem project (Coppedge et al., 2019). Data regarding military spending was taken from the Correlates of War Project (Sarkees and Wayman, 2010). Finally, data on the ideology of the head of state was coded by myself. Heads of state inclined to the political left received a dummy with the value of 1, while heads of state inclined to the political right received a value of 0.

Results

I constructed the synthetic Colombia as the combination of countries in the donor pool that most closely resembled the country prior to 1951 in foreign aid predictors. The results can be seen in Table 2, which compares pre-treatment characteristics of Colombia with that of the synthetic Colombia as well as with the average of the 21 countries in the donor pool. The average of states that did not send troops to Korea does not provide an adequate control group for Colombia. Synthetic Colombia, on the other hand, is very similar to Colombia.

Table 2
Balance: Colombia *versus* Synthetic Colombia

	Colombia	Synthetic Colombia	Average
Foreign Aid (1000000)	4.06	4.03	16.27
GDP (1950)	24955	24937	18476
Liberal Democracy Index (1950)	0.47	0.47	0,89
Ideology (1950)	0	0	0,27
Miliyary Spending (1000000)	19670	19679	28743

10 This is suggested by (Abadie, Diamond, and Hainmueller, 2010:495).

Table 3 shows the weights of each control country in the synthetic Colombia. The weights reported indicate that foreign aid trends in Colombia prior to 1951 are well reproduced by a combination of several countries.

Table 3
Weights of the Synthetic Colombia

Country	Weight
Argentina	0
Bolivia	0.18
Brazil	0
Chile	0.058
Costa Rica	0.006
Cuba	0.008
Dominican Republic	0.161
Ecuador	0.01
El Salvador	0
Guatemala	0
Haiti	0.17
Honduras	0.13
Jamaica	0.01
Mexico	0.001
Nicaragua	0.012
Panama	0
Paraguay	0.019
Peru	0.094
Trinidad and Tobago	0.009
Uruguay	0
Venezuela	0.564

Figure 2 displays foreign aid given by the US for Colombia and synthetic Colombia during the period between 1946 and 1953. It is clear that foreign aid received in synthetic Colombia very closely reproduces the trajectory of the same variable in actual Colombia for the period before 1951. Combining this with the high degree of balance on the foreign aid predictors, we can come to the conclusion that synthetic Colombia is a suitable counterfactual for the amount of foreign aid received that would have appeared in Colombia had the country not sent troops to the Korean War.

I estimate the effect of the participation in the Korean War on foreign aid received by Colombia as the difference between the amount of aid received by Colombia and its synthetic counterpart. Instantly after the sending of troops to Korea, the lines begin to prominently diverge. Colombia shows a more intense increase in aid received from the US. The discrepancy between the lines suggests a large positive effect of sending troops to Korea. Results suggest that Colombia received more than three times the amount of aid than the synthetic Colombia in the next two years.

Figure 2
Total Aid From the US in millions of dollars:
Colombia *versus* Synthetic Colombia (1946-1953)

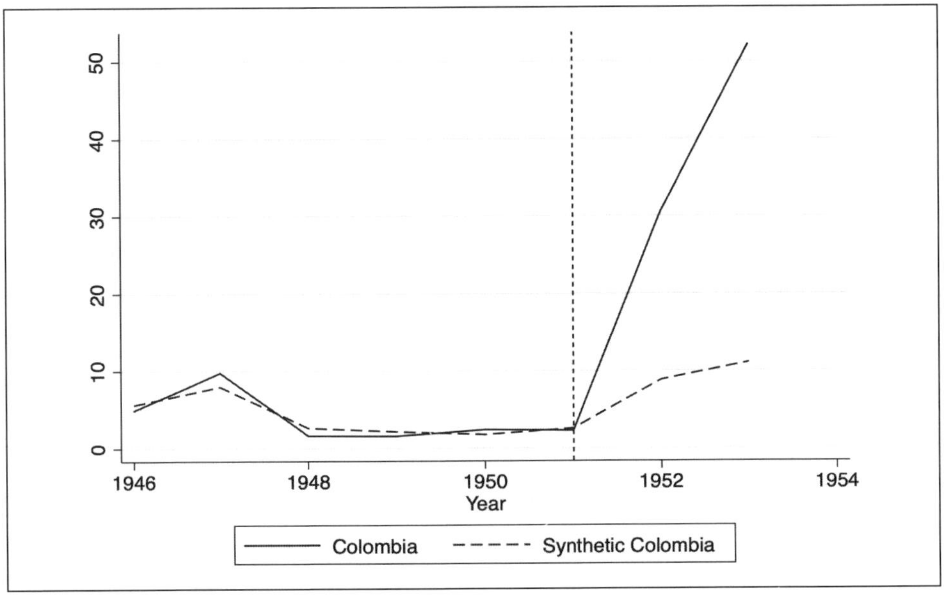

How often would we obtain similar results had we chosen a state at random for the study? This question is answered through the use of placebo tests. I applied the synthetic control method to every state in the donor pool, shifting Colombia to the donor pool in each of these tests. If the placebos created similar results to the one estimated for our treated state, the analysis would not provide significant evidence of a positive effect of sending troops to Korea. Nevertheless, this was not the case. Colombia presents the largest ratio of post/pre-treatment Mean Squared Predicted Error (RMSPE) among the 22 countries analyzed.

The RMSPE ratio is calculated by dividing the post-treatment RMSPE by the pre-treatment RMSPE. The former is calculated by squaring the differences in aid between Colombian and synthetic Colombia after the treatment, taking their mean and taking the squared root of this mean. The latter is calculated with the same process, this time using the pre-treatment years. This is a good measure of statistical significance because it "punishes" countries that do not present a good pre-treatment fit. Hence, as proposed by Abadie, Diamond, and Hainmueller (2010), since Colombia has the largest RMSPE ratio, the probability of finding a result like this randomly in a set of 22 countries is 1/22, or 4 percent.

In sum, the results above suggest a positive effect on foreign aid for Colombia. However, a few caveats are in order. One important point is that the increase in aid to Colombia took place in the context of increased aid for the region. Again, I have provided evidence that aid to Colombia increased more than it would had it not gone to Korea. But it is worth emphasizing that joining military coalitions is far from being a necessary condition for receiving aid or having it increased. Several countries in Latin America which refused to send troops to Korea still received considerable increases in aid. Thus, from this data, there is no reason to believe that countries that say no to these requests from great powers will be punished. Brazil, for example, received much more aid than Colombia after the Korean War. Although Brazil also received much more aid prior to the war as well, this further suggests that Brazil was not punished in any sense. Figure 3 shows Brazil and Colombia in comparison with the average of the region.

Also, these findings go counter some studies that suggest no effects on aid from joining coalitions. However, this might be due to some scope conditions. First, Colombia's participation coincided with an influx of aid to the region. It could very be that when great powers decide to prioritize a region more, they take recent compliance into account. Second, Colombia heavily pressured the US for aid after the sending of troops, as shown in the previous sections. Finally, Colombia's president at the time had a poor relationship with the US, and it was the sending of troops that opened the door for aid requests. This makes the counterfactual even more powerful – without Korea, it would make no sense for the US to prioritize a country from which the president was not even allowed to visit Washington. Among these three scope conditions, smaller powers have no control over the first. However, my findings suggest that sending troops to join coalitions could be especially effective when 1) the concession is followed by pressure and requests for aid, and 2) the relationship with the US needs improvement.

Figure 3
Colombia and Brazil *versus* Region Average, Foreign Aid

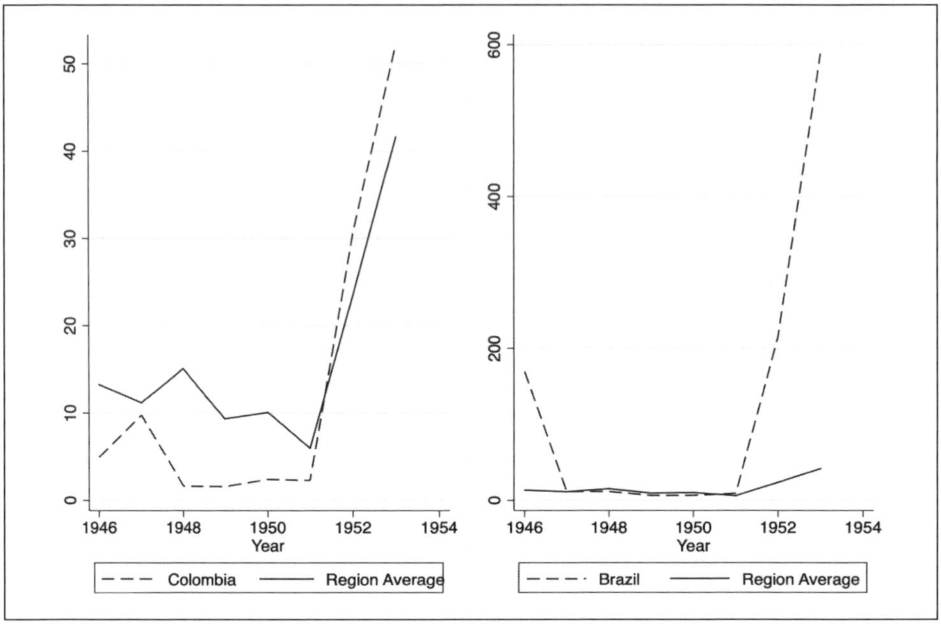

Source: USAID <www.uasid.gov>.

Conclusion

This chapter addressed the causes and consequences of the participation of smaller powers in important conflicts alongside great powers. Regarding the first question, I have shown that small powers are transactional and decide to do so when leaders perceive that they are going to be rewarded by the great power. This attempt to gather benefits consists of the demand for the (usually material) benefit and the perceived likelihood that sending troops abroad will generate it. Also, where there is no civilian control over the armed forces, they will be a veto player.

These findings have significant broader implications both for theory and policymaking. First, they reaffirm the autonomy of small powers in the international system and show that they frequently have the agency to make decisions that are often consequential.

My arguments also shed light on what motivates states and the nature of their preferences. Namely, it suggests that states often use foreign policy to satisfy domestic preferences and that these preferences can be predominantly material. It also becomes clear that context can heavily influence rationality and the quest for material gains. Although elites are not always rational, it is useful to treat rationality as "a 'sometimes-true theory' that is restricted to the analysis of particular actors or particular settings in which the theorist has reason to consider the rationality assumption appropriate" (MacDonald, 2003). Because of the nature of the decision-making processes explained here, leaders have the opportunity to engage in deliberate decision-making, which allows them to be rational and focus on material gains. This study also tells us much about the behavior of small powers, which should often be transactional and expect rewards in exchange for alignment.

There is also much that policymakers can learn from this study. Great powers such as the US are continually struggling to make allies contribute more to the cost of their defense and make themselves available to provide military assistance when crises arise. This chapter reaffirms that security is not the only good at stake when collective security is under negotiation. Thus, great powers can convince allies to contribute more to collective security by offering them other goods that they might be interested in. Negotiations should be broader and more direct and can become less expensive for these powers while also generating benefits for every state involved. There is no reason not to treat them as explicit transactions. Also, gathering allies to fight wars is seemingly not a goal that can be successfully achieved in the short term and solely based on promises of future assistance. The cases of Brazil and Colombia have shown that small powers tend to infer their future gains based on their past relationship with great powers. Thus, keeping a minimum amount of benefits flowing to important regional allies can be a cost-effective strategy in the long run. On the other hand, when demand for external assistance is remarkably high, as was the case in Colombia during the Korean War, the great power can successfully recruit an ally to send troops to a major war regardless of past behavior. Nonetheless, one should not expect this to be the case frequently.

Finally, the findings presented here are also important for recent developments in international politics, and especially for the US, given that the recent Trump administration has given attention to burden sharing and shown increasing skepticism towards formal alliances. Again, in this context, one can expect that future coalitions could depend even more on a *quid pro quo* logic – therefore, if the US decides to weaken its formal alliances, the country should be ready to "open the wallet" to be able to form military coalitions in the future.

As for the consequences of sending troops, there are important implications for the literature on side payments, foreign aid, and military coalitions, which often present conflict findings from study to study. I show, alternatively, that joining coalitions can, in fact, increase the resources a country receives under certain scope conditions.

Moreover, important policy implications can arise from this work. From the perspective of smaller powers, knowing the consequences of joining such coalitions can better inform their future decisions on whether to do it or not or how to negotiate their support. With this in mind, one could expect not only more cohesive and efficient military coalitions but the minimization of post-conflict tensions between allies as a result of unfulfilled expectations of rewards.

References

ABADIE, Alberto; DIAMOND, Alexis; HAINMUELLER, Jens. Synthetic Control Methods for Comparative Case Studies: Estimating the Effect of California's Tobacco Control Program. *Journal of the American Statistical Association*, 105(490), 2010, p. 493-505.

________. Comparative Politics and the Synthetic Control Method. *American Journal of Political Science*, 59(2), 2015, p. 495-510.

________; GARDEAZABAL, Javier. The Economic Costs of Conflict: A Case Study of the Basque Country. *American Economic Review*, 93(1), 2003, p. 113-132.

ALESINA, Alberto; DOLLAR, David. Who Gives Foreign Aid to Whom and Why? *Journal of Economic Growth*, 5(1), 2000, p. 33-63.

ALVES, Vagner Camilo. *Da Itália à Coréia:* decisões sobre ir ou não à guerra. First Edition. Belo Horizonte, Minas Gerais: UFMG, 2008.

AMSTRUP, Niels. The Perennial Problem of Small States: A Survey of Research Efforts. *Cooperation and Conflict*, 11(3), 1976, p. 163-182.

BLAND, Elizabeth; KILBY, Christopher. *Informal Influence in the Inter-American Development Bank*. Villanova School of Business Department of Economics and Statistics. 2012. Retrieved from https://ideas.repec.org/p/vil/papers/22.html. August 24, 2019.

Brooks, Risa A. Civil-Military Relations and Military Effectiveness: Egypt in the 1967 and 1973 Wars. In *Creating Military Power:* The Sources of Military Effectiveness. Palo Alto, California: Stanford University Press, 2007.

BUENO DE MESQUITA, Bruce; SMITH, Alastair. The Pernicious Consequences of UN Security Council Membership. *Journal of Conflict Resolution*, 54(5), 2010, p. 667-686.

________. Domestic Explanations of International Relations. *Annual Review of Political Science*. 2012. Retrieved from https://www.annualreviews.org/doi/abs/10.1146/annurev-polisci-070209-174835. August 24, 2019.

BUSHNELL, David. *The Making of Modern Colombia:* A Nation in Spite of Itself. Berkeley: University of California Press, 1993.

CARVALHO, J. M. *Forças Armadas e política no Brasil*. Rio de Janeiro: Zahar, 2005.

COLEMAN, Bradley Lynn. *Colombia and the United States:* The Making of an Inter-American Alliance, 1939-1960. First Edition. Kent, Ohio: The Kent State University Press, 2008.

COLTON, Timothy J. *Commissars, Commanders, and Civilian Authority:* The Structure of Soviet Military Politics. First Edition. Cambridge, Mass: Harvard University Press, 1979.

CORBETTA, Renato; DIXON, William J. Multilateralism, Major Powers, and Militarized Disputes. *Political Research Quarterly*, 57(1), 2004, p. 5-14.

Desch, Michael C. *Civilian Control of the Military:* The Changing Security Environment. Baltimore, Md.: Johns Hopkins University Press, 2001.

DREHER, Axel; NUNNENKAMP, Peter; SCHMALJOHANN, Maya. *The Allocation of German Aid:* Self-Interest and Government Ideology. Kiel Institute for the World Economy (IfW). Kiel Working Paper, 2013. Retrieved from https://econpapers.repec.org/paper/zbwifwkwp/1817.htm. August 24, 2019.

________; ________; THIELE, Rainer. Does US Aid Buy UN General Assembly Votes? A Disaggregated Analysis. *Public Choice*, 136(1), 2008, p. 139-164.

________; STURM, Jan-Egbert; VREELAND, James Raymond. Development Aid and International Politics: Does Membership on the UN Security

Council Influence World Bank Decisions? *Journal of Development Economics*, 88(1), 2009a, p. 1-18.

________. Global Horse Trading: IMF Loans for Votes in the United Nations Security Council. *European Economic Review*, 53(7), 2009b, p. 742-757.

DUNNING, Thad. Improving Process Tracing: The Case of Multi-Method Research. In *Process Tracing:* From Metaphor to Analytic Tool, Cambridge University Press, 2014.

FALLETI, Tulia G.; LYNCH, Julia F. Context and Causal Mechanisms in Political Analysis. *Comparative Political Studies*, 42(9), 2009, p. 1.143-1.166.

FEAVER, Peter D. Civil-Military Relations. *Annual Review of Political Science*, 2(1), 1999, p. 211-41.

________. *Armed Servants:* Agency, Oversight, and Civil-Military Relations. Revised edition. Cambridge, Mass.: Harvard University Press, 2003.

FINER, Samuel. *The Man on Horseback:* The Role of the Military in Politics. New Brunswick, N.J: Routledge, 2002.

FOX, Annette Baker. *The Power of Small States Diplomacy in World War II*. Franklin Classics, 2018.

GEDDES, Barbara. *Paradigms and Sand Castles:* Theory Building and Research Design in Comparative Politics. University of Michigan Press, 2003.

GERRING, John. *Case Study Research:* Principles and Practices. 1st ed., New York: Cambridge University Press, 2006.

GOERTZ, Gary; MAHONEY, James. *A Tale of Two Cultures:* Qualitative and Quantitative Research in the Social Sciences. Princeton University Press, 2012.

HENKE, Marina E. The Politics of Diplomacy: How the United States Builds Multilateral Military Coalitions. *International Studies Quarterly*, 61(2), 2017, p. 410-424.

________. The Rotten Carrot: US-Turkish Bargaining Failure over Iraq in 2003 and the Pitfalls of Social Embeddedness. *Security Studies*, 27(1), 2018, p. 120-147.

________. Buying Allies: Payment Practices in Multilateral Military Coalition-Building. *International Security*, 43(4), 2019, p. 128-162.

HERNANDEZ, Diego. *Does Inclusion Guarantee Institutional Autonomy? The Case of the Inter-American Development Bank*. Discussion Paper Series.

Working Paper, 2013. Retrieved from https://www.econstor.eu/handle/10419/127362. August 24, 2019.

HUNTINGTON, Samuel P. *The Soldier and the State:* The Theory and Politics of Civil-Military Relations. Cambridge, Mass.: Harvard University Press, 1957.

________. Armed Forces and Democracy: Reforming Civil-Military Relations. *Journal of Democracy*, 6(4), 1996, p. 9-17.

KEOHANE, Robert O. *After Hegemony:* Cooperation and Discord in the World Political Economy. 1st Princeton Classic Ed edition. Princeton, N.J: Princeton University Press, 2005.

KIM, Tongfi. *The Supply Side of Security:* A Market Theory of Military Alliances. Stanford: Stanford University Press, 2016.

KRUGLANSKI, Arie W. Goals as Knowledge Structures. In *The Psychology of Action: Linking Cognition and Motivation to Behavior*, New York, NY: Guilford Press, 1996, p. 599-618.

KUZIEMKO, Ilyana; WERKER, Eric. How Much Is a Seat on the Security Council Worth? Foreign Aid and Bribery at the United Nations. *Journal of Political Economy*, 114(5), 2006, p. 905-930.

LIM, Daniel Yew Mao; VREELAND, James Raymond. Regional Organizations and International Politics: Japanese Influence over the Asian Development Bank and the UN Security Council. *World Politics*, 65(1), 2013, p. 34-72.

LISKA, George. *Alliances and the Third World*. The Johns Hopkins University Press, 1968.

MACDONALD, Paul K. Useful Fiction or Miracle Maker: The Competing Epistemological Foundations of Rational Choice Theory. *American Political Science Review*, 97(4), 2003, p. 551-565.

MAHONEY, James. Beyond Correlational Analysis: Recent Innovations in Theory and Method. In HEDSTRÖM, Peter; SWEDBERG, Richard; RAGIN, Charles C. (eds.). *Sociological Forum*, 16(3), 2001, p. 575-593.

________. Process Tracing and Historical Explanation. *Security Studies*, 24(2), 2015, p. 200-218.

________; VANDERPOEL, Rachel Sweet. Set Diagrams and Qualitative Research. *Comparative Political Studies*, 48(1), 2015, p. 65-100.

MCCANN, Frank D. *Brazil and the United States During World War II and Its Aftermath:* Negotiating Alliance and Balancing Giants. 2018a, ed., New York, NY: Palgrave MacMillan.

MORROW, James D. Alliances: Why Write Them Down? *Annual Review of Political Science*, 3(1), 2000, p. 63-83.

MOUSSEAU, Michael. Democracy and Militarized Interstate Collaboration. *Journal of Peace Research*, 34(1), 1997, p. 73-87.

NIELSEN, Richard A.; SIMMONS, Beth A. Rewards for Ratification: Payoffs for Participating in the International Human Rights Regime? *International Studies Quarterly*, 59(2), 2015, p. 197-208.

NORDLINGER, Eric A. *Soldiers in Politics:* Military Coups and Governments. Englewood Cliffs, N.J: Pearson College Div., 1976.

PALACIOS, Marco. *Between Legitimacy and Violence:* A History of Colombia, 1875-2002. Durham: Duke University Press Books, 2006.

PERLMUTTER, Amos. *The Military and Politics in Modern Times:* On Professionals, Praetorians, and Revolutionary Soldiers. 1st ed., New Haven: Yale Univ Press, 1977.

PILSTER, Ulrich. Are Democracies the Better Allies? The Impact of Regime Type on Military Coalition Operations. *International Interactions*, 37(1), 2011, p. 55-85.

PION-BERLIN, David. Military Autonomy and Emerging Democracies in South America. *Comparative Politics*, 25(1), 1992, p. 83-102.

POAST, Paul. Does Issue Linkage Work? Evidence from European Alliance Negotiations, 1860 to 1945. *International Organization*, 66(2), 2012, p. 277-310.

RICE, Condoleezza. *The Soviet Union and the Czechoslovak Army, 1948-1983:* Uncertain Allegiance. Princeton, NJ: Princeton University Press, 2016.

ROTHSTEIN, Robert L. *Alliances and Small Powers*. Columbia University Press, 1968.

RUBIN, Donald B. Causal Inference Using Potential Outcomes. *Journal of the American Statistical Association*, 100(469), 2005, p. 322-331.

RUESCHEMEYER, Dietrich. Can One or a Few Cases Yield Theoretical Gains? In *Comparative Historical Analysis in the Social Sciences*. 2003. Retrieved from /core/books/comparative-historical-analysis-in-the-social-sciences/can-one-or-a-few-cases-yield-theoretical-gains/DCAEAA3B87669F1C-137BCEE9BECBC906. September 19, 2019.

SKIDMORE, Thomas E. *Brasil. De Castelo A Tancredo. 1964-1985*. São Paulo: Paz e Terra, 1999.

SLATER, Dan; ZIBLATT, Daniel. The Enduring Indispensability of the Controlled Comparison. *Comparative Political Studies*, 46(10), 2013, p. 1.301-1.327.

SNYDER, Glenn H. *Alliance Politics*. 1st ed., Ithaca, NY: Cornell University Press, 2007.

STEPAN, Alfred. *Os militares na politica*. Rio de Janeiro: Editora Artenova, 1975. Retrieved from https://www.estantevirtual.com.br/livros/alfred-stepan/os-militares-na-politica/371176874. August 14, 2019.

________. *Rethinking Military Politics:* Brazil and the Southern Cone. Princeton, N.J: Princeton University Press, 1988.

SVARTMAN, Eduardo Munhoz. Brazil-United States Military Relations during the Cold War: Political Dynamic and Arms Transfers. *Brazilian Political Science Review*, 5(2), 2011, p. 75-93.

________. Da II Guerra Mundial à Guerra Fria: conexões entre os exércitos do Brasil e dos Estados Unidos. *Latin American Research Review*, 49(1), 2014, p. 83-103.

TAGO, Atsushi. Why Do States Join US-Led Military Coalitions?: The Compulsion of the Coalition's Missions and Legitimacy. *International Relations of the Asia-Pacific*, 7(2), 2007, p. 179-202.

________. Is There an Aid-for-Participation Deal?: US Economic and Military Aid Policy to Coalition Forces (Non)Participants. *International Relations of the Asia-Pacific*, 8(3), 2008, p. 379-398.

TELHAMI, Shibley Z.; BARNETT, Michael (eds.). *Identity and Foreign Policy in the Middle East*. 1st ed., Ithaca: Cornell University Press, 2002.

TETLOCK, Philip E.; BELKIN, Aaron. *Counterfactual Thought Experiments in World Politics:* Logical, Methodological, and Psychological Perspectives. Princeton University Press, 1996.

URÁN, Carlos H. Colombia e Los Estados Unidos En La Guerra Da Corea. *Working Paper 069*. Helen Kellogg Institute for International Studies, University of Notre Dame, 1986.

U.S. Agency for International Development (USAID). Foreign Aid Explorer: The Official Record of U.S. Foreign Aid. Retrieved from https://aidscape.usaid.gov/aid-trends.html. August 14, 2019.

VREELAND, James Raymond; DREHER, Axel. *The Political Economy of the United Nations Security Council:* Money And Influence. New York, NY: Cambridge University Press, 2014.

VUCETIC, Srdjan. Bound to Follow? The Anglosphere and US-Led Coalitions of the Willing, 1950–2001. *European Journal of International Relations*, 17(1), 2011, p. 27-49.

WALDNER, David. What Makes Process Tracing Good? Causal Mechanisms, Causal Inference, and the Completeness Standard in Comparative Politics. In *Process Tracing:* From Metaphor to Analytic Tool, Cambridge University Press, 2014.

WALT, Stephen M. *The Origins of Alliances*. New edition. Ithaca: Cornell University Press, 1990.

WEIS, W. Michael. *Cold Warriors & Coups D'Etat:* Brazilian-American Relations, 1945-1964. Albuquerque: Univ of New Mexico Pr., 1993.

WELCH, Claude (ed.). *Civilian Control of the Military:* Theory and Cases from Developing Countries. Albany: SUNY Press, 1976.

WOLFORD, Scott. *The Politics of Military Coalitions*. Reprint edition. New York, NY: Cambridge University Press, 2016.

Conclusion: Bolsonaro and Beyond: The Future of Defense Studies in Brazil

Octavio Amorim Neto

Throughout the 20th century Brazil's defense policy was largely made and implemented by the armed forces. It is thus no wonder that the study of defense affairs was monopolized by members of the military profession. However, by the mid-1980s the country transited to democracy. Two decades later democracy was thriving. Not surprisingly, civilian politicians began to participate more intensely in the direction of national defense (Amorim Neto, 2019; Duarte, 2022). Moreover, since the 1990s social sciences graduate programs began to be institutionalized and grew apace up to the first half of the 2010s. Not surprisingly, by the first half of the 2010s defense became the object of investigation by many civilian scholars, departments, and research centers (Marques and Fuccille, 2015).

The picture drawn in the paragraph above is, overall, one of positive change from a macro-historical perspective. However, if one zooms in on the details of 21st-century Brazil, one also sees fits and starts, roller coasters, bumps on a winding road, and backsliding. To begin with, the quality of democracy in the country has been going down since 2016 (Lührmann et al., 2020). Since 2018, the military has returned to the center of the political arena and are is again in charge of defense policymaking (Amorim Neto and Acácio, 2020; Villa and Passos, 2022).[1] Finally, Brazil's armed forces continue to play an active role in many areas that are of civilian nature. The chapters in this book provide evidence of all these trends.

When looking into the future, should Brazilian civilian scholars be optimistic about civil-military relations and the study of defense policy? What should

1 On a more positive note, Duarte (2022:2) argues that Brazil has incorporated several actors in its defense policymaking, including "representatives of the private sector, subnational units, academics, and organized civil society". According to this author, defense policy should be no longer thought of with a clear division between civilians and the military but rather as based on "[...] dialogue, negotiation, mutual influence, cooperation, contradiction and conflict between diverse actors [...]."

they expect to take place in the 2020s? A first step to answer these questions is to probe into what civilian defense scholars have published.

Studies on defense in Brazil have undergone substantial changes in the last two decades. Brazil went from 12 research centers or groups focused on defense in 2010, as described by Figueiredo (2010), to almost 50 exclusively civilian research groups registered with Brazil's National Research Council (CNPq) in 2022. In addition to the creation of these groups, there are new graduate programs. In 2005 the Brazilian Association of Defense Studies (ABED) was created. In 2014 ABED published the first issue of *Revista Brasileira de Estudos de Defesa* (Brazilian Journal of Defense Studies).

That said, this conclusion provides a brief and selective evaluation of defense studies in Brazil based on these scholarly articles and then offers some insights into what to expect regarding these studies after the Bolsonaro presidency. The chapter is organized as follows. The next section examines keywords related to the study of defense and the armed forces in Brazil's social sciences publications. The third section analyzes the articles published in *Revista Brasileira de Estudos de Defesa.* The final section deals with the challenges facing defense studies after Bolsonaro.

Defense and armed forces studies in Brazil's social sciences

This section maps the output of Brazil's social sciences on themes directly or indirectly related to the investigation of the armed forces and defense. To do so, articles published in periodicals registered in the Scientific Electronic Library Online (SciELO) were identified on the basis of the following keywords: civil-military relations, defense policy, international security, military coup, military regime, military dictatorship, and peacekeeping. All issues of these periodicals are available online and in Portuguese. Articles published in any year by Brazilian journals associated with areas classified as human sciences or applied social sciences were examined. Keywords were used as search terms for the title or abstract. In the end, 143 articles published between 1989 and 2022 were selected.[2]

Table 1 below shows that, in terms of keywords, studies on "military regime,""military dictatorship," and "military coup" are the most frequent. This

[2] The Online Scientific Electronic Library was launched in 1997. Articles prior to this date were included in SciELO after journals digitized their publications prior to the date of each journal's inclusion in SciELO.

is no surprise and has, obviously, to do with researchers' acute concern with Brazil's military regime from 1964-1985. Then there are "international security," "civil-military relations," and, to a lesser extent, "defense policy" and "peacekeeping." The first two are classical topics, their position in the hierarchy of themes being expected. The position of "defense policy" on the pecking order is also to be expected. Finally, as pointed out by Anselmo (this volume), peace operations began to appear in Brazilian publications due to the country's participation in MINUSTAH from 2004-2017.

The frequency of themes discussed in the paragraph above is perfectly aligned with Brazilian history in the past 50-60 years and with trends in the employment of the armed forces in the past two decades.

Table 1
Thematic frequency of the Brazilian bibliography on the Armed Forces and Defense by keyword

Keyword	Frequency	%
Civil-Military Relations	18	12.6
Defense Policy	11	7.7
International Security	26	18.2
Military Coup	23	16.1
Military Regime	30	21.0
Military Dictatorship	27	18.9
Peacekeeping	8	5.6
Total	143	100%

Figure 1 below displays the frequency of articles over time. Interestingly enough, as time went by, there was a marked increase in works on "military regime" and "military dictatorship," especially in studies on the 2011-2014 National Truth Commission, the latter's monitoring by Congress (Barros, 2020), and on truth commissions in subnational contexts (Hollanda and Israel, 2019). As Brazil belatedly tried to review its authoritarian past, research into the military regime grew in the 2000s and 2010s. However, this trend relates to all social sciences. As far as the area of comparative politics in Brazil is concerned, publications on the military regime declined in the first decade of the 21st century (Amorim Neto, 2010). Articles on civil-military relations, defense policy, and peacekeeping remained relatively stable. Articles on international security grew at a moderate rate in the first two decades of the 21st century.

Figure 1
SciELO articles by keywords associated with the military and defense in 1990-2020

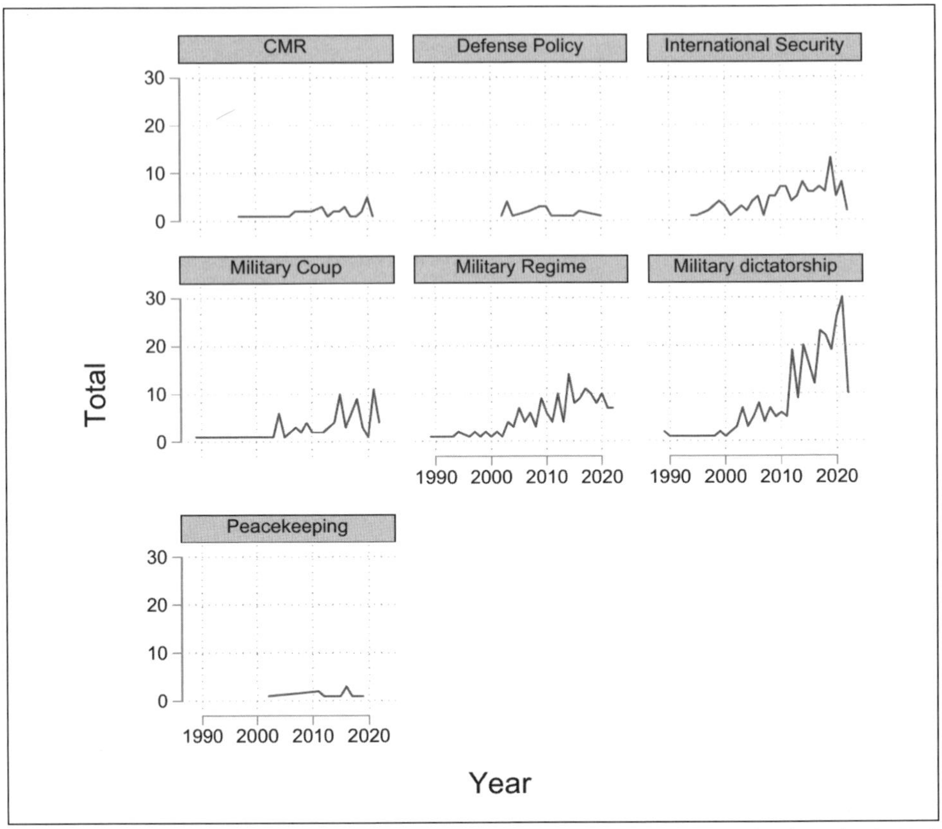

Source: *Scientific Electronic Library Online*. Each of the keywords was searched on the SciELO search engine (https://search.scielo.org/), in Brazilian journals in the areas of Humanities and Social Sciences.

That said, one can speculate that the growing frequency of studies on the military regime or military dictatorship in the 2000s and 2010s, while legitimate and necessary, tended to divert civilian interest in research into defense policy. For a democracy striving to consolidate civilian direction of the defense sector, that was not the optimal allocation of scarce academic resources, time, and energy. Tragically, the Final Report of the Truth Commission, published in December 2014, naming and shaming many former military officers allegedly associated with violations of human rights in 1964-1985, became one of the starting points in the re-politicization of the Brazilian armed forces (Amorim Neto and Acácio, 2020).

The output of *Revista Brasileira de Estudos de Defesa*

Despite the preponderance of research into the military regime in Brazil's social sciences, defense studies are characterized by the diversity of their themes but also by the regional concentration of authors. To demonstrate these points, this section maps the output of *Revista Brasileira de Estudos de Defesa* (henceforth RBED) in 2014-2021 by identifying authors' attributes: if civilian or military; if military, of which service; state of residence, institutional affiliation; and themes/keywords of their publications. One hundred forty-four articles were published in RBED over that period.

Table 2 below shows data on the type of author over time. The authors are massively civilians, which is the pattern to be expected. Authors who are members of the military profession are only 24 out of 241 authors (10.0%).

Table 2
Civil-Military *status* of authors publishing in *Revista Brasileira de Estudos de Defesa* in 2014-2021

Year	Civilian	Army	Air Force	Navy	Total
2014	13				13
2015	25	2	4		31
2016	33		1	1	35
2017	27	3		1	31
2018	33	3			36
2019	28	4			32
2020	34	1	1	1	37
2021	24	1	1		26
Total	**217**	**14**	**7**	**3**	**241**

Source: https://rbed.abedef.org/rbed/index.

Table 3 below shows the distribution of RBED authors by state of residence. The states of São Paulo (25.4%) and Rio de Janeiro (22%) account for almost half of the authors who published in the journal. This is no surprise, given the role played by both states in Brazil's economy, population, and academic and cultural life. However, Rio Grande do Sul (12.4%) and Santa Catarina (8.13%) come in third and fourth place, respectively, despite having the 6th and 10th biggest populations (also respectively). This mismatch between, on the one hand, the frequency of

RBED articles by scholars residing in Rio Grande do Sul and Santa Catarina and, on the other, state size has to do with history and geography. They are very close to Argentina, Brazil's main rival from the end of the Paraguay War in 1870 up to the Falklands/Malvinas War in 1982. Rio Grande do Sul, in particular, has always had many troops and military units and a strong military culture even in society. Such attributes ended up encouraging civilian interest in defense studies and military affairs in this state's universities. Symmetrically, some big and politically and culturally important states, such as Minas Gerais and Bahia, are underrepresented in the RBED output. While Brazil is an unequal country on many social, economic and political dimensions, the regional concentration of RBED authors contributes to the attention deficit in defense issues on the part of Brazilian civilian elites in general.[3]

Table 3
State of residence of authors publishing in *Revista Brasileira de Estudos de Defesa* in 2014-2021

State	Authors (N)	percentage
Amapá	3	1.4%
Bahia	1	0.5%
Ceará	2	1.0%
Federal District	12	5.7%
Mato Grosso	1	0.5%
Mato Grosso do Sul	2	1.0%
Minas Gerais	11	5.3%
Pará	3	1.4%
Paraíba	15	7.2%
Paraná	7	3.3%
Pernambuco	7	3.3%
Rio de Janeiro	46	22.0%
Rio Grande do Sul	26	12.4%
Santa Catarina	17	8.1%
Sao Paulo	53	25.4%
Sergipe	3	1.4%
Total	**209**	**100.0%**

Note: Countries of residence of RBED authors other than Brazil include: Argentina (12), El Salvador (1), Ecuador (1), Spain (1), United States (2), France (1), England (1), New Zealand (1), Portugal (2), Uruguay (1) and Venezuela (1). Source: https://rbed.abedef.org/rbed/index.

---

3 See the discussion of this "attention deficit" in Latin America in the pioneering article by Pion-Berlin and Trinkunas (2007).

Finally, by counting the keywords of the 144 articles published in RBED in 2014-2021, one finds a total of 576. The 25 keywords that appeared the most are listed in Table 4 below.

Table 4
Frequency of keywords (in Portuguese) in the articles published in *Revista Brasileira de Estudos de Defesa* in 2014-2021

Keywords	Word count	%
Brasil (Brazil)	12	2.08
América do Sul (South America)	11	1.91
Defesa (Defense)	11	1.91
Geopolítica (Geopolitics)	11	1.91
Estados Unidos (United States)	8	1.39
Forças Armadas (Armed Forces)	8	1.39
Relações Civil-Militares (Civil-Military Relations)	8	1.39
Política de Defesa (Defense Policy)	7	1.22
Argentina	6	1.04
Russia	6	1.04
Segurança (Security)	6	1.04
Estudos de Defesa (Defense Studies)	5	0.87
Indústria de Defesa (Defense Industry)	5	0.87
Defesa Cibernética (Cybernetic Defense)	4	0.69
Estratégia (Strategy)	4	0.69
Operações de Paz (Peacekeeping Operations)	4	0.69
Relações Internacionais (International Relations)	4	0.69
Segurança pública (Public Security)	4	0.69
Epistemologia (Epistemology)	3	0.52
Espaço Cibernético (Cybernetic Space)	3	0.52
Estudos Estratégicos (Strategic Studies)	3	0.52
Fronteira (Border)	3	0.52
Guerra (War)	3	0.52
Militarização (Militarization)	3	0.52
Pacificação (Pacification)	3	0.52
Segurança Nacional (Nacional Security)	3	0.52
Total	148 (out of 576)	100

Source: https://rbed.abedef.org/rbed/index.

The raw numbers displayed in Table 4 certainly limit what one can say about the real content of the RBED articles.[4] At any rate, note the strikingly low number of the theme "guerra" (war in Portuguese). It is even on par with epistemology. While this may surprise scholars from big powers that are usually involved in military conflicts, historically speaking, this is a typically Brazilian and Latin American feature (Centeno, 2002). Moreover, Brazil and Spanish-speaking Latin American countries have become non-war-fighting nations since the end of WWII for many reasons, mostly domestic (Jenne, 2021).[5] This obviously has affected the topics to which civilian defense intellectuals are attracted in Brazil. While this makes historical sense, such pattern also implies that civilian scholars in Brazil do not conduct enough research into a phenomenon whose knowledge is key for them to feel confident when interacting with members of the military profession. This lack of civilian confidence in debating warfare fosters civilian timidity vis-à-vis the military and negligence of defense issues, which, in turn, weaken civilian capacity to control the military and direct defense policy.

The previous paragraph is not a plea for hawkishness or war-mongering. But why should civilian scholars of a non-war-fighting nation study war? Even pacifist scholars of a peaceful country should study war, so they can properly and confidently inform defense policy debates and, thus, help strengthen civilian control of the military.[6]

Surprisingly, Brazilian diplomats also refrain from studying war-related issues. The consequence is that the country's highly professional diplomatic corps does not have an in-depth thinking about the use of force in international relations (Alsina Júnior, 2009). Given the cultural influence of Brazilian diplomats on the country's elites (Costa e Silva, 2001), it is plausible to speculate that this pacifism on the part of diplomats ends up percolating down to civilian academia. By this logic, Accorsi (this volume) offers a blueprint to study war-related topics associated with Brazil's historical experience from a comparative perspective.

---

[4] For in-depth analyses of defense studies in Brazil, see Diniz (2015), Marques and Fuccille (2015), Saint-Pierre (2015), and Soares (2015).

[5] The interstate wars in Latin America after 1945 are the Falkland/Malvinas War in 1982 and the Cenepa War in 1995.

[6] Brazil is peaceful as far as external war is concerned; otherwise, Brazilian society is very violent.

Finally, Table 5 below deals with the methodological choices of the RBED articles published in 2014-2021. Each piece was categorized according to its main methodology: essay/conceptual work, descriptive work, qualitative/historical analysis, basic quantitative analysis, and regression analysis. Table 5 indicates the prevalence of studies of an essayistic or conceptual nature, the standard form of writing in Brazil's political science until the early 1990s (Soares, 2005). Studies that either make use of basic quantitative analysis or adopt regression analysis are rare in the journal, unlike the trend that has recently been consolidated in the country's political science (Figueiredo et al., 2021).

Table 5
Methodology adopted by the articles published in *Revista Brasileira de Estudos de Defesa* in 2014-2021

Methodology	N	%
Essay/Conceptual	76	52.8
Qualitative case study	12	8.3
Descriptive	12	8.3
Qualitative/Historical analysis	42	29.2
Basic quantitative analysis	1	0.70
Regression analysis	1	0.70
Total	**144**	**100**

Source: https://rbed.abedef.org/rbed/index.

All said, in Brazil there is a keen need to expand the publication of defense studies based on quantitative research. The works by Acácio (this volume) and Pimenta (this volume) offer good models to do so.

Bolsonaro and After

The Bolsonaro government, with its extensive militarization of the executive branch and politicization of the military, is a turning point in Brazil's civil-military relations under the democratic regime initiated in 1985. Whether reelected or not in 2022, Bolsonaro is likely to have a major impact on the study of civil-military relations and defense policy in Brazil. Why?

First off, Bolsonaro will draw more scholars to conduct research into military politics, civilian control of the military, and the relations between democracy and the armed forces. These are classical topics but they had lost salience on the research agenda of Brazilian social scientists up to the rise of Bolsonaro to the presidential office in 2019. Therefore, no longer will international relations and defense scholars are the ones who will pay close attention to civil-military relations, as became the pattern in the 2000s and 2010s. Anthropologists, constitutional lawyers, historians, political scientists, and sociologists are likely to stage a comeback to an issue – the political role of the military – that used to be key to the study of Brazilian politics and society.

Brazilian social scientists – and Brazilianists too – are likely to spend the next years trying to understand why the Brazilian military became so enthralled by a traditional politician, Jair Bolsonaro, who had been expelled from the Army and had been considered a "bad officer" by former general-president Ernesto Geisel (D'Araújo and Castro, 1997:235). Many other questions relating to the Bolsonaro presidency will be investigated. Here are some of them: to what extent and why have the military's preferences over their participation in domestic politics changed between, say, 2010 and 2018? Do retired officers differ from active-duty ones as regards their political preferences and behavior in and out of the government? During the Bolsonaro presidency, to what extent did officers holding civilian positions coordinate with active-duty officers working in the armed services? To what extent did the military affect the content of policies other than defense in 2019-2022? What is the impact of the Army generals who have been heading Brazil's Ministry of Defense since February 2018 on civilian control of the military, defense policymaking, the content of defense policy, and transparency on defense issues? What is the effect of the militarization of government and the politicization of the military under Bolsonaro on the quality of Brazil's democracy?

International relations and defense scholars will certainly be prodded to investigate the issues mentioned previously, but this will likely divert them from research agendas that are closer to their hearts, such as international security, foreign policy, regional integration, and the defense industry. Ominously, given that the Brazilian military has recently reaffirmed its historical predilection for participating in domestic politics, the study of warfare, already weak in the

Brazilian academia, is likely to be further weakened. Therefore, the vicious cycle depicted above will be further strengthened: civilian scholars will be unlikely to invest enough time and resources in the study of warfare; thus they will feel less confident when interacting with the military; consequently, civilian diffidence in debating warfare will further enhance civilian timidity vis-à-vis the military and civilian negligence of defense issues, which, by their turn, will further erode civilian capacity to control the military and direct defense policy.

To break the vicious cycle depicted above, vigorous research programs conducted by the country's civilian academic institutions and funded by the federal and state governments will be necessary. However, these funds will only be made available under governments committed to removing the military from politics and turning the Ministry of Defense into a civilian-led agency. To achieve the latter goal, it is simply indispensable that the promise made by the 2008 *National Defense Strategy*, an official publication of the Ministry of Defense, be fulfilled: "The Ministry of Defense will conduct studies about creating a staff of civilian defense experts to prepare them for career paths in the civil and military administration, such that it would create a labor force capable of managing defense policy, working in programs and projects in the field of defense, as well as interacting with government agencies and society, integrating political and technical points of view" (Brazil 2008:50).

Fourteen years later, Brazil has yet to design an exam and a career for civilian defense experts. It is not because of a dearth of money that this career has so far not been created. Likewise, there is no dearth of excellent candidates for such positions. Therefore, with a simple bill of law, a president could easily make that career a reality. But it takes far-sightedness and a strong political will to do so. In the long run, civilian defense experts would enable the democratization of civil-military relations' essential institution, the Ministry of Defense – by breaking up the monopoly that the military has on the knowledge of and information on defense issues and strategic affairs. Argentina and Chile undertook this process some decades ago (Pion-Berlin and Martinez, 2017). It is high time Brazil catches up with its neighbors in this regard.

References

ALSINA JÚNIOR, João Paulo Soares. *Política externa e poder militar no Brasil:* universos paralelos. Rio de Janeiro: Editora FGV, 2009.

AMORIM NETO, Octavio. A política comparada no Brasil: a política dos outros, p. 321-40. In LESSA, R. (ed.). *Horizontes das ciências sociais no Brasil:* São Paulo: Anpocs/Editora Barcarolla/Discurso Editorial/ICH, 2010.

________. The Impact of Civilians on Defense Policy in New Democracies: The Case of Brazil. *Latin American Politics and Society*, 61(3), 2019, p. 1-28. Doi: 10.1017/lap.2019.3.

________; ACÁCIO, Igor. De volta ao centro da arena: causas e consequências do papel político dos militares sob Bolsonaro. *Journal of Democracy em Português*, 9, 2020, p. 1-29. Retrieved from http://www.plataformademocratica.org/Arquivos/nov-20/01_De_volta_ao_centro_da_arena.pdf.

BARROS, Antonio Teixeira de. O debate parlamentar sobre a comissão nacional da verdade no congresso nacional brasileiro. *Revista Brasileira de Ciências Sociais*, 35, 2020. Doi: 10.1590/3510401/2020.

BRAZIL – Ministry of Defense. *Estratégia Nacional de Defesa*. Brasília: Ministério da Defesa, 2008.

CENTENO, Miguel. *Blood and Debt:* War and the Nation-State in Latin America. University Park: Pennsylvania University Press, 2002.

COSTA E SILVA, Alberto (ed.). *O Itamaraty na cultura brasileira*. Brasília: Instituto Rio Branco, 2001.

D'ARAÚJO, Maria Celina; CASTRO, Celso. *Ernesto Geisel*. Rio de Janeiro: Editora FGV, 1997.

DUARTE, Rubens de S. Trajetória sinuosa: surgimento de uma dimensão pública na formulação da política de defesa no Brasil? *Dados* 65, 2022. Doi: 10.1590/dados.2022.65.4.278.

FIGUEIREDO, Dalson; FERNANDES, Antônio; BORBA, Lucas; AGUIAR, Thaís Helena. Metodologias de pesquisa em ciência política: uma breve introdução. *BIB – Revista Brasileira de Informação Bibliográfica em Ciências Sociais*, (94), 2021. Retrieved from https://bibanpocs.emnuvens.com.br/revista/article/view/175.

FIGUEIREDO, Eurico de Lima. Os estudos estratégicos, a defesa nacional e a segurança internacional. In LESSA, R. (ed.). *Horizontes das Ciências*

Sociais, a Ciência Política. São Paulo: Anpocs/Editora Barcarolla/Discurso Editorial/ICH, 2010.

HOLLANDA, Cristina Buarque de; ISRAEL, Vinícius Pinheiro. Panorama das Comissões da Verdade no Brasil: uma reflexão sobre novos sentidos de legitimidade e representação democrática. *Revista de Sociologia e Política*, 27, 2019. Doi: 10.1590/1678-987319277006.

JENNE, Nicole. The Domestic Origins of No-War Communities. *Journal of International Relations and Development*, 24(1), 2021, p. 196-225. Doi: 10.1057/s41268-020-00188-7.

LÜHRMANN, Anna et al. Autocratization Surges – Resistance Grows. In *Democracy Report 2020*, Varieties of Democracy Institute (V-Dem), 2020. Retrieved from https://www.v-dem.net/static/website/files/dr/dr_2020.pdf.

MARQUES, Adriana A.; FUCCILLE, Alexandre. Ensino e pesquisa em defesa no Brasil: estruturação do campo e desafios. *Revista Brasileira de Estudos de Defesa*, 2(2), 2015. Doi: 10.26792/rbed.v2n2.2015.64674.

MEDEIROS, Sabrina Evangelista. Da epistemologia dos estudos de defesa e os seus campos híbridos. *Revista Brasileira de Estudos de Defesa*, 2(2), 2015. Doi: 10.26792/rbed.v2n2.2015.63034.

PION-BERLIN, David; MARTÍNEZ, Rafael. *Soldiers, Politicians, and Civilians:* Reforming Civil-Military Relations in Democratic Latin America. Cambridge: Cambridge University Press, 2017.

________.;TRINKUNAS, Harold. Attention Deficits: Why Politicians Ignore Defense Policy in Latin America. *Latin American Research Review*, 42(3), 2007, p. 76-100. https://www.jstor.org/stable/i405012.

SAINT-PIERRE; LUIS, Héctor. Ensaio sobre os estudos de defesa e a comunidade que os pratica. *Revista Brasileira de Estudos de Defesa*, 2(2), 2015. Doi: 10.26792/rbed.v2n2.2015.63747.

SOARES, Gláucio Ary Dillon. O calcanhar metodológico da ciência política no Brasil. *Sociologia, Problemas e Práticas*, (48), 2005, p. 27-52. Retrieved from https://sociologiapp.iscte-iul.pt/pdfs/48/512.pdf.

SOARES, Samuel Alves. Por uma nova ontologia da defesa. *Revista Brasileira de Estudos de Defesa*, 2(2), 2015. Doi: 10.26792/rbed.v2n2.2015.65447.

VILLA, Rafael Duarte; PASSOS, Anais M. Engagement of Military Peacekeepers in Brazilian Politics (2011-2021). *Armed Forces & Society*, on-line first version, 2022. doi: 10.1177/0095327X221087254.

About the Authors

André Anselmo holds a law degree from Universidade Federal Fluminense (UFF), an MSc in Administration from the Brazilian School of Public and Business Administration (FGV EBAPE) and is a PhD candidate in political science at Syracuse University. His research interests are civil-military relations and grand strategy. He seeks to understand how states – especially developing countries – align goals and means, integrating defense and foreign policies to achieve long-term objectives.

Camila Scheidegger Farias is a PhD student in Political Science at the University of British Columbia. Her research interests broadly lie in the comparative politics of developing countries, including the politics of public policy, state-society relations, and indigenous politics in Latin America. She obtained her BA in Administration from the Federal University of Pernambuco, Recife, and her MSc in Administration from the Brazilian School of Public and Business Administration (FGV EBAPE).

Gabriel Alves Pimenta holds an MSc in Administration from the Brazilian School of Public and Business Administration (FGV EBAPE), Rio de Janeiro, Brazil, and is a Ph.D. candidate at the department of political science at the University of California at Riverside. His research deals with new approaches to civil-military relations within government defense institutions with a particular focus on the contribution of civilians. He is particularly interested in institutional development and how the relationships between groups influence this process.

Igor Acácio was a Research Assistant at the Brazilian School of Public and Business Administration (FGV EBAPE) in 2013-2016. Currently, he is a Post-doctoral Fellow at Tulane University's Center for Inter-American Policy and Research and a Hans J. Morgenthau Fellow at the Notre Dame International Security Center. He obtained a Ph.D. in Political Science at the University of California, Riverside. His research focuses on civil-military relations, military missions, defense, and security issues. His recent work has appeared in *Comparative Politics, Democratization, Journal of Democracy, Armed Forces and Society,* and *Public Opinion Quarterly.*

Karina Furtado Rodrigues is Adjunct Professor in the Post-Graduate Programme in Military Sciences at the Brazilian Army Command and General Staff College and Research Leader of the Laboratory of Governance, Management and Public Policy in National Defense. She holds an MSc and a PhD in Administration from the Brazilian School of Public and Business Administration (FGV EBAPE). Her research interests are state secrets, freedom of information, defense governance, defense policy, and historical-comparative methodology.

Octavio Amorim Neto is a full professor of political science at the Brazilian School of Public and Business Administration (FGV EBAPE). He is a comparativist whose work has appeared in several international journals. He is the author of *Presidencialismo e Governabilidade nas América* (FGV Editora, 2006) and *De Dutra a Lula: A Condução e os Determinantes das Política Externa Brasileira* (Campus, 2011).

Pedro Accorsi is a PhD Candidate in Political Science at the University of Minnesota, and an MSc in Administration from the Brazilian School of Public and Business Administration (FGV EBAPE). He was previously a Managing Editor of Security Studies and Hans J. Morgenthau Fellow at the Notre Dame International Security Center. His research interests lie broadly in international conflict and civil-military relations, including themes such as military effectiveness, military coalitions, US foreign policy, grand strategy, deterrence, and defense policy.

Este livro foi impresso nas oficinas gráficas da Editora Vozes Ltda.,
Rua Frei Luís, 100 – Petrópolis, RJ.